D1547430

JEAN-NOËL ALETTI

The Birth
of the Gospels
as Biographies

With Analyses of Two Challenging Pericopae

Translated by Peggy Manning Meyer

Pontificia Università Gregoriana
Pontificio Istituto Biblico

ROMA 2017

Cover: Serena Aureli
Impaginazione a cura dell'Autore

© 2017 Pontifical Biblical Institute
Gregorian & Biblical Press
Piazza della Pilotta, 35 - 00187 Roma, Italy
www.gbpress.org - books@biblicum.com

ISBN: 978-88-7653-**702**-8

TABLE OF CONTENTS

PART TWO
THE NARRATIVE ANALYSIS OF TWO PERICOPAE

FOREWORD

This essay would have never come about if Jean-Pierre Sonnet, director of the collection "Le livre et le rouleau", had not asked me to write it. In 1999, one of my articles, entitled "Le Christ raconté. Les évangiles comme littérature?", was published in a collected work, *Bible et littérature*[1]. In it, I explored the question of the genre – biographical or not? – of the Gospels, of their similarities but also, and above all, of their differences from the writings of their era, that is, whether or not one could give them the appellation of *literary works*. But I did not think of developing the ideas that I then succinctly put forward. Not that I was disinterested in the Gospel narratives: two previous monographs, using the narratological approach, had provided keys for the reading of the Gospel of Luke and the Acts of the Apostles[2]; the study of Gospel characters[3] had supplemented this work and had shown the influence that the narrators' techniques have on the Christology and theology of their narratives. But my research on the Pauline letters required a great deal of time and did not allow me to revisit the genre and purpose of the New Testament narratives at greater length.

Having had, during the past few years, the opportunity of giving numerous lectures on the subject that is going to occupy us and of seeing how very different audiences – experienced biblical scholars, students in biblical theology, theologians and the general public – were passionate

---

[1] Fr. Mies (ed.), *Bible et littérature. L'homme et Dieu mis en intrigue* (Bruxelles/Namur ; Lessius 1999) 29-53.

[2] J.N. Aletti, *L'art de raconter Jésus-Christ. L'écriture narrative de l'évangile de Luc*, Seuil, Paris, 1989; Id., *Quand Luc raconte. Le récit comme théologie* (Cerf, Paris, 1998).

[3] Cf., among others, "La construction du personnage Jésus dans les récits évangeliques. Le cas de Mc", in C. Focant and A. Wénin (ed.), *Analyse narrative et Bible. Deuxième colloque international du RRENAB. Louvain-la-Neuve – avril, 2004* (BETL 191 ; Leuven, Peeters 2005) 19-42; "Analyse narrative de Mc 7,24-30. Difficultés et propositions", in *Biblica* (2012) 357-376.

about the questions tackled, I thought it good to undertake the route that the reader, in his turn, must follow from the first chapter to the last, for the argumentation is very linear.

The article on the narrated Christ, responding in part to the challenges encountered in the Gospels by specialists, merited being extended: do these narratives describe the real Jesus? Are they reliable? By taking up these long-standing questions, beginning with the necessity of showing that the genre of the Gospels is biographical, it will be possible to clarify and to resolve some enigmas and, let us hope, to make clear the literary and theological genius of these anonymous narrators who for a longtime have been thought to be storytellers without talent, even if it were necessary to believe them to be inspired.

To Sylvie and Louis
Gracious Hosts
Le Paren (Orthez), 2015

FOREWORD TO THE ENGLISH EDITION

As the narrative approach to the Gospels first appeared in the United States, it seemed to me that many in the English-speaking world would appreciate a translation of my latest essay on the way in which the first Christian narrators overcame the challenge of writing biographies [*bioi*], even though everything seemed to prohibit their doing so.

Unlike the French and Italian editions, this one has two parts. To the first, which is a faithful translation of the original by Peggy Manning Meyer, who has my sincere thanks for her valued collaboration, have been added two examples of the narrative approach that analyze Gospel episodes that until recently were erroneously interpreted: Jesus' encounter with the Syrophoenician woman in Mark 7:24-30 and the parable of The Father and the Two Sons in Luke 15:11-32. May this second part allow the reader not only to see in a concrete way the importance of sound procedures for the narrative approach but also to become aware that, unfortunately, the consensus among exegetes was too quickly considered as certain and definitive.

The first part of this work was originally published by Editions Lessius and the second chapter of the second part by Editions du Cerf.

ABBREVIATIONS

Acts	Acts of the Apostles
AnBib	Analecta Biblica
ANRW	Aufstieg und Niedergang der römischen Welt
BETL	Bibliotheca Ephemeridum Theologicarum Lovaniensium
Bib	*Biblica*
BJ	Bible de Jérusalem
FzB	Forschung zur Bibel
JBL	*Journal of Biblical Literature*
John	Gospel According to John
JSNT	*Journal for the Study of the New Testament*
JSNTSS	JSNT Supplement Studies
JGRChJ	*Journal of Greco-Roman Christianity and Judaism*
Luke	Gospel According to Luke
LD	Lectio Divina
LNTS	Library of New Testament Studies
Mark	Gospel According to Mark
Matthew	Gospel According to Matthew
NovT	*Novum Testamentum*
NovTS	NovT Supplements
NT	New Testament
NTS	*New Testament Studies*
OT	Old Testament
RHPR	*Revue d'histoire et de philosophie religieuses*
RRENAB	Réseau de Recherche en Narratologie et Bible
RSR	*Recherches de Science Religieuse*
SBL	Society of Biblical Literature
SBLMS	SBL Monograph Series
SNTS	Societas Novi Testamenti Studiorum
SNTSMS	SNTS Monograph Series
TANZ	Texte und Arbeiten zum neutestamentlichen Zeitalter
TOB	Traduction Œcuménique de la Bible
WUNT	Wissenschaftliche Untersuchungen zum Neuen Testament

PART ONE

THE DECISIVE ROLE OF THE *ANAGNÔRISIS* IN THE WRITING OF THE SYNOPTICS

INTRODUCTION

Exegetes, as a whole, think that, before the appearance of the Gospels as continuous narratives, a series of episodes from the life of Jesus and some of his sayings (in Greek, *logia*) were read in liturgical assemblies – in particular, the narratives of his Passion, death and resurrection during the Easter vigil – and were used for catechesis. These texts for liturgical and catechetical use, probably utilized by most, indeed all, of the communities, assuredly sufficed to nourish and reinforce the faith and piety of believers. So, when and why was it judged useful, indeed necessary, to link these micro-narratives and *logia* and make of them continuous macro-narratives of the biographical type? The question further merits being asked since, given the conventions of the era regarding the writing of lives (in Greek, *bioi*), the first Christians, as one will see in the course of the analyses, would never have had to write lives of Jesus. In other words, the Gospel narratives, in principle, never had to come into being.

One has, of course, pertinently responded "that the evangelists chose the genre of biography because it was the genre that was best suited to present the words and deeds of Jesus to the largest possible audience. This potential audience would include both a primary (Christian) audience and a broad secondary audience, including any who became interested in the person and work of Jesus[4]". And why was this genre the most suitable? Because "[t]he benefit of biography was that its focus was on the subject. The narrative structure of the gospels as biographies allowed for an incredible amount of diversity in the arrangement and presentation of the Jesus materials. The genre provided the evangelists with a literary structure that gave them the room and flexibility to express their individual theological outlooks, while keeping the focus on Jesus[5]".

Well enough! But how did the evangelists do this so as to respect the Greco-Roman requirements to which biographies had to submit?

---

[4] J.M. SMITH, *Why Βίος? On the Relationship Between Gospel Genre and Implied Audience* (LNTS 518; London, Bloomsbury 2015) 202. An assertion repeated in almost identical words, p. 212.

[5] *Ibid.*, p. 212.

Indeed, the protagonists of the biographies of that time were known and recognized as great men, whereas Jesus was to a great extent rejected by his coreligionists because of his death on the cross as a blasphemer and a seducer of the people. To write his life was thus an apparently impossible challenge to take up. After having presented the characteristics of literary, historical and popular Greco-Roman biographies (chap. I), we will see why and how the evangelists wanted and were able to write, in their turn, lives of Jesus, and we will show, by following Mark, that the genre of the Gospels is biographical[6]. Some exegetes still refuse to admit that this is their genre. This can only be out ignorance of the numerous studies made in recent decades on the subject (chap. II). The genre of the narratives having been highlighted, it will then be necessary to see why the issues are the same for Matthew (chap. III) and for Luke (chap. IV and V) and to draw conclusions for the interpretation of these narratives. The results of the inquiry, as one will see, will be interesting to say the least. The last chapter will broaden the horizon by proposing some orientations and suggestions.

The present inquiry is limited to the synoptic Gospels (Mark, Matthew and Luke). It has already been shown that John also belongs to the biographical genre, and the reader can consult the authoritative monographs on the subject[7]. But the difficulties confronted by the Synoptics and the solutions that they provided sufficed for our purpose, as the reader will be able to realize at the end of the journey.

That the Gospel biographies were aimed at a large audience and not only the believers of a community has also been shown[8]. But one can ask if Mark and those who followed also did not think that others, not just potential Christian readers, would be interested in and able to get to know Jesus in a way other than by the caricatural rumors that began to be spread

---

[6] The reader will have undoubtedly noted the route's paradox, which opens with the narrative of Mark, the most distant from Greco-Roman biographies and yet is here presented as the initiator of the genre, and ends with Luke, definitely much closer than Mark to the biographies of that time. The reason for this arrangement will progressively become apparent.

[7] R.A. BURRIDGE, *What Are the Gospels? A Comparison with Graeco-Roman Biography* (Grand Rapids, MI; Eerdmans 2004[2], original 1992), and D. FRICKENSCHMIDT, *Evangelium als Biographie. Die vier Evangelien im Rahmen antiker Erzählkunst* (TANZ 22; Tübingen, Francke Verlag 1997).

[8] Quite recently by J.M. SMITH, Why *Βίος*?, who relies upon the works of Richard BAUCKHAM, *The Gospels for All Christians. Rethinking the Gospel Audiences* (Edinburg, T&T Clark 1998), and others.

among the Jews and the pagans[9]. If apologia is not absent from the Gospels, it is made not only in order to confirm believers but also to present to those who are not reasons to believe.

The present essay is original – said in all humility, as must be – on the subject and on the way of treating it, not because studies on the biographical genre are lacking or are not reliable but because the relationship between biography and *anagnôrisis*[10] has not yet been studied in its conditions and its consequences and because one has not seen the influence that this had on the writing of Mark, Matthew and Luke, whose narratives are influenced and structured by this problem.

---

[9] Cf. G.N. STANTON, *Jesus and Gospel* (Cambridge, Cambridge University Press 2004) 127-161.

[10] We will return to the meaning of this term and to the importance that it has in the Ancients throughout this essay.

CHAPTER I

BIOGRAPHIES
AT THE TIME OF THE GOSPELS
GENRE AND COMPONENTS

I. TOWARDS AN UNDERSTANDING OF THE GENRE

In search of a Literary Genre

Before examining whether or not the Gospel narratives belong to literature, it is important to place them in relation to the biographical narratives of their time. With what type of narrative are we dealing? As one knows, there are still some exegetes for whom the Gospels do not belong to any then-known genre: according to them, any attempt at a comparison with the prevailing literature remains unfruitful and useless, for the Gospels are in reality the direct product of the faith of the primitive Church[1]. One has thus quite naturally come to speak about the "Gospel genre", as one does about a being or thing, by saying it is *sui generis*, this genitive discreetly indicating that one is not very clear about the genre in question[2].

In our day, it is true, those who rank the Gospels among biographies are more and more numerous[3]. But this stance does nothing to advance the

---

[1] The most marked representative of this point of view is probably Rudolf Bultmann, in his *History of the Synoptic Tradition* (Oxford, Blackwell 1972, original 1921), and his *Theology of the New Testament* (New York, Scribner 1951-1955).

[2] Thus, even recently, E.M. BECKER, *Das Markus-Evangelium im Rahmen antiker Historiographie* (WUNT 194; Tübingen, Mohr Siebeck 2006), after having presented a complete *status quaestionis* on the genre of Mark, then concludes that it is "ein Werk *sui generis*" (p. 65).

[3] Already C.W. VOTAW, "The Gospels and Contemporary Biographies", in *American Journal of Theology* 19, (1915) 45-73; but the idea truly took hold after 1960, with M. HADAS and M. SMITH, *Heroes and Gods. Spiritual Biographies in Antiquity* (Religious Perspectives 13; New York, Harper & Row 1965); C.H. TALBERT, *What is a Gospel? The Genre of the Canonical Gospels* (Philadelphia, Fortress 1977); Ph.L. SHULER, *A Genre for the Gospels: The Biographical Character of Matthew* (Philadelphia, Fortress 1982). The

research if one does not immediately add that it is important to know exactly what the *biography* genre encompasses[4]. Some designate the Gospels as popular biographies, differentiating them from historical biographies; others, following Plutarch's example[5], distinguish between biographies (*bioi*) and histories (*historiai*), classifying the Gospels among the first and the Acts of the Apostles among the second. But in order to avoid anachronistically characterizing the genre in question, it is absolutely necessary to begin with the traits that are present in the biographies (more or less) contemporary to the New Testament narratives[6].

To say that there were biographies during the era when the Gospel narratives came about can, moreover, seem anachronistic, to the extent that the Greek substantive *biographia* only appeared for the first time in the Vth century of our era, in the *Life of Isidore* written by the Byzantine philosopher Damascius, his disciple. But if the word did not yet exist, the number of narratives called *lives (bioi)* began to be considerable: lives of poets, philosophers, great generals, famous orators, etc. And as the two terms designated the same type of narrative, specialists have not hesitated to speak uniformly of *biographies*, a usage that we will follow throughout the present essay.

Some Characteristics

The reader familiar with biblical narratives will possibly think that, in writing lives of Jesus, the first Christian generations simply followed the example of the sacred writers to whom we owe the lives of Abraham, Isaac, Jacob, Joseph, Moses, Samson, Samuel and David. As the pages that follow will show, the requisites that were in force in the I[st] century of our era, however, seemed to prohibit the writing of a life of Jesus. Before seeing why this was so, it is no doubt necessary to refer to the research on the traits that characterize the biographies of that time.

For a long time, it has been noted that, in Antiquity, a definition of biography did not exist[7]. But the Ancients did not need a definition in

---

idea is being accepted more and more; about this, see the history of the research in R.A. BURRIDGE, *What Are the Gospels?*

[4] BURRIDGE, *What Are the Gospels?*, 6, also 38-54.

[5] PLUTARCH, *Life of Alexander*, 2: "My design is not to write histories (*historias*), but lives (*bious*)". This statement has been commented upon many times by specialists.

[6] BURRIDGE, *What Are the Gospels?*, 70-81.

[7] On the absence of a definition, see H. SONNABEND, *Geschichte der antiken Biographie. Von Isokrates bis zur Historia Augusta* (Stuttgart, J.B. Metzler Verlag, 2002).

order to call *bioi* the narratives that narrate the life of a historical man[8] – which distinguishes them from fictional narratives[9] –, by uniformly placing the emphasis on his words and deeds. These are the formal elements that characterize biographies and allow speaking of the genre: (1°) the function of these narratives is to highlight (2°) the words and deeds – including the death – (3°) of a known historical person[10]. In short, these biographies all have in common narrating the life, from the near or distant past, of a man, the principle character of the narrative, the one in relation to whom the other persons and events are mentioned.

The protagonist, as just said, is described by his words and his deeds. But do the narratives proceed by accumulation or by selection? A quick overview of the ancient lives (*bioi*) shows that never or almost never do the narrators aim to be exhaustive, for, as Plutarch declares in the prologue to his already mentioned *Life of Alexander*, when he is explaining his choice of themes, of episodes but also his omissions, "my design is not to write histories [*historiai*] but lives [*bioi*], and the most glorious exploits do not always furnish us with discoveries of virtue or vice". Even if it is necessary to provide deeds by which virtue and vice can be recognized, biographers refuse to accumulate episodes, preferring to keep only those that they judge the most representative. What Plutarch's statement indicates as well is that the biographies of the era do not describe a political, social, psychological or spiritual itinerary, but a man in whom vices or virtues are manifested. The moral component is thus primary, all the others being subordinated to it, and its raison d'être varies as well according to what is needed: apologia, praise, imitation, conversion, a life inspired by superior values, etc. In short, as interested as the biographies

---

[8] To my knowledge, there were no biographies of women in the writings that precede those of the N.T. Incidentally, and notwithstanding the opinion of Armin D. BAUM, "Biographien im alttestamentlich-rabbinischen Stil. Zur Gattung der neutestamentlichen Evangelien", in *Bib* 94 (2013) 534-564, the books of Judith and Esther are not biographies, for they do not cover the entire life – including the death – of their heroines, only some events limited in time.

[9] Narratives generally called *novels*, the designation itself also being anachronistic, for this word was used much later, when one passed from Latin to vernacular (Romance) languages.

[10] Cf., for example, J.M. SMITH, *Why Bioς?*, 203: "[C]ertain formal elements remain consistent throughout the roughly 800-year period of Graeco-Roman biographical development. The emphasis on the words and deeds of a particular individual is the hallmark of this literature. Fundamentally, a work can be understood to be a biography *if* the focus of the work is the presentation of the life of an individual of importance (and often one worthy of emulation) via their works and deeds".

of that time are in the protagonist, they are equally interested in what he represents. That is why these narratives are constituted from episodes relatively independent of each other; they do not form a progressive plot in a continuous manner but rather illustrate a thesis or an entire project.

As they deal with *lives*, one will not be surprised to see most of these narratives beginning with the birth and ending with the death of the protagonist. This being said, even if the chronological cadre often decides the arrangement of the narrative, it does not constitute an essential component, for if some biographies closely follow the order of major events, others proceed more by themes, others still – like Xenophon's *Agesilaus* and *Moses* by Philo of Alexandria – begin with the chronology and end with the themes.

If, as the biographers of that time notice, it is the words and deeds that principally characterize the protagonist, most of these narratives, nevertheless, begin by briefly describing the origin and the education[11]. The origin (in Greek, *genos*) is personal (the birth and what preceded it – visions, celestial phenomena; physical and human qualities), familial (the parents, more widely known ancestors) and geographical (the city and its reputation, the region, when it is worth being mentioned). The education (in Greek, *paideia*), scholastic as well as practical, equally aims at highlighting the protagonist's ability. If all the lives do not begin with the birth[12] and do not necessarily mention the education, they emphatically develop the words and the deeds – subsumed under the term *praxeis*:

genos (origin)	ancestors, city, country, personal assets	short part
paideia (education)	formation and acquisition of knowledge and skill	short part
praxeis (words and deeds)	words and deeds *wanted* by the protagonist; deeds *sustained* by him	long part

---

[11] Cf., for example, the *Progymnasmata* of HERMOGENES in G.A. KENNEDY, *Progymnasmata. Greek Textbooks of Prose Composition and Rhetoric Translated with Introductions and Notes* (SBL Writings from the Greco-Roman World 10; Leiden, Brill 2003) 81-82.

[12] All do not begin with the birth. Cf., for example, the very beginning of the life of Caesar by Suetonius: "Caesar was sixteen years old when he lost his father. The following year, he was designated a flamen of Jupiter; and although he had been engaged, since his childhood, to Cossutia, from a modest, but very rich, equestrian family, he repudiated her, in order to marry Cornelia, the daughter of Cinna, with whom he had four times been Consul. He soon had a daughter, named Julia...". According to specialists, the beginning of the life of Julius Caesar (title, dedication and chap. 1) has probably been lost. The book would thus now begin with chap. 2.

Biographies and Their Sub-Genres

As the praise (in Greek, *egkômion* or *epainos*) was one of the narratives that school children had to write over the course of the *progymnasmata*[13] and consisted of the same arrangement (*genos, paideia* and *praxeis*), it is not always easy to distinguish between biography and praise[14]. Thus, for the Ancients, the *Evagoras* of Isocrates and the *Agesilaus* of Xenophon were (above all) praises. But as the same *genos–paideia–praxeis* schema is found in some biographical narratives not having as their primary purpose to praise their protagonist, it was quite necessary to admit that *lives* (*bioi*) formed a genre with diverse purposes and that because of this they touched upon numerous genres: some indeed emphasize the occurrence of events, others are didactic, others are closer to the praise or, on the contrary, more critical. They can even incorporate several genres: history – if need be, fictionalized –, (moral) example, apologia, philosophical and religious teaching, dialogue, discourse and debate[15]. One will thus not be surprised, in reading an ancient biography, to encounter discourses, teachings, arguments, etc. The biographical genre is flexible enough to encompass others, without losing its identity. Burridge has shown this with the help of some significant examples that, for this reason, are pointless to repeat and that the following diagram ideally represents[16]:

---

[13] Literally "preparatory exercises" that the teachers (grammarians and rhetors) had their young students do.

[14] Cf. the comment of M. LEDENTU, in her article "Les Vies de Cornélius Népos. Une nouvelle manière d'écrire l'histoire à Rome?", in *Interférences* 5, 2009, § 8 (http://interferences.revues.org/886): "For the Ancients, the *de uita moribusque* narrative is doubly located, with regard to epidictic eloquence and the tradition of praises (*laudationes*) and with regard to *historia*, that is to historiography intended as a narration of the events that on a large scale comprise the history of a people. This comparison with other types of narration is a constant in the discourse of the Ancients on "biography", which is otherwise perceived as a totally separate genre, at least as a type of text that is located on the periphery of other forms of discourse constitutive of its identity. It is in some way a grafted genre that is nourished by the potentialities of other genres and deepens them. An absolute distinction between *uita, historia* and *laudatio* is thus impossible, which notably accounts for the fact that some texts that we classify either as *historia* or as praise have been received as "narratives of life".

[15] Cf. BURRIDGE, *What Are the Gospels?*, 66 and 149-152.

[16] *Ibid.*, 64.

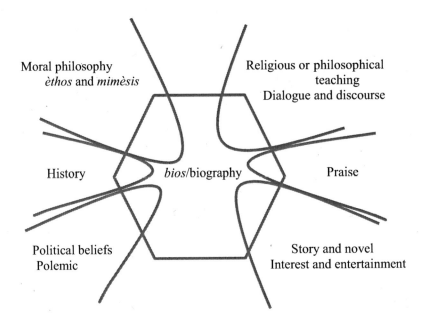

Literary Biographies and Popular Biographies

One has recently reproached Burridge for having only considered literary biographies and for having omitted others, popular because of their protagonists and the readers to whom they are addressed[17].

Some, it is true, have denied the existence of popular biographies, for, they said, the common man was for the most part uneducated and did not know how to read. But if during the era, the individual reader was very rare, there were educated people whose services could be used at private and public gatherings. In fact, Greek tragedies and comedies were not first written to be read but to be heard by the greatest possible number of spectators. Borrowing Smith's categories, we will say that they aimed at an "*open audience*[18]". Several works, one of which is the biography of Aesop the fabulist[19], are clear evidence of the existence of the "popular

---

[17] A.D. BAUM, „Biographien", 534-564.

[18] J.M. SMITH, *Why Βίος?*, 53-55.

[19] That Aesop had a violent death – he was pushed from atop a steep rock by the inhabitants of Delphi –, does not prevent the narrative of which he is the hero of being a

biography" genre. These narratives are even more interesting because they have several traits in common with the Gospels:
- their authors are anonymous;
- the protagonist is not from an upper social milieu[20];
- these narratives are formed from episodes that are independent of each other[21];
- direct discourse is favored, and dialogues are numerous;
- the protagonist narrates stories as well[22].

Another trait also distinguishes literary biographies from popular biographies: the latter do not cite the witnesses or sources at their disposal and say nothing about their reliability, whereas the first do not hesitate to distance themselves from rumors, gossip or accounts concerning their protagonists' actual deeds and motivations. Often, Plutarch declares as false the common opinion about one of the illustrious men whose life he is recounting and gives another version of the true motivations that are his. Thus, speaking of the friendship that Cicero had for the young Caesar, he declares: "These were the reasons spoken of [about this affection], but it [the true motives of this attachment] was principally Cicero's hatred of Antony and a temperament unable to resist honor, which attached him to Caesar[23]." In short, if in popular biographies the critical spirit is little present, in literary biographies, it is, and the historical intention is clearly affirmed.

Following the example of popular biographies, the Gospel narratives – at least Matthew, Mark, and Luke – do not give their sources and do not give their opinion on their soundness. This trait seems to reinforce the similarities that they have with these biographies. It will be necessary for us to determine the reasons for this silence: is this due to a lack of interest in the reliability of their sources and to the absence of a historical intention?

Having briefly presented some characteristics of ancient biographies, it remains to complete the picture with the help of the lives written by a Jew, Philo, and by two pagans, Plutarch and Suetonius, that are useful for responding to our own questions on the Gospel narratives.

---

comic biography, as C. JOUANNO shows "La vie d'Ésope: une biographie comique", in Revue des études grecques 118 (2005) 391-425.

[20] Thus, Aesop is a slave/doulos.

[21] What one calls the episodic style.

[22] Fables for Aesop, parables for Jesus.

[23] Life of Cicero, 45:1.

II. A FEW BIOGRAPHIES FROM THE ERA.
A PRELIMINARY COMPARISON WITH THE GOSPELS

Philo and His Heroes

That Philo is the author of biographies, he himself says in *De Josepho*, 1:1, in which he refers to the patriarchs Abraham, Isaac and Jacob thus: "[I have written about] the man who arrived at excellence in consequence of instruction [Abraham], and him who was self-taught [Isaac], and him [Jacob] who attained to the proposed end by practice."[24] If the lives of Isaac and Jacob were very early on lost, we still have those of Abraham, Joseph and Moses.

Philo's statement, just cited, points out as well that, for this author, the biographical interest is arranged by the description of models, that is, of morally or religiously representative men. His life of Joseph (*De Josepho*) confirms this, being a reflection on the political man, the one who must manage the interests of the city. The beginning of *De Abrahamo* is also quite instructive, for it is devoted, as often occurs at the beginning of these ancient works, to the author's project. By grouping the patriarchs into threes, he associates each of them with a virtue; those of the first triad refer to spiritual attitudes: Enos to hope, Enoch to repentance and conversion, Noah to justice; as for the second group, comprised of Abraham, Isaac and Jacob, it allegorically represents the qualities that are the fruits of study, of nature and of practice. For Philo, a biography allows concretely showing how a man lived in conformity with the ideals of that time, that of the Jew, whose task is to obey the Torah, and that of the Greek, for whom reason must dominate the passions. A passage from *De Abrahamo* excellently summarizes these two ideals when it states that the patriarchs are "living laws and full of reason[25]".

The *Vita Mosis*, which is also a biography, as Philo notes at the beginning of the first book – he is going "to write the life [*bios*] of Moses" (1:1) –, shows at every possible opportunity that, even if followed *grosso modo*, the chronological order does not necessarily become an all-encompassing cadre. Philo seems to want to respect it, since, in the first

---

[24] Transl. C.D. YONGE, *The Works of Philo Judaeus, the Contemporary of Josephus* (London, Henry G. Bohn, 4 vols. 1854-1855).
[25] In Greek, *empsychoi kai logikoi nomoi*.

expositions, he peremptorily declares: "I will begin where it is necessary to begin[26]", that is, with the beginning of the life of Moses. The summary of the first book that he gives in the prologue of the second[27] confirms the presence of a chronological central thread, since he tells of having recounted the birth, the early childhood, the education, and the deeds of Moses in Egypt, at the time of the crossing of the Red Sea, and in the desert (2:1). But this cadre is neither the only one nor the most important since the author also points out that the division into two books is for principally thematic reasons[28]: the first recounts what Moses did as king, and the second treats his responsibilities as legislator (2:8-65), as high priest (2:66-186) and as prophet (2:187-292). The chronological and logical arrangements thus complement each other more than they conflict.

If Moses is a moral model, he also has exceptional physical and intellectual qualities: he is the most beautiful (1:9)[29], the most intelligent (1:21) and his formation is complete, scientifically and philosophically (according to the Greeks; cf. 1:23), but he also receives the education of a king (1:8; 1:20); his temperament is quite noble, since he does not enjoy jokes, laughter and sport and only pays attention to talks and entertainments profitable to the soul (1:20). But it is undoubtedly upon moral traits that Philo places the emphasis: Moses rejects lying in order to seek only the truth (1:24) and comes to dominate all the passions and his desires perfectly (1:26; 1:29). His behavior is such that all wonder if the mind (in Greek, *nous*) that dwelt in such a body is human or divine (1:27).

Moses' moral excellence is not, moreover, emphasized for itself but in relation to his role as the guide of a people who themselves have an extraordinary vocation: "God, who in His providence directs the universe, judged it good to give him [Moses] the kingship of a more numerous and stronger nation [Israel] that, among all, had to serve as priests[30] in order to pray unceasingly for the human race, in order to eliminate evil, to convey the good" (1:149). Furthermore, Philo especially highlights the modalities by which Moses accomplished his task as king, for example, by wanting

---

[26] *Vita*, 1:5. The French translation followed here is that of R. ARNALDEZ, Cl. MONDÉSERT, J. POUILLOUX and P. SAVINEL, *Les œuvres de Philon d'Alexandrie*, vol. 22 (Paris, Cerf 1967).

[27] Note the analogy with Acts 1:1-5, which constitutes the prologue of the second book of Luke.

[28] See *Vita*, 1:334, and 2:3-7.

[29] Just like Hebrews 11:23 and Acts 7:20, here Philo repeats Exodus 2:2.

[30] In Greek, *hierasthai*.

only to serve: "He proposed for himself a single goal, the most necessary: to serve those whose leader he was, doing everything with a view to being useful to them, by deed and by word, without allowing any occasion to pass that could lead the community to act well" (1:151). This royal service Moses rendered without ostentation, but rather in extreme poverty and humility: "He is the only one of all those who have ever governed, who amassed neither gold nor silver, who did not levy taxes, who owned neither houses nor estates, nor flocks, nor personal servants, nor revenues, nor anything of splendor or superfluous luxury; and yet he could have had it all in abundance" (1:153). What one demands of a king is that he be just, give justice to all, with impartiality: impartial, Moses is, but he also shows great humanity[31] for those over whom he has charge, this people who murmurs in the desert, for he knows that a crowd is a naturally fickle thing (1:197). A humanity that went to the extreme since it exerted itself in favor of those towards whom it was not required, namely the enemies of his people (1:245; 1:249): "Our kindness must overcome their malice", he declares to those of his race (1:245). Far from oppressing those over whom he has charge, he unceasingly only promotes their dignity, which is theirs by their election: "You are all equal, one race, you have the same fathers, you are from one house, you have the same customs, you have in common the same laws and innumerable other things" (1:324).

With all these traits, Moses combines the qualities required by the Greeks and by the Jews. In other words, he is a perfect, accomplished man. That there are analogies between the Jesus of the Synoptics and the Moses of Philo jumps out. Both have a kindness and humanity that are extended even to enemies. The major difference comes, however, from the slight attention paid by the Synoptics to the physical qualities and intellectual formation of Jesus. It is rather the contrary that is emphasized since all those who knew him during his youth, the crowds that follow him and the learned among the people wonder how a man with a quite rudimentary education is able to teach as he does[32]. It will be necessary for us to determine why the Gospels also have so little to say about Jesus' physical appearance, his intellectual and religious formation. Is this silence a specific element?

---

[31] In Greek, *philanthrôpia*.

[32] Cf., among others, Matthew 13:53-58 and parallels; Matthew 21:23-27 and par.; Matthew 22:15-37 and par.

The Illustrious Men of Ancient Biographies

If Philo writes, it is also in order to remediate a lack, namely the Greek writers' omission of Moses, who, however, merited being regarded as one of the great men[33]. This does not necessarily mean that Philo makes the Greeks his primary readers but that his project in part connects to theirs, to the extent that *De viris illustribus* is a *topos* of which Suetonius, of course, was not the creator. That the praise had been principally developed by Hellenism, no one can deny; that its influence, moreover, had reached as far as the Jewish literature from before our era, numerous passages from Sirach and the Wisdom of Solomon show[34]; that lastly ancient biographies always gave a greater place to the praise – or to the blame, its opposite –, those written by Plutarch fully confirm, which, being subsequent to the Philonian and New Testament narratives, all the more attest to the continuity of the biographical genre and its purpose, which is to cause reflecting upon the essential qualities or virtues that each man[35] must possess in order to lead a life worthy of this name.

Plutarch and the Technique of the *synkrisis*[36]

Everyone knows the *Parallel Lives* of Plutarch; parallel because they come in pairs – each time the author couples a Greek and a Roman: the lives of Theseus and Romulus, of Lycurgus and Numa, of Pericles and Fabius Maximus, of Alcibiades and Coriolanus, of Pyrrhus and Marius, of Lysander and Sulla, of Alexander and Caesar, etc. And if this is so, it is very much in order that the reader may compare the individuals paralleled, as Plutarch himself suggests several times: "Now that we have finished journeying through the life of [Lysander], that of [Sulla], let us pass on to

---

[33] Cf. *De vita Mosis*, 1:1-2.

[34] Cf. the praise of ancestors in Sirach 44–50, and that of wisdom in Wisdom 6–9. The very fact that the Hebrew text for Sirach 44–50 also exists clearly indicates as well that during the era when these chapters were composed, the praise was a known and used genre, even by those who did not write in Greek.

[35] Political men, of course, form an emblematic echelon, for, when these qualities are lacking in them, the effects are catastrophic for them *and* for the nations over which they have charge.

[36] A technique very much used by Plutarch but that one also finds elsewhere in Greek and Roman writers. For Cornelius Nepos, see M. LEDENTU, "Les vies de Cornélius Népos", §25.

the comparison[37] of the two" (Sulla, 39:1)[38]. What then did Lysander, the excellent Spartan from all points of view, and Sulla, the unscrupulous Roman dictator, choleric and cruel, have in common? Nothing or very little, as Plutarch himself emphasizes (*Sulla*, 39–43), for the *synkrisis* does not aim only to show the similarities; it serves equally to highlight the differences, in particular moral. If, on the other hand, Alexander and Caesar are presented together, would it rather not be because of what they have in common? They were the two greatest conquerors of Antiquity, both were thought to have gods for ancestors, both harbored an ambition, a love of great deeds that did not allow them to enjoy in peace the successes achieved. In them, Plutarch saw and described the instability of the human condition, the vanity of ambition and its deadly effects. Going through all these *lives*, the reader must thus continually wonder about the reason for paralleling them, for, with Plutarch, the *synkrisis* becomes the favored instrument of moral judgment and discernment[39].

How does the *synkrisis* help us to understand the Gospel narratives? For in these, one can also note its diverse presence[40]. First, in all the parables that highlight two groups in order to contrast them: the ground that receives the Gospel and makes it fruitful or not[41], the servants who see

---

[37] In Greek, *sygkrisis*, which is written *synkrisis*.

[38] The formulation is similar to that at the end of the lives of Romulus: "Here are the facts worthy of being remembered that we have been able to learn on the subject of Romulus and Theseus" (*Romulus*, 30:1); of Numa: "Now that I have recounted the life of Numa and that of Lycurgus and that I have depicted both of them, it is not necessary to shrink before the task, however difficult, of noting the differences [in Greek, *diaphorai*] between them" (*Numa*, 23:1); of Publicola: "Does not the parallel of these two men [Solon and Publicola] offer something singular and that is not encountered in any of the others about whom we have written, namely that one was the imitator of the other and this one was the guarantor of the other?" (*Pubicola*, 24:1); of Fabius Maximus: "That is what history teaches us of the life of these two men [Pericles and Fabius]" (*Fabius*, 28:1); of Coriolanus: "Now that we have expounded the deeds of these two men [Alcibiades and Coriolanus] ..." (*Coriolanus*, 40:1); of Cato the Elder: "Now that have I reported on these two men [Aristides and Cato] the facts worthy of being remembered, if one compares [in Greek, *paratihèmi*] the entire life of one with the entire life of the other, it is not easy to see the differences that are hidden under numerous and great similarities" (*Cato the Elder*, 28:1).

[39] The technique, very widespread during the era, is systematically used by Plutarch. On this subject, see C.B.R. PELLING, "Synkrisis in Plutarch's Lives", in *Quaderni del Giornale Filologico Ferrarese* 8 (1986) 83-96.

[40] For the technique in Luke/Acts, see J.-N. ALETTI, *Quand Luc raconte, passim*.

[41] See Matthew 13:1-9 and the parallels Mark 4:2-9; Luke 8:4-8.

themselves entrusted with talents and do or do not add to them[42], the travelers who, finding in route a man half-dead, continue on their way without stopping or caring for him with their goods[43], the Pharisee and the publican at prayer[44], or even the rich and the poor with opposite fates[45], etc. The *synkrisis* is also notable in other parables, this time in order to highlight similarities, as in Luke 15:3-10, in which the reaction of the shepherd and the woman are identical. And, despite appearances to the contrary, it is the same with the subsequent parable, that of the Father and the two sons[46], for, as I have shown elsewhere[47], if the elder son and the younger had totally different itineraries, the first wisely remaining close to his father and the second sowing his wild oats as far away as possible from his family home, they reason according to the same principles, those of retributive justice, the limits of which the narrator shows and which he invites leaving in order to enter into the baffling logic of God the Father.

In addition to the parables, the *synkrisis* also structures several episodes of the primary Gospel narrative, by highlighting the similarities or the differences between the actors, their attitudes or reactions, etc. May it suffice to point out here some differences: between John the Baptist and Jesus in Luke 1–2[48], between Martha's reactions and those of Mary in Luke 10:38-42, between the respective interrogations of Jesus and Peter during the Passion, well placed in contiguity by Mark in order to emphasize the opposite responses of the two actors[49]. As for the similarities, it is especially all those established by the Lucan narrator between Peter and Paul (Acts), but above all between Jesus and his disciples, that must be considered, as they highlight the important place of

---

[42] See Matthew 25:14-20; Luke 19:12-26.

[43] Luke 10:29-37.

[44] Luke 18:9-14.

[45] Luke 16:19-31. For a parable highlighting a contrast (or a heightened difference) more than an outright opposition, see the parable of the two debtors in Luke 7:41-42.

[46] Luke 15:11-32.

[47] For a narrative approach to the parable, see ALETTI, *Quand Luc raconte*, 219-267.

[48] These parallels being noted by all commentators, there is no point in focusing on them at length; let us only note that beyond some similarities between John and Jesus, the goal of the *synkrisis* is to show the superior status of Jesus.

[49] See Mark 14:53-72 and parallels. This *synkrisis* between Jesus and Peter was narratively analyzed by A. BORRELL I VIADER, *The Good News of Peter's Denial. A Narrative and Rhetorical Reading of Mark 14:54.66-72* (Atlanta GA, Scholars 1996), who, moreover, points out other uses of the technique in Mark.

the *synkrisis* in the Luke-Acts diptych[50]. Without going back over the reasons for which Luke caused the disciples, especially Paul, to resemble their master and Lord[51], it is now important to ask if the *synkrisis* of the Gospel narratives comes from a Hellenistic influence. The response must be nuanced. If it is impossible to prove for the parables – in particular those that present two groups of actors (three opposed to one) and that seem actually to copy a type of older narrative, the most characteristic example of which is the apologue of Jotham in Judges 9:7-15[52] –, for the Lucan narrative, on the other hand, the Hellenistic influence seems to be accepted.

Perhaps it should be pointed out that Plutarch and Luke are not the only ones to use this technique. Present in other biographies of the era, but to a lesser degree, it had to have been understood by almost all those who went through the *progymnasmata*, as it was a part of its program. And if the *synkrisis* alone does not mean that the Synoptics, Matthew, Mark and Luke, are biographies, adding it to the preceding clues strongly invites the reader to head in this direction.

Suetonius and His Idea of the Biography

Among the ancient biographers, Cornelius Nepos is possibly the most representative of the genre, from the Roman world, of course[53]. But he is the counterpart of the Greek biographers. With Suetonius, on the other hand, whose *De viris illustribus* and *The Twelve Caesars* appeared a little after the Parallel Lives of Plutarch[54], a new concept of the biography

---

[50] On the extent and function of the *synkrisis* in Luke-Acts, see ALETTI, *Quand Luc raconte*, 69-112.

[51] The *synkrisis* between Jesus and Paul has already been pointed out in an almost exhaustive way by A.J. MATTILL, "The Paul-Jesus Parallels and the Purpose of Luke-Acts", in *NovT* 17 (1975) 15-46, and W. RADL, *Paulus und Jesus im lukanischen Doppelwerk* (Berne-Francfort 1975), but its ultimate function remained to be determined, which I have precisely done in *Quand Luc raconte*, 100-103 and 103-111.

[52] With the commentators, let us note the bipartite composition of the passage, with a clear contrast between a first group (the olive tree, the fig tree, the vine) and a second, constituted by the buckthorn. On this type of division, running through the Hebrew Bible, see the analyses of S. BAR-EFRAT, *Narrative Art in the Bible* (Sheffield, Academic Press 1989) 111-140.

[53] He lived in the 1st century B.C. and wrote *De excellentibus ducibus*, in which the praise surfaces on each page.

[54] The two works of Suetonius here mentioned were written in 113 and circa 120 C.E, respectively.

can be glimpsed. Not that the former had renounced the chronological cadre, but, like those of Plutarch, his expositions follow a thematic as well as chronological logic. Of course, the *Life of Augustus* allows seeing that, on at least one point, Suetonius actually does not differ from the biographers of his time. The book indeed begins with a summary (1–8), which the remainder is going to take up in detail, not by following a chronological order but by presenting the events according to categories: wars, political activity and family life.

Having in some way presented the summary of his [Augustus'] life, I am going to examine one by one the different parts, not by following the chronological order [*per tempora*] but [by grouping the facts] by categories [*per species*], in this way making clearer their account and their study. (9)

The arrangement is thus logical, by types of activities, which number 61 adequately highlights by distinguishing between public life and domestic (or family) life. In it, it is clearly apparent that the presentation is principally thematic and that the chronological thread can be completely identified in each of the areas considered:

Having recounted who Augustus was in his commands, in his public offices, and in the administration of his public affairs throughout the whole world, in peace and in war, I am now going to describe his domestic and family life, by recounting what were his conduct and his fate, in his home and in the midst of his own, from his youth until the last day of his life.

Suetonius, furthermore, does not differ from the biographers of that time in his way of treating the marvelous. He in no way hesitates to report visions, as an emblematic episode, that of the crossing of the Rubicon, shows:

As he [Caesar] hesitated, he received a sign from above. A man of extraordinary height and beauty suddenly appeared, seated very close and playing a reed; some shepherds having rushed to hear him as well as a crowd of soldiers from nearby posts, and among them also some trumpeters, this man took the instrument from one of them, rushed towards the river and, sounding the charge with a powerful blast, crossed to the other side. Then Caesar said, "Let us go where the signs of the gods and the injustice of our enemies call us. *Iacta alea est*[55]. "

Suetonius mentions the vision because it is a divine sign: its purpose is thus emphasized; as to its reality, it is indirectly pointed to by the numerous shepherds and soldiers who, in addition to Caesar, are its recipients. This no doubt points to the objective attitude of Suetonius, who, even when he is recounting the intervention of the divine, of the numinous, is looking for objective information – here the number of those who witnessed the event.   For, unlike Plutarch and many other biographers, Suetonius does not want to form the moral judgment of his reader, nor to orient his choices by presenting him with men to imitate or not, possibly because the Caesars whose lives he is writing are exceptional cases; but there is more to it: what interests him is not the moral purpose, but much rather the creation of a true work, by narrating everything about an individual, the good and the bad, so that the portrait is consistent with reality. In this respect, one wanted to charge Suetonius with immorality, for he recounts some racy, to say the least, episodes: actually, it is neither to offend the prudish nor to tantalize the depraved but in order that one may know exactly what happened. Suetonius' project is amoral, in the sense of its being outside of the moral, and veridical: it is through the accumulation of information that, according to him, one can better see how to draw a personality, in its complexity and its truth.   Of course, the veridical project is never absent in the other biographers prior to or contemporary with Suetonius, but they proceed by drastic selection; let us not forget Plutarch's observations mentioned above, according to which it is not necessary to say everything, but to choose the deeds that best show vice or virtue[56]. With Suetonius, it is the description itself that becomes its own goal.

The Gospel narratives find themselves equidistant from those of Plutarch and those of Suetonius. If they are not attempting to recount everything that Jesus did or said, their project is not above all moral. But, conversely, they go further than only a superficial and purely objective presentation of Jesus' behavior: by choosing some episodes from his ministry, they do not aim above all or only to convince the reader that they are speaking the truth, but much rather to inspire his faith or to confirm

---

[55] *Caesar*, 32.
[56] See *Alexander*, 1:2.

it[57]. One will possibly retort that by being accompanied by a radical change of life, the adherence to the faith to which the Gospel narratives invite one is fundamentally connected to Plutarch's moral project. But this is not so, for the Gospels really emphasize the fact that it is the faith in Jesus that causes entering into life. The moral change is described in them as the effect of the acceptance of the teaching of the Master and of the strength received from above. Jesus is less the example of a virtue it is necessary to follow or to imitate than the only one by whom we receive salvation and divine blessings. It is thus the recognition of who he is, Christ and Son of God, in other words faith in him, that the narratives emphasize.

These observations point to where it is necessary for us to look for the most important difference that exists between the Gospel narratives and those of the biographies of pagan authors. For, Cornelius Nepos, Plutarch and Suetonius narrate the lives of men known by all, whether or not paragons of virtue. Yet, at the time when the Gospel narratives were written, Jesus is recognized as a great man neither in the pagan world – where he is not even known –, nor above all in Israel, except by a small group of men who say they are his disciples. Does the evangelists' project thus connect with that of the *Vita Mosis*, in which the extraordinary grandeur of the one who guided the Israelites out of Egypt towards Canaan is shown at length? No, for Moses' grandeur remains undisputed in the eyes of the Israelites of all times, whereas they still contest that of Jesus. If one must thus admit that there is apologia in Philo and in the evangelists, have not the latter, as is commonly said, had to exaggerate the portrait of Jesus in order to make sure that their readers would change the image they had received from the Jews? For such is really the paradox, as already noted above: the Gospel narratives say nothing of the physical appearance, the culture, the scientific and philosophical formation, or even of the remarkable virtues of Jesus. It is less the moral, intellectual and religious excellence of the man that is at stake, but his role and the reason for which

---

[57] Matthew 28:20 implicitly points out that, in order to observe what Jesus prescribed and thus become his disciple, it is necessary to read the preceding micro-narratives that recorded this teaching. Cf. J.P. SONNET, "De la généalogie au "Faites disciples" (Mt 28, 19). Le livre de la génération de Jésus", in C. FOCANT and A. WÉNIN (eds)., *Analyse narrative et Bible. Deuxième colloque international du RRENAB, Louvain-la-Neuve, avril 2004* (BETL 191 ; Louvain, Peeters 2005) 199-209. In the same way, John 20:30-31: the signs written in the book were "that you may believe that Jesus is the Christ, the Son of God, and that believing you may have life in his name". If Mark and Luke do not have the same formulations, the intention of the narrative is clearly from the same order.

it is not recognized by his coreligionists either before or after his death. The narratives thus aim to provide a guide for reading, thanks to which the true identity of Jesus can be accepted; better: confessed.

But this goal is not at all incompatible with the biographical genre, for the different lives written at the time rather point out that the genre in question, as we saw above, is sufficiently flexible to authorize different projects. The real question is another: can the Gospels simply be called *Vitae Jesu*, in other words, does the biographical genre suffice to explain the Gospel project? Of course not, but it gives to it a commodious cadre. Moreover, by choosing this genre, as we will see, the evangelists have confronted some redoubtable difficulties. However, do the clues accumulated up to now suffice to conclude that the Gospels are biographies?

Before providing a more systematic response to this question, we can already reach a decision on what was formulated above regarding the absence of a critique of sources and witnesses in the synoptic Gospels: unlike popular biographies, the Gospel narratives are historiographic works. The historiographers of the era indeed claimed (1°) to research the causes of events, in particular the death of their heroes, (2°) to present the evidence capable of confirming the authenticity of the narrated events in order to separate the true from the false, (3°) to make the present intelligible with the help of the past[58]. That the evangelists depended upon reliable witnesses, namely the disciples chosen by Jesus, today is admitted to by all – but it was not the same at the end of the I[st] century, and one will see further on how the narratives had to show the reliability of Jesus' disciples. As for the search for the causes and the intelligibility of events, it is omnipresent, the Gospels variously explaining why Jesus was not recognized by most of his coreligionists.

Having presented the major traits of the biographies of the era and after broadly comparing them with those of the Gospel narratives, we can directly tackle the question of the genre of the latter.

---

[58] On these two last points, see F. HARTOG, *Évidence de l'histoire. Ce que voient les historiens* (Folio Histoire; Paris, Gallimard 2005) 91-108.

CHAPTER II

HOW DID THE LIVES OF JESUS
COME TO BE WRITTEN?

I. THE NARRATIVE OF MARK AS BIOGRAPHY

Mark, A Biography

The findings of Burridge's monograph, mentioned several times in the preceding chapter, have possibly had the most influence on the research and have furthered a new paradigm. Not only does this work examine the different external[1] and internal[2] traits by which the ancient, Greek or Roman, biographical genre can be recognized, but it also shows that the Gospel narratives belong to this genre, for they have its principal traits, in particular those of the lives of Plutarch[3].

Of the three Synoptics, Mark is the one that least resembles Greco-Hellenistic biographies, so it is important to see whether or not appearances are misleading. This narrative indeed lacks the *genos* and the

---

[1] These *bioi* (1) are narrative prose writings, (2) having as a protagonist (the subject of the majority of the verbs) a well-known man (3) characterized by his words (*logia*) and deeds (*praxeis*), (4) generally in a chronological cadre, (5) that by using various accounts and sources, (6) are able to accommodate sub-genres (discourses, histories, etc.) as well, and (7) that lastly have between 5,000 and 25,000 words. BURRIDGE, *What Are the Gospels?*, 194, adds: "We would do better to search for a genre for the gospels among works of medium length. In fact, Matthew and Luke are comparable to the longest of Plutarch's Lives, such as *Alexander* or *Antony*, while Mark is similar to Plutarch's average length for his *βίοι* of 10,000-11,000 words."

[2] Narratives that go from the birth (or from the beginning of the public life) to the death and that emphasize the *praxeis*, the most developed part of the greatest length. It is interesting to note that in the IInd century, the title given to the second book of Luke, *Praxeis apostolôn*, the *Acts of the Apostles*, reflects the biographical model (the part of the *praxeis*).

[3] BURRIDGE, *What Are the Gospels?*, 105-184. Also see his article, which achieves the same result: "The Problem of the Markan Genre. The "Gospel of Mark" and the Jewish Novel", in *Expository Times* 115 (2004) 244-245. Burridge's monograph was endorsed and extended by that of D. FRICKENSCHMIDT, *Evangelium als Biographie*.

paideia[4], two parts found in almost all the ancient Greco-Roman biographies. The time span of the journey described is short as well. Indeed, from his baptism (Mark 1:10-11) to his death and the announcement of his resurrection (Mark 16:6-7), Jesus celebrated only one Passover, which reduces the time of his ministry to one year at the most. But is this period of time sufficient to make the narrative a biography? Later we will see why the parts devoted to the *genos* and the *paideia* are absent from Mark. To the narrative's time frame being only one year and not the length of a life, we can respond that Mark is not the only one to provide this temporal cadre, the other two Synoptics doing the same. And if that is the duration of Jesus' ministry in Mark, Matthew and Luke, it is not because the narrators have ignored Jesus' prior activity but because their protagonist did not live longer! One can also be surprised that, compared with the contemporary biographies of equivalent length, which extend the words and deeds (*praxeis*) of their protagonists over many more years, the synoptic narratives have proportionally recounted infinitively more of theirs.

By comparing the distribution of the words and deeds (*praxeis*) in the Greco-Hellenistic lives (*bioi*) of that time and those in Mark, Burridge ascertains that it is quantitatively more or less equivalent[5]:

CHAPTERS	VERSES	SUBJECTS	%
1:1-13	13	Preparation and beginnings	2.0
1:14 – 3:6	66	Ministry in Galilee	9.9
3:7 – 6:6	119	Call of the disciples and ministry	17.9
6:7 – 8:26	113	Mission and blindness of the disciples	17.0
8:27 – 10:52	113	Journey to Jerusalem	17.0
11 – 13	114	Ministry in Jerusalem	17.1
14:1 – 16:8	127	Last Supper, Passion, death & resurrection	19.1
Total:	665		100.0

Even if it says nothing about Jesus' birth or education, the Markan narrative, like the Greco-Hellenistic biographies, virtually has for its only subject the *praxeis*[6] of its protagonist throughout his peregrinations, *praxeis* that, like those in the ancient Greco-Roman biographies, are of two

---

[4] The origin (familial, geographical), the birth and the education.
[5] BURRIDGE, *What Are the Gospels?*, 192.
[6] The term generically includes the *words* and the *deeds* of Jesus.

types: those wanted (Mark 1:1 – 14:52) and those sustained[7] (Mark 14:53 – 15:47).

Burridge's table also shows how exaggerated is Martin Kahler's famous statement (at the end of the XIXth century), according to which the Gospels were a narrative of the Passion and death of Jesus preceded by a long introduction; if Mark 14 – 16 only corresponds to 19% of the macro-narrative, one hardly sees how the remaining 80% would be its introduction – an unthinkable proportion according to the biographical canons of the era.

The two elements noted so far, the protagonist and his words and deeds (*praxeis*), are essential to the biographical genre, but they do not suffice. Another formal element is required: in order to be a life (*bios*), a narrative must be autonomous, in other words must not be a part of a macro-narrative into which it could be inserted and without which it would be difficult to understand. For in a narrative like that of Genesis 37 – 50, Joseph's words and deeds (*praxeis*) cover nine decades, from his early youth to his death[8] and provide a temporal cadre that could cause it to resemble a life (*bios*), but the first verses (Genesis 37:1-12) implicitly refer to the history of Jacob, which thus does not need to be presented, nor Joseph's either, his birth having been mentioned in Genesis 30:22-24. Thus, the first sentences of a narrative are often decisive for determining whether its genre is biographical or not. Nevertheless, on their own, they do not suffice, for some narratives, such as those of Tobit, Judith and Esther, begin like lives (*bioi*), but the words and deeds (*praxeis*) of their characters are not extended over an entire life. Mark, being an autonomous narrative describing the words and deeds of Jesus, the protagonist, from the beginning of his ministry until his death, can thus be designated as a biography

---

[7] *Praxeis* that were attributed to fate, considered at that time as a deity (Fortune; in Greek, *Tychè*).

[8] Joseph is seventeen years old when the narrative begins (Genesis 37:2) and one hundred ten when it ends (Genesis 50:22). But of these ninety-three years, fifty-five are mentioned in only four verses (Genesis 50:22-26). The narrator of the history of Joseph develops only the episodes useful to his project. Let us not forget that the Greco-Roman biographers, in particular Plutarch, proceed in a similar way. On the manner in which Genesis 37 – 50 covers the time narrated and makes its choices, one may consult the analyses of A. WÉNIN, *Joseph ou l'invention de la fraternité*, Lessius, coll. Le livre et le rouleau n° 21, Bruxelles, 2005, in particular the chronological table on p. 341-342. Cf. as well M. STERNBERG, *La grande chronologie. Temps et espace dans le récit biblique de l'histoire* (Le livre et le rouleau 32 ; Bruxelles, Lessius 2008) 96-102.

Mark, A Popular Biography

Without denying that Mark is a biography, A.D. Baum, as previously noted, has criticized Burridge's approach[9], which uses only literary or historical biographies as models. In his opinion, the Gospels, and Mark in particular, are not lives (*bioi*) like those of Xenophon, Cornelius Nepos or Plutarch, written for cultured, indeed even well-read, persons but are popular lives (*bioi*), written for ordinary people. Thanks to the findings of the preceding chapter, we will admit with him that Mark and the other two Synoptics belong to the category of popular Greco-Hellenistic biographies. But they are also inspired by narratives from the Old Testament. One could schematize this dual influence by saying that on the formal level Mark and the other Synoptics belong to the Greco-Roman biographical genre and that on the thematic level – that of characterizations, of typology, etc. – they owe much to the Old Testament[10], which it will, of course, be necessary for us to prove. Baum rightly thinks that the first sentences of the Gospels are indicative of this Old Testament influence[11]:

THE BEGINNING OF SOME BOOKS OF THE OLD TESTAMENT	THE BEGINNING OF MATTHEW, MARK, LUKE AND JOHN
The book (*biblos*) of the words of Tobit (son) of Tobiel (son) of Hananiel… (Tobit 1:1).	The book (*biblos*) of the genealogy of Jesus Christ, son of David… (Matthew 1:1)
The beginning (*archè*) of the word of the Lord to Hosea (Hosea 1:2)	The beginning (*archè*) of the Gospel of Jesus Christ… (Mark 1:1)
And there was (*egeneto*) (a word) in the days of Jehoiakim, son of Josiah (Jeremiah 1:3)	There was (*egeneto*) in the days of Herod, king of Judea, a priest… (Luke 1:5)
In the beginning (*archè*), God created the heavens and the earth (Genesis 1:1)	In the beginning (*archè*) was the Word, and the Word was with God (John 1:1)

It is, nevertheless, immediately necessary to add that these lexicographical echoes do not allow determining the genre, historical or popular, of the Gospels, for the borrowed words are found in prophetic

---

[9] A.D. BAUM, "Biographien im alttestamentlich-rabbinischen Stil. Zur Gattung der neutestamentlichen Evangelien", 534-564.

[10] On this dual influence and about the author of the book of Acts, see D. Marguerat's very correct observation: "Luke, all the while fulfilling the mold of Greco-Roman narrative procedures, makes the thematic choice of biblical historians", *La première histoire du christianisme* (LD 180; Paris, Cerf 1999) 36.

[11] The table is BAUM'S, "Biographien", 554.

books (Jeremiah and Hosea) and in narratives that are not biographical (Genesis and Tobit). And if the popular aim of Mark and the other Gospels can be highlighted thanks to the lexicographical echoes and the stylistic turns, it is also, and above all, based on narrative criteria. The table that summarizes Baum's position, of course, points out the dual influence (Greco-Roman and biblical/Jewish) exercised on the Gospels but has for a primary objective emphasizing that the latter have many more traits in common with the biblical and rabbinic narratives rather than with the literary and even popular Greco-Roman bibliographies[12]:

CHARACTERISTICS	PAGAN HIGH *VERSUS* LOW-LEVEL LITERATURE		GOSPELS	JEWISH OLD TESTAMENT RABBINIC	
autonomous form	+	+	+	-	-
anonymous	-	+	+	+	+
no narrator's aside	-	+	+	+	+
opening sentence	-	-	+	+	-
prologue/epilogue	+	*	*	-	-
ordinary prose	-	+	+	+	+
Semitisms	-	-	+	+	(+)
parallelisms	-	-	+	+	+
chiasma	-	-	+	+	+
episodes	*	*	+	*	+
numerous discourses	-	+	+	+	+
direct discourse	-	+	+	+	+
dialogues	-	+	+	+	+
parables	-	-	+	*	+
miracle narratives	-	-	+	+	+
vocation narratives	-	-	+	+	+
didactic project	+	*	+	+	+

With the shading, the table seems to indicate that the Gospels are much closer to biblical narratives[13], but it is misleading, for the left-hand column is composite: if one takes into account only those traits that relate to the genre, it is with the popular Greco-Roman biographies that the

---

[12] BAUM, "Biographien", 562. The traits in common with the Gospels and with the other writings are in gray. The meaning of the symbols: + = frequently; * = from time to time; - = rarely or never.

[13] I am not taking into consideration the rabbinic narratives, far more recent than the Gospels and whose genre would call for a separate study.

Gospels have the most traits in common[14].   And, actually, Baum's criticisms of Burridge must be minimized, for the latter author in his monograph has clearly shown that the biographical genre includes numerous sub-genres; and the table's elements that are common to the Gospels and the writings of the Old Testament, like the miracle and vocation narratives, are in this category.   Moreover, whether or not the author of a biography is anonymous does not change the latter's genre.   In short, one can summarize the preceding expositions by simply saying that the Gospels are popular lives (*bioi*) – whose model is Greek – influenced by the Old Testament for the contents and stylistic/rhetorical formulations.

The last line of Baum's table implies that the goal of the Gospel lives (*bioi*) is didactic.   There are undoubtedly some didactic traits in the Gospels, but one must not forget that the ancient biographies could have other purposes, for example: historical, apologetic or encomiastic – these three characteristics are present in the majority of ancient biographies, even if the praise is more frequent.   The goal of popular biographies is itself also varied: to the praise it is necessary to add entertainment.   The biographical genre of the Gospels being accepted, the question asked of the exegete is then the following: why did the first Christian generations judge it necessary to write popular lives of Jesus?   In order to respond, it is important to determine the dominant trait of each Gospel: historicity, teaching, apologia, or praise?   Here is where the difficulties begin.

II. THE CONDITIONS OF A BIOGRAPHY OF JESUS

The Necessity of a Final Recognition

In his monograph, D. Frickenschmidt compares the Gospels with (almost) all the ancient biographies, pagan and Jewish.   Yet, the protagonists of these narratives were known and even recognized as great men, whether they were politicians, orators, philosophers, writers, military men, legislators, religious…   Although a slave, Aesop was himself also recognized as an eminent fabulist.   In order to be the protagonist of a life (*bios*), a man *had* to be – a condition *sine qua non* – acknowledged to be a great man by his generation and by those that followed.   It is, nevertheless, necessary to add that the recognition of the identity and/or of the value of

---

[14] Namely, an autonomous form, an anonymous author who does not make critical remarks on his sources or on his protagonist, ordinary prose, numerous discourses and dialogues.

the protagonist is not necessarily incompatible with a violent death. Although put to death by the people of Delphi, Aesop was recognized throughout all of Antiquity as one of the greatest fabulists. Similarly, if Epaminondas was falsely accused by the Thebans, his fellow citizens, and threatened with death, he was also recognized after his death as a great general by all Greeks[15]. A rejection or a violent death does not prevent a man of value from then regaining a real fame. But for Jesus, the difficulty came from his coreligionists' rejection of his identity as Messiah and eschatological prophet, even for a long time after his death. The discredit of which he was the subject came not so much from his humble Galilean origins nor from his not having been a great politician, writer, philosopher, military man, legislator, etc., but from his death on the cross for blasphemy and rebellion – a death that furthermore is not announced (at least explicitly) by the Scriptures: the death on the cross of the Messiah was not a part of what was expected, it was even unthinkable. To attempt to write a life of Jesus was thus a challenge, all the more so because a great many literary and popular lives (*bioi*) take after the praise – and one does not write the praise of a man crucified for blasphemy!

Of course, there already existed narratives on Jesus, on his sufferings and his death, on his miracles, on his controversies with legalists; several discourses, parables and aphorisms – that are referred to as *logia* (sayings) – were put down in writing as well; all these texts were used in catechesis and read during the liturgical assemblies of the Churches, at the time of feasts, in particular Easter. Their reading, of course, assumed that Jesus was recognized as Messiah, Prophet and Son of God by the faithful[16], but, conversely, if he were recognized as such by the first communities, it is most certainly because the existing narratives themselves provided keys for reading and responded in their way to the challenge posed by the necessity of a final recognition. How were the narrators, in particular those of the narratives of the Passion and death of Jesus, able to respond to such a challenge?

The Final Recognition in Mark

The narrator of the second Gospel has apparently not succeeded in meeting the challenge. His narrative indeed ends with the death on the cross of a Jesus abandoned by his disciples, rejected by the religious elite

---

[15] CORNELIUS NEPOS, *Vie d'Épaminondas*, 7-8.
[16] Ecclesial reading, *ad intra.*

of his people and even by the crowds that had followed and cheered him throughout his ministry. But, will one object, is there not the beautiful declaration of the centurion (Mark 15:39)? Let us admit that this verse may be an *anagnôrisis*[17]. Nevertheless, according to the literary canons of that time, this recognition does not suffice, for in order to become the protagonist of a biography it was necessary to have been recognized as a man of great value by many: the recognition by a single person could have had value if it had come from someone of importance, who himself was also admired by all; but one could not construct a biography solely on the recognition of a centurion, a foreigner, moreover anonymous. Would not the resurrection, because of its divine origin, be the ideal final recognition? Certainly, but the narrator seems to have cut the ground out from under our feet, for if the resurrection is clearly announced to the women who came to the tomb in order to embalm Jesus (Mark 16:6), they say nothing to any one, and the narrative ends with fear, the reason for their silence, a silence that seems to exclude not only the disciples' recognition but also that of all others. What does a divine recognition that is not transmitted and broadly diffused by human voices signify?

Does this final paradox indicate that the narrator of Mark is not interested in the question of the recognition? It suffices to follow the

---

[17] The recognition – in Greek, *anagnôrisis*, or, beginning with the Hellenistic period, *anagnôrismos* – can be understood in the technical sense or in the broad sense. In the technical sense, in narratives or the theater, it is the recognition of a person previously unrecognized or different in appearance; it can be (1) physical, like Ulysses, when he returns to Ithaca, recognized by his dog and his servant, or even like Chariclea who, on the point of being offered as a prisoner in sacrifice, is recognized by her parents, the queen Persinna and the king Hydaspes of Ethiopia (HELIODORUS, *The Ethiopian Story*, book X), even indeed Joseph who was recognized by his brothers in Egypt (Genesis 45:1-15) or Jesus by the disciples of Emmaus (Luke 24:31), (2) axiological, negatively, like Oedipus at Thebes, finally recognized as responsible for the disastrous situation of the city, whose king he is. In the same way, one will say that there is an *anagnôrisis* for Jesus, whose hidden identity as Messiah and Son of God is recognized by the disciples, whereas his coreligionists in the end recognize him as a blasphemer who seduces and misleads the people. I also use the term in a broad sense in order to designate the recognition of the value and grandeur of the protagonist of Greco-Roman biographies. – Mark 15:39 is interpreted by commentators on the whole as a confession and thus a recognition (*anagnôrisis*). But as in the Septuagint, the expression *ex enantias* is almost always used in battle narratives, some think that, "… the spatial description of the centurion as standing opposite Jesus (*ex enantias autou*), if it has any symbolic or metaphorical force at all, may well signify the initial role of the centurion as an enemy of Jesus or as one who afflicts him". A. YARBRO COLLINS and H.W. ATTRIDGE, *Mark. A Commentary on the Gospel of Mark*, Fortress (Hermeneia; Minneapolis 2007) 765.

narrative thread in order to ascertain that the problem is actually very present, implicitly evoked in the summaries by the narrator[18] and explicitly stated after the miracles (in Greek, *dynameis*) by the crowds[19]. P. Mascilongo has, furthermore, brilliantly shown that the first eight chapters of Mark progressively lead to the declaration at Caesarea (Mark 8:27-30), which makes the recognition of the crowds and the disciples known[20]. This intermediate recognition is not the only one: the reader encounters another, collective as well as shared, at the time of the entrance into Jerusalem (Mark 11:8-10). The narrator of Mark has thus neither forgotten nor avoided the question of the recognition; his multiple mentions give it even more importance than do the Greek and Roman biographies[21]. But the declarations of recognition that Mark accumulates during Jesus' ministry do not suffice, for one could object that these repeated recognitions are those of the crowds and that they have perhaps been obtained by seduction[22] – the crowds allowing themselves to be easily manipulated –, whereas the religious elite do not let themselves be fooled. Yet, Mark in no way indicates a final recognition on the part of the elite or the crowds, but much rather the opposite, a massive rejection. How to interpret this final situation?

The Markan Paradox

Thus, instead of showing that Jesus was recognized as innocent by the other characters, the Passion narrative in Mark retains only the final

---

[18] Mark 1:22, 27-28; 2:13; 3:8; 6:2, 14-16, 55-56; 9:15.

[19] Mark 2:12; 4:41; 7:37.

[20] Paolo MASCILONGO, *"Ma voi, chi dite che io sia?"*. *Analisi narrativa dell'identità di Gesù e del cammino dei discepoli nel Vangelo secondo Marco, alla luce della Confessione di Pietro (Mc 8, 27-30)* (AnBib 192; Rome, Gregorian and Biblical Press 2011).

[21] On this, J.P. Sonnet has pointed out to me a passage from M. Sternberg that I had forgotten and in which the place and the role of the *anagnôrisis* are emphasized: "[...] anagnorisis gets promoted [in the Bible] from an optional to an omnipresent and foregrounded element of plot...", *The Poetics of Biblical Narrative. Ideological Literature and the Drama of Reading* (Indiana Literary Biblical Series; Bloomington IN, Indiana University Press 1985) 177.

[22] An opinion that one finds in John 7:12, 47. Repeated in JUSTIN, *Dialogue with Trypho*, 69:7: "They [the Jews] dared to say that he [Jesus] was a magician [*magos*] and deceived the people [*laoplanos*]." It is difficult to know if Justin is reporting a rumor that arose at the time of Jesus or if it echoes what was said among the Jews of his day. On the subject, see G.N. STANTON, *Jesus and Gospel*, 127-147, according to whom the rumor was already contemporaneous to Jesus.

rejection of which he was the object[23]. Worse still, instead of minimizing or relativizing this rejection, Mark has accentuated it. For what purpose?

Those who study the Markan Passion narrative admit that the motifs of the supplications of the unjustly persecuted faithful have determined the choice of the episodes. The hypothesis was recently proposed for the entirety of the Passion, namely Mark 14 – 15[24]. I myself had already shown that the scenes at the foot of the cross echo in reverse order the motifs of Ps 21/22[25]:

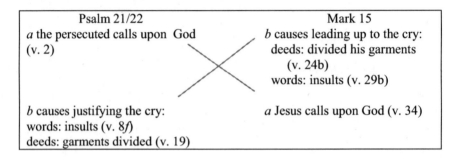

Psalm 21/22	Mark 15
a the persecuted calls upon God (v. 2)	*b* causes leading up to the cry: deeds: divided his garments (v. 24b) words: insults (v. 29b)
b causes justifying the cry: words: insults (v. 8*f*) deeds: garments divided (v. 19)	*a* Jesus calls upon God (v. 34)

The order had to be reversed, for the logic of the Psalm is to formulate the cry (a) and, only afterwards, its motivations, namely the life or death situation of the supplicant (b), whereas, in a narrative, the enemies' deeds and words (b) have the effect of provoking the reaction of the one who is assaulted (a): in the narrative, the cry and the call necessarily follow what has provoked them. In addition to their presence in the scenes at the foot of the cross, the motifs of the supplications of the innocent, as was just said, run throughout Mark 14 – 15. Let us see how!

---

[23] The authorities Mark 14:53, 64; 15:31; Peter and his denial 14:66-72; the passers-by 15:29. Let us note on this point that in Mark, Pilate does not explicitly make a pronouncement on the innocence of Jesus (15:14).

[24] See F. DE CARLO, *"Dio mio, Dio mio, perché mi hai abbandonato?" (Mc 15, 34). I Salmi nel racconto della passione di Gesù secondo Marco* (AnBib 179; Rome, Gregorian & Biblical Press 2009).

[25] J.N. ALETTI, "De l'usage des modèles en exégèse biblique. Le cas de la mort de Jésus dans le récit marcien", in V. COLLADO BERTOMEU (éd.), *Palabra, prodigio, poesìa. In Memoriam P. Luis Alonso Schökel, S.J.* (AnBib 151; Rome, Gregorian & Biblical Press 2003) 337-348.

The Model of the Supplications in Mark 14 – 15.

Two relationships are principally highlighted in the supplications of the persecuted innocent, the one between the supplicant and other men, and that between him and God, as the following two tables show, paralleling the corresponding verses from Mark:

a) The Supplicant and Other Men

- plot of the enemies: Psalm 30/31:14; 63/64:5-7; 70/71:10-11	Mark 14:1-2
- betrayal of a friend: Psalm 40/41:10	Mark 14:10-11
- estrangement or abandonment of friends: Psalm 30/31:12; 37/38:12; 68/69:9; 87/88:19; - isolation of the faithful: Ps 24/25:16; 70/71:11; 141/142:5	Mark 14:50-52 Mark 14:66-72 Mark 14:32-42
- false witnesses, false accusations: Psalm 26/27:12; 34/35:11; 37/38:21; 108/109:4, 29	Mark 14:53-59; 15:3
- the enemies want the death of the faithful: Psalm 12/13:4; 21/22:16; 69/70:3	Mark 14:64; 15:13-14
- insults, sarcasms and provocations: Psalm 21/22:7-9; 30/31:14; 101/102:9	Mark 14:65; 15:16-20, 29, 31
- the supplicant does not respond to the accusations nor to the enemies' sarcasms	Mark 14:60-61; 15:4-5
- the supplicant's religious identity disputed: Psalm 3:3; 41/42:4, 11	Mark 15:31-32
- poison, etc.: Psalm 68/69:21	Mark 15:36

b) The Supplicant and His God

the supplicant assiduously turns towards God alone (and not towards his enemies): all the supplications of the innocent	Mark 14:32-42
God declared as deaf, aloof, or absent: Ps 6:4; 10:1; 12/13:2; 21/22:2	Mark 15:34
the supplicant declares himself to be honest and righteous: Ps 7:9; 16/17:3-4; 25/26:1-8; 58/59:4-5; 85/86:2	

the supplicant does not offer his sufferings to God for the conversion and forgiveness of his enemies[26]	
the supplicant does not know if God loves him nor if He considers him as being faithful: Ps 76/77:8-11	Mark 15:34
what is at stake is divine, for the death of the faithful places God Himself in question, He who promised to protect His faithful. He must save them, so that they may praise Him. Praise being necessary so that God may be recognized as a righteous and all-powerful savior: Ps 6:6; 87/88:11-13; 141/142:8.	

From the tables emerge some important points. (1°) Almost all the episodes of the Passion in Mark contain at least one motif of the supplications of the persecuted faithful; (2°) Mark clearly uses the motifs of these supplications as a narrative thread, in an increasingly dramatic rhetorical ascent, from the initial plot to the death. For Mark, Jesus integrally lived the persecution and the temptation to which the faithful of the Psalms were submitted. (3°) In the already cited article on the death of Jesus on the cross in Mark, I have shown that the motifs echoing the supplications belong to an organized dynamic and form a model, (4°) in some way the final cry must be interpreted in relationship to the entire model. The motifs of Psalm 21/22 echoed by Mark in the scenes at the foot of the cross implied that the cry of Jesus was that of the supplicant from the same Psalm. In technical terms, we will say that Mark constructed and developed a structure. Some exegetes have examined the Greek words *eis ti* from the cry (Mark 15:34) and translate it "to what goal?"; but whatever the nuance of *eis ti* may be, the cry must be interpreted based on all the motifs that precede it and that are its motivations, reasons. The relationship of Jesus on the cross to the innocent of the supplications is clearly *typological*, and the exegete must ask why the narrator of Mark chose the figure of the persecuted innocent of the supplications in order to narrate the Passion/death of Jesus.

Of course, the typological relationship does not prohibit differences between the figure (the type) and the figured (the antitype). Some of the motifs of the supplications are, moreover, absent from the narratives of the

---

[26] In the Markan narrative of the public Passion, which goes from the arrest to the death on the cross, Jesus at no time says that he is offering his life and his sufferings for his enemies. The oblative component is found only at the Last Supper, in Mark 14:24.

Passion in Mark, such as the plea for the total destruction of the enemies[27]. As for the other motifs of the supplications, they are particularly used with regards to the salvific goal of Jesus' death. Indeed, in each episode of the public Passion, in particular when he is hung on the cross, the Jesus of Mark does not offer himself for the forgiveness of his enemies. This does not mean that for Mark the death of Jesus is not salvific, as the words of Jesus over the cup in Mark 14:24[28] show, but that the episodes of the public Passion in Mark faithfully follow the model of the supplications of the innocent up to the final cry of Jesus, a Jesus who experiences the same dereliction, the same rejection, but also the same faith as the innocent of the supplications. The model has prevailed over the other semantic fields[29].

The Psalmic Model and Its Effects on the *anagnôrisis* in Mark

The model faithfully followed by Mark having been highlighted, it is possible to reformulate our astonishment. In the supplications, the innocent is not recognized by any one; all his friends, and seemingly God Himself, have abandoned him. Yet, by using this model and by emphasizing the extreme isolation of Jesus, Mark does not seem to respond to the requirements of biographies concerning the recognition of the protagonist's value. As for the model used by the narrator, it prohibits the protagonist Jesus from being recognized by the other characters in the narrative *because the non-recognition of all other men is an integral part of the model.* Instead of writing an explicitly apologetic life (*bios*) in which Jesus would in the end be recognized by his coreligionists, the narrator of Mark gives the impression of destroying what he wanted to defend.

This being said, the chosen model and the absence of recognition that seem to discredit the Markan Passion narrative are actually a brilliant innovation. The Markan narrative indeed shows that there was not a final recognition on the part of the other human actors *because there did not have to be one.* He overcame the difficulty by highlighting that Jesus,

---

[27] The supplicant's enemies are in fact those of God – Psalm 16/17:13; 27/28:4; 30/31:18-19; 34/35:3-8; 58/59:14; 69/70:3-4; 140/141:7,10.

[28] "This is my blood of the covenant, which is poured out for many". (RSV)

[29] The semantic field of the kingdom is equally present throughout the Passion of Mark (and of Matthew/Luke) but is *narratively* subordinated to the model of the innocent of the supplications.

being in the same situation as the innocent of the supplications, could not and must not be the object of human recognition and, thus, that his narrative could not end with such a recognition. In Mark, as in the Old Testament model that it follows, it is not the human characters who determine the protagonist's value and status *but God alone*. The narrator of Mark has thus found a model in which the final recognition of the human characters does not have a raison d'être. The only recognition that the model calls for and requires is divine[30]. In order to show the existence of this divine recognition, first – that of the public Passion –, the narrator enumerates all the motifs that show that the death of Jesus is that of the supplicants of the Psalms, a truly innocent death *that only needs the divine recognition and that calls for it insistently*; secondly, from the mouth of the young man in Mark 16:6-7, a divine herald, he explicitly mentions the resurrection of Jesus as an effect of this recognition. The final recognition is thus really there. The genius of Mark is not to have eliminated it but, thanks to the choice of the model chosen in order to develop all its characters, that of the supplications of the persecuted innocent of the Psalms, to have by-passed the recognition of the human characters (a horizontal recognition, essential according to the Greek canons) for that of God (a vertical recognition).

The Passion Narrative and Mark as Biography

The recognition (*anagnôrisis*) is thus doubly present in Mark, (1°) horizontally, that is from human voices, those of the crowds and the disciples, up to the entrance into Jerusalem, and, (2°) vertically, prepared for in the Passion narrative and affirmed by the announcement of the resurrection.

Having reached this conclusion, the reader cannot but wonder if writing a biography of Jesus was possible only after the question of the *anagnôrisis* was resolved. From the *praxeis* sustained by Jesus – rejection, suffering and death –, one could then pass to the *praxeis* of which he had been the initiator, in other words his ministry, by showing that the Passion

---

[30] It goes without saying that the centurion's declaration in Mark 15:39 is a solitary (horizontal) recognition, complementary to Peter's in Mark 8:29b. It is thus important to see why the Markan narrator has not omitted it given the Old Testament model followed for the Passion narrative. Some very beautiful studies have been published on this declaration and its Christological function. Let us only repeat here that given the model chosen by Mark, it does not suffice as a final *anagnôrisis*.

and death brought to an end an itinerary with a continuous coherence. Modifying Kahler's statement, we will say that the Passion narrative of Jesus called for a narrative of what had preceded it, in order to show that already at the time of the baptism of John, Jesus acted anonymously in the midst of penitent sinners, that he had then not wanted to be praised for his acts of power (in Greek, *dynameis*[31]), that he had come to call sinners, that he said he had to suffer and be rejected, etc. In doing this, the Markan narrator wanted to show that there was a real continuity between the events of the Passion and the decisions made during the ministry. In short, the Passion narrative in Mark has in large part determined the choice and the dynamic of the episodes of Jesus' ministry, and not the opposite.

There are numerous commentators who question – without finding a decisive answer – why the original ending of Mark is so short and concludes with the mention of the women's fear (Mark 16:8). Without here enumerating all the reasons why this is so, let us only say that this ending is nothing less than logical given the model chosen for the Passion narrative. We have indeed ascertained that the model followed by the Markan narrator for these episodes was that of the Psalms of the persecuted innocent, in which all human – or horizontal – recognition is excluded. If the recognition must only be divine, the message of the resurrection announced to the women by the young man (in Greek, *neaniskos*) representing God suffices. The other, horizontal and collective, recognition by the disciples and/or the other characters of the narrative, consequently does not have a raison d'être. Mentioning it would have quite simply disregarded the chosen structure and model.

One can ask the same question about the absence of a *genos* and a *paideia* at the beginning of the Markan macro-narrative. The answer must be similar to that of the preceding paragraph. The narrator did not need these two parts – in fact, always brief in the ancient Greco-Roman biographies – for what he wanted to show: emphasizing as he does the will of Jesus to avoid all triumphalism during his ministry and to live the rejection of the persecuted faithful during his Passion, these two initial parts, essentially laudatory in most of the biographies of that time, would have been counter-productive and even in contradiction with the rest of the Markan project.

---

[31] On the narrative and theological function of the injunctions to silence in Mark, see S. DE VULPILLIÈRES, *Nature et function des injonctions au silence dans l'évangile de Marc* (EB NS n° 62, Pendé, Gabalda 2010).

The result attained is at the least paradoxical: having at the beginning recalled that the first Christian generation, in principle, neither had to nor could write biographies of Jesus, we come to see that the model brilliantly used by Mark in order to narrate the Passion and death of Jesus had to rely upon words and deeds (*praxeis*) capable of preparing for and justifying these extreme ways, in short, it had to sooner or later give birth to a biography.

III. FOR WHICH READERS WAS MARK WRITTEN?

The narrative of Mark, as just seen, looks like a biography that lacks the *genos*, the *paideia* and the final collective recognition, that of Jesus' coreligionists. The Markan narrative has indeed only kept the words and deeds (*praxeis*), wanted (the ministry) and sustained (Passion and death). Thus, for which readers was such a biography written? Would a Greek be able to accept the absence of a final collective recognition? In chapter IV, we will see why the narrator of Luke inserted into his narrative these three components – the *genos*, the *paideia* (in part) and the final horizontal *anagnôrisis*. Who can thus be the first reader of Mark[32]? The response is not uniform, for the reading could be public or private[33]. Thus, the Gospel episodes read during the liturgical celebrations[34] were then explained, the commentators most probably pointing out the allusions made to the holy Scriptures and their raison d'être. One cannot thus *a priori* say that the faithful of Jewish origin, with a better knowledge of the holy books, were the only ones capable of grasping the allusions to the Psalms of the persecuted innocent in the Markan Passion narrative. One can, on the other hand, speculate that the use of the Psalms as a hermeneutic model for the Passion of Jesus by the narrator of Mark spoke

---

[32] Even if the Gospel episodes were read during the liturgical assemblies within the communities, with Smith, it seems more *ad rem* to examine which reader(s) – and not which community(ies) – the evangelists were aiming at. The ancient *bios* genre was indeed considered by all as open to several categories of readers and not only to a closed or limited audience. Cf. J.M. SMITH, *Why Bíος?*, 132-201.

[33] On this subject, also see SMITH, *Why Bíος?*, *passim*.

[34] Cf., for example, JUSTIN, *First Apology*, 67, that refers to an already well-established practice. In this paragraph, the texts read are called *apomnèmoneumata tôn apostolôn*, "memoires of the Apostles", an expression that clearly designated the Gospels as books, according to the same JUSTIN, *Apology*, 66:3: "The apostles, in the memoires that were written by them and that one calls Gospels [*euaggelia*], …".

more to these faithful and showed them in a convincing way that Jesus had wanted to undergo the extreme and ultimate ordeal of the innocent of the Psalms. By noting in episode after episode of his Passion narrative that Jesus experienced the sufferings of these faithful until his last breath, Mark provided the Jewish disciples of Jesus with keys for reading and a pertinent response to their difficulties concerning the rejection of their coreligionists and the ignominious death of their master.

The disciples of Jewish origin were more familiar with the keys for reading provided by the Passion in Mark. One can, henceforth, assume that the narrative was first written for them. There are, however, one or two places where the narrator addresses his readers as if they were not Jews[35]. It is, however, necessary to avoid proceeding by exclusion, for, even if the first readers of Mark were not Jews, the commentary that accompanied the public reading of the Passion allowed all the hearers, Jewish or not, to recognize the allusions to the Psalms of supplication and to grasp their purpose.

Can one say as well that in addition to these readers, the Markan macro-narrative indirectly aims at non-Christians, in order to correct the erroneous image that they had of Jesus, or, if they had not yet heard him spoken of, to make him known to them? Without a doubt, the apologetic component is present in Mark, for it was incumbent on the first Christian generations to defend the memory of a man unjustly accused and misunderstood[36]. And if it is true that during that era, to write a biography consisted of presenting the value of a man and of offering it for the judgment of the greatest number, the narrator of Mark could not but have had an equivalent project[37]. With the narrative of his life, Jesus could henceforth go beyond the circle more or less closed/open to Christian readers[38].

---

[35] Cf. Mark 7:3.

[36] Some ancient biographies have a pronounced apologetic tone. Cf., for example, Tacitus's *Agricola*.

[37] Like Bauckham and others, G.N. STANTON has recently recalled in his *Jesus and Gospel*, 193, that the evangelists did not write for only one community but "for *all* Christians everywhere" (author's italics).

[38] In his *Evagoras*, 74-75, ISOCRATES was one of the first to state the relationship existing between the spread of biographies (for him the equivalent of praises) and their usefulness: "These [discourses] I prefer to statues because I know, in the first place, that honorable men pride themselves not so much on bodily beauty as they desire to be honored for their deeds and their wisdom: in the second place, because I know that images must of necessity remain solely among those in whose cities they were set up, whereas portrayals in words may be published throughout Hellas, and having been spread abroad in the

IV. CONCLUSIONS

In this chapter, our voyage began with investigating the genre of Mark, a stage necessary for determining its project. Having ascertained that the genre was biographical, we had to see why the evangelist opted for this genre that was apparently prohibited to him, and how, thanks to the model of the supplications of the persecuted innocent, he was able to do without the final collective recognition of Jesus by his people.

What methodological and semantic results does this route put to the fore?

1. It no doubt is useful to recall the importance of literary models, Greco-Hellenistic and biblical. Before investigating the historicity of a pericope, its historical background, the usage of a Christological title, etc., it is important to single out the models that structure it. In other words, the literary analysis is the basis upon which all the others rest.

In contrast to historians who interpret the facts of the Passion narrative without taking into consideration the models at work, it is thus necessary to recall that identifying the model followed by the Markan narrator is necessary in order to avoid misinterpretations. And yet, highlighting a model does not suffice; it is also important to determine its exact function in order for it not to say what it does not. If the last cry of Jesus in Mark only has meaning in relation to the model to which it belongs, one cannot, however, draw apodictic historical conclusions and declare, for example, that in dying the Jesus of history pronounced the phrase mentioned in Mark: "My God, my God, why have You forsaken me?": One cannot pass, except with caution, from one level of interpretation (or of meaning) to another – an elementary rule, unfortunately often forgotten.

Mark is not reporting all the episodes and details of the Passion but chooses the pertinent elements for the meaning that he intends to promote. Not that he has distorted or mutilated the reality, but he is presenting a key for reading it, by integrating the details into a semantic structure that

---

gatherings of enlightened men, are welcomed among those whose approval is more to be desired than that of all others; [75] and finally, while no one can make the bodily nature resemble molded statues and portraits in painting, yet for those who do not choose to be slothful, but desire to be good men, it is easy to imitate the character of their fellow-men and their thoughts and purposes—those, I mean, that are embodied in the spoken word" (Translation G. Norlin, 1980). A part of this passage is cited by J.M. SMITH, *Why Bίος?*, 170.

reveals its meaning. For whomever knows the models used by the four narratives of the Passion/death of Jesus, the differences and contradictions do not come from erroneous sources or from lacuna that make the narratives unreliable but from the respect that each narrator has for the chosen model(s).

2. The difficulty raised by the necessary presence of a final *anagnôrisis* was smoothed over thanks to typology, in other words, by recourse to the motifs of the supplications of the innocent persecuted faithful. The typology used by Mark in order to describe the Passion of Jesus is structuring, and one cannot overly emphasize its importance.

3. Let us return, in order to conclude, to the hypothesis formulated above: the facts presented strongly invite admitting that the development of the macro-narrative of Mark was made based on his narrative of the Passion and death of Jesus. Let us go further: the narrative of the Passion/death in Mark was not only written before that which narratively precedes it, namely Mark 1 – 13, but it also determines the presentation and the development of the Christology of these first thirteen chapters, in particular the importance of the injunctions to silence, the increasing incomprehension of the disciples, etc.

If this is so, we find ourselves faced with a final paradox: the narrative approach must, in principle, follow the thread of the macro-narrative from the beginning to the end; nevertheless, the most respectful presentation of the Markan project seems to have to begin with the end. This is what we have actually done here. In short, if the model of the supplications of the persecuted innocent ordered the Markan Passion narrative, it has also had its influence on the configuration and on the physiognomy of the remainder of the macro-narrative.

CHAPTER III

THE GOSPEL OF MATTHEW
AND THE BIOGRAPHIES OF ITS TIME

I. INTRODUCTION

The preceding chapter has set out how the Markan narrator succeeded in overcoming the handicap that seemed to prohibit the disciples of Jesus from writing the life of their master. But does this mean that this essay opts for the anteriority of Mark over Matthew and is ignoring the debates on the synoptic problem, in particular the reasons of those for whom Matthew would have been the first Gospel[1]? Before locating ourselves in the spectrum of positions, let us recall that if it is necessary to make minute comparisons between the pericopae of Matthew/Mark, it is also necessary not to lose sight of the social, cultural, political and religious environment of the second half of the Ist century of our era: the opposition and attacks were not the same in the 60s, the 80s and at the end of the century. The criticisms of which the leaders of the Christian movement were the subject in the 80s led Luke to write the book of Acts in order to show that there was not a break between Jesus and his disciples, that they were faithful to their master's teaching, etc. It is wrong to imagine that in such circumstances the Markan redactor would have been able to write a narrative in which the negative performance of these disciples carried water to the well of those who denigrated them. The portrayal of the disciples in Mark assumes a time in which one could still have emphasized their increasing incomprehension, their fears and their dispersal during the Passion, possibly because most of the Twelve were

---

[1] Several exegetes are still in favor of the priority of Matthew over Luke and Mark. Among the most known at the end of the XXth century, W.R. FARMER, *The Synoptic Problem. A Critical Analysis* (Dillsboro NC, Western North Carolina Press 1976); B. ORCHARD, *Matthew, Luke & Mark (The Griesbach Solution to the Synoptic Question I)* (Manchester, Koinonia Press 1976); D.L. DUNGAN, *A History of the Synoptic Problem. The Canon, the Text, the Composition, and the Interpretation of the Gospels* (Anchor Bible Reference Library; New York, Doubleday 1999).

still living and could have given believers the reasons for their pre-Pascal poor performance. That is why it seems improbable that Mark was written after Luke/Acts. But what about Matthew and Mark? Their Passion narratives, as we will see, do not allow deciding between them chronologically. Might the infancy narrative in Matthew 1 – 2, which corresponds to the *genos* section of Greek and Roman biographies? As a positive or negative response does not immediately impose itself[2], it will be necessary to review the characteristics and the purpose of each narrative, in particular the role played by the problem of the final *anagnôrisis*.

Whatever the dating may be, specialists of the Gospels on the whole accept that "Matthew is undoubtedly closer to Mark than to any other ancient biography[3]", even if it has more traits in common with the latter than Mark: "By his addition of infancy narratives and his fuller passion and resurrection narratives, Matthew links his gospel even more closely to the ancient biographical tradition[4]." This result was only recently established, but for a minority of specialists, Matthew belongs to the *gospel* genre, a new genre, *sui generis*, for reasons that it will suffice to recall briefly. Jesus indeed says at the beginning of the discourse on the end of time (in Matthew 24:14):

This Good News of the Kingdom [*touto to euaggelion tès basileias*] will be preached throughout the whole world; all the pagans will have it as a testimony. And then will come the end.

Also, in response to the disciples who, at Bethany, are indignant at seeing the expensive perfume poured out (Matthew 26:13), he declares:

Wherever is preached this Good News [*to euaggelion touto*] in the whole world, what she has done will be told in memory of her.

If one can question whether in Matthew 24:14 the expression *this Good News* is designating Matthew in its entirety, it is not the same with

---

[2] For, as was pointed out in the preceding chapter, given his project and the chosen model, the Markan narrator did not need the *genos* part of biographies and could have simply by-passed it. The presence or absence of this part is in and of itself not decisive for the dating of the macro-narrative.

[3] Thus, for example, G.N. STANTON, *A Gospel for a New People*, 66.

[4] *Ibid.* The author clearly opts for the anteriority of Mark.

Matthew 26:13, where Jesus seems to present the Matthean narrative as the basis of the Gospel or the means by which it is known, and as the appellation *euaggelion* comes from Jesus himself, it seems apodictic. To this interpretation, it has quite rightly been objected that, even if Jesus were thus designating the Matthean narrative – an all the more extravagant hypothesis as the text had not yet even been written when Jesus makes this statement –, he is not alluding to the genre (gospel) but to the message (of the Gospel).

The "gospel" hypothesis being ruled out, let us ask if Matthew has the traits of Greco-Roman biographies. And if the answer to this question is positive, why was this genre preferred to others?

II. THE BIRTH AND INFANCY NARRATIVE. MATTHEW 1 – 2

According to the opinion of Stanton noted above as well as that of numerous other specialists, it is first of all because of the episodes referred to as the infancy that the Matthean narrative has in the end been considered as belonging to the biographical genre. One has, nevertheless, asked whether the genre of these first two chapters were not biblical or Jewish, more precisely *biblos geneseôs*[5], for the narrative begins thus: *biblos geneseôs Ièsou Christou hyiou David hyiou Abraam* (Matthew 1:1); a nominal phrase that is difficult to translate: "The book of the *genesis* of Jesus Christ, son of David, son of Abraham" (JB) or "The book of the *origins* of Jesus Christ..." (TOB)? If today one admits that the expression *biblos geneseôs* does not have the function of indicating the genre of the macro-narrative, we still wonder about its import: is it announcing the entire Gospel of the Infancy, in other words Matthew 1 – 2, or only the genealogy of Matthew 1:1-17?

Matthew 1:1-17: The literary Genre

With the commentators, let us note that this first sentence of Matthew clearly mirrors the biblical genealogies, which have diverse

---

[5] Thus, G.N. STANTON, "Matthew: *biblos, euaggelion* or *bios*?", in F. VAN SEGBROECK et al. (ed.), *The Four Gospels. Festschrift Frans Neirynck* (BETL 100; Leuven, Leuven University Press 1992) 1187-1201, for whom Matthew belongs to the *bios* genre.

functions according to where they are found[6]. Which raises another question: is the model of Mathew 1 – 2 Greek or biblical? As such, the genealogy of Matthew 1:1-17 copies those of the Old Testament that precede the birth and history of Noah (Genesis 5:1-32) and that of Abraham (Genesis 11:10-32). The two genealogies indeed respectively connect these patriarchs to the most distant human past, but they also point out that each time a new era is about to begin. Matthew 1:1-17 as well has the function of connecting Jesus to the history of Israel at the same time as it indicates that he is going to be the royal/messianic protagonist of the narrative that is going to follow. But if the genealogies of Genesis just mentioned explain the form and the function of Matthew 1:1-17, one, nevertheless, must not exclude the influence of Greek biographies. For if, unlike the biblical books, there is not a genealogy – in the strict sense – in these Greco-Roman narratives, one often finds in them a brief equivalent: before the presentation of the protagonist of a life (*bios*), mention is made of his ancestors, in order to show that the hero's excellence was preceded by that of his ancestors. Two examples from writers contemporary to Matthew, one Greek, Plutarch, and the other Roman, Tacitus, will illustrate the fact:

> Pericles was of the tribe Acamantis, of the deme Cholargus, and of the foremost family and lineage on both sides. His father, Xanthippus, who conquered the generals of the King at Mycale, married Agariste, granddaughter of that Cleisthenes who, in such noble fashion, expelled the Peisistratidae and destroyed their tyranny, instituted laws, and established a constitution best tempered for the promotion of harmony and safety. [2] She, in her dreams, once fancied that she had given birth to a lion, and a few days thereafter bore Pericles.
> PLUTARCH, *Pericles*, 3,1-2[7].

Cnaeus Julius Agricola was born at the ancient and famous colony of Forum Julii. Each of his grandfathers was an Imperial procurator, that is, of the highest equestrian rank. His father, Julius Graecinus, a

---

[6] On the biblical genealogies and their function, see, for example. L. RAMLOT, "Les généalogies bibliques. Un modèle oriental", in *Bible et vie chrétienne* 60 (1964) 53-70; R.R. WILSON, "The Old Testament Genealogies in Recent Research", in *JBL* 94 (1975) 168-169, and M.D. JOHNSON, *The Purpose of the Biblical Genealogies with Reference to the Setting of the Genealogies of Jesus* (SNTSMS 8; Cambridge UK, Cambridge University Press 1988; original 1969).

[7] Transl. of B. PERRIN, *Perseus Library*.

member of the Senatorian order, and distinguished for his pursuit of eloquence and philosophy, earned for himself by these very merits the displeasure of Caius Caesar. He was ordered to impeach Marcus Silanus, and because he refused was put to death. His mother was Julia Procilla, a lady of singular virtue. Brought up by her side with fond affection, he passed his boyhood and youth in the cultivation of every worthy attainment.

    TACITE, *Agricola*, IV, 1-3[8].

These examples are typical: all or almost all of the biographies of that time devote at least one or two sentences to the parents and/or ancestors of their protagonists. It is thus not necessary to reason by exclusion: if the genre of Matthew 1:1-17 is clearly biblical, it also has the function of the first elements of the *genos* of the Greco/Roman biographies. What about the other pericopae of Matthew 1 – 2?

Matthew 1 – 2 and Ancient Greek Biographies

These chapters were and still are the subject of numerous studies. Here, it is not a question of making a commentary on them but only of seeing if they have the characteristics of the part of the ancient biographies that concern the origin (*genos*) of their protagonist and of highlighting the original manner in which the Matthean narrator has followed the model.

What characteristics make Matthew 1 – 2 a part devoted to the *genos*?
1. Specialists note that the parts reserved for the *genos* and the *paideia* are relatively brief in the Greco-Roman biographies contemporary to the Gospels. It is similar in Matthew and in Luke[9].
2. The excellence of the ancestors is indicated in the genealogy not only by the status of kings, but it is also shown to be moral and religious in the person of Joseph, a righteous man, obeying the will of his God and fully accepting the paternal role confided to him.
3. The coming and status of the protagonist were certainly wanted by God, but several times the narrator emphatically declares – thus clearly stating

---

[8] Transl. of A.J. CHURCH and W.J. BRODRIBB, 1877.

[9] According to the statistics, Matthew 1:1 – 2:23 would represent 4.5% of the macro-narrative, and Luke 1:5 – 2:52, 11%. Let us recall that this part is lacking in Mark, and that in John, the prologue on the origin (John 1:1-18) makes up 2% of the whole. See R.A. BURRIDGE, *What Are the Gospels?*, 191-192.

his point of view – that they fulfill prophecies, in other words that the events described refer to the divine word from the past and show its efficacy: God has not lost His memory! The protagonist's journey is thus inseparable from the prophecies and, with them, the history of Israel.

4. The protagonist and his parents are located geographically as well: Jesus is born in Bethlehem (Matthew 2:1), a royal city, but is going to spend his childhood in Nazareth, a city of Galilee without fame (2:23).

5. What is mentioned in the origin is generally encomiastic, and Matthew does not make an exception to the rule. The reading of Matthew 1 – 2 does not allow knowing if the parents of Jesus are rich or poor, for nothing is said of their social condition[10], unlike Luke who, although he also accentuates the divine origin of Jesus, once or twice implies that the parents are from humble circumstances[11]. However, if the royal origin of Joseph, and thus of Jesus, is accentuated in the genealogy and in the remainder of this section, Joseph associates neither with kings nor princes, since Jesus is not born in a royal palace and, if there had not been the visit of the Magi, his birth would have passed unnoticed in Judea.

6. In addition to the royal and messianic identity of Jesus stated by the narrator (Matthew 1:16), which combines the origin and purpose, the infancy narrative provides through the voice of the angel a decisive complement: Jesus will be the son of God for, "that which is conceived in her [Mary] is of the Holy Spirit" (Matthew 1:20) and savior, for "he will save his people from their sins" (1:21); Jesus is placed in relationship to God and to mankind – he will always be with them, Emmanuel –, two traits about which only Joseph and the reader are informed. The narrative thus begins with a high Christology, furthermore: revealed by God Himself. Matthew 1 – 2 thus provides the reader with the dual origin of Jesus: he is both the son of man, more specifically king/Messiah, and the son of God, savior. In Matthew 1, the first identity is provided by the narrator (to the reader), the second, by the angelic voice (to Joseph and the reader). To these two voices is added in Matthew 2 that of the Magi (to Herod, to the inhabitants of Jerusalem and to the reader), who state the royal identity (*king of the Jews*)[12] in their own way. One will have noted

---

[10] It is necessary to wait for Matthew 13:55 in order to learn that Joseph was a manual laborer, a carpenter.

[11] Cf. Luke 2:7 and 24, as well as note 7 in the next chapter.

[12] The expression "the king of the Jews/Judeans" can come only from non-Jews/Judeans. For members of the elect people would have said "the king of Israel", a difference that one also encounters in the narrative of the Passion (compare Matthew 27:29, 37 and 27:42).

the difference existing between the divine statement and that of the Magi. The first is a revelation, the second an *anagnôrisis*.

7. This last word is of importance, for, as we will have to demonstrate, the question of the recognition is going to be one of the guiding themes of the Matthean narrative. Matthew 2 sets in motion the problem of the recognition of the royal or messianic identity of Jesus and the rejection of which he will be the object. From his birth, the king/Messiah is recognized *and* rejected – recognized by foreigners and rejected by the highest political authority of his people. Threat and death constitute from the beginning the background of the narrative. In presenting the drama, the Matthean narrator still indirectly makes his point of view known. Indeed, neither the Magi nor Herod have seen the infant; they thus do not know the king/Messiah of whom they are speaking, the first only having had a sign, a star, directing them to go and worship him[13], and the second having only the information from the holy Scriptures of Israel for knowing where he was born. Learning that the newborn object of the coming of the Magi is the Messiah, Herod wants him to die and, in order to be sure of achieving his goals, orders putting to death all the children of the same age in the region of Bethlehem. Herod's rejection, which shows a will of non-reception, announces that of the religious authorities of Israel.

All the traits that have just been noted show as well that Matthew 1 – 2 is the introduction in due form of the Matthean macro-narrative; thanks to the intervention of the angel of God, these chapters indeed provide, in a completely reliable manner, the identity of the protagonist, in his origin and his role; they announce as well the drama that will run throughout the narrative: why did Israel not recognize in Jesus its Messiah?

The existence of a part dedicated to the *genos* of Jesus, the protagonist, certainly does not suffice to assure the Matthean macro-narrative's fully belonging to the biographical genre. But by declaring from the first lines that Jesus is the Messiah of Israel (Matthew 1:1, 16, 18) and that he is because God has wanted it to be so (Matthew 1:20-21), the narrator indirectly points out that, by his royal/messianic and divine dignity, *he has the right to a biography*. If there is a figure whose excellence is recognized by all the Israelites of that time, it is that of the

---

[13] In Matthew 2:11, the Greek reads *prosekunèsan* ("worship", "to bow down to"), a verb that one encounters 13 times in this narrative (2 times in Mark, 3 times in Luke and 7 times in John, respectively) and that has a strong meaning, as Jesus' response to Satan in Matthew 4:10 shows, which positively repeats ("You shall worship the Lord your God") what Deuteronomy 5:9 said negatively ("You shall not worship [idols]").

Messiah. The difficulty, however, comes from the discrepancy that exists between the status of Jesus – reported by the narrator – and his rejection, his ignominious death, as it is known by the Jewish contemporaries of the Matthean narrator. He is thus going to have to show that the death on the cross of Jesus in no way ruins the grandeur nor the value of his protagonist.

III. THE MODEL OF THE MATTHEAN PASSION NARRATIVE

Recognition and Rejection in Matthew

Before seeing how Matthew confronts the question of the recognition, it is necessary to show that he did pose it and that it has a role in the unfolding of the narrative. Can one note throughout the episodes some clues that authorize a reliable response?

During the ministry of Jesus, the narrator points out numerous reactions of recognition. The problem is thus very much present, made known by the narrator but also explicitly stated by the characters. Jesus' renown reaches the surrounding regions[14], and the crowds, hearing him spoken of, come from everywhere to meet him, they bring to him their sick[15], give thanks for his miracles[16], follow him assiduously[17], are struck by the authority of his teaching[18], and see in him a great prophet[19], their

---

[14] Matthew 4:24, the narrator (Nr): "So his fame spread throughout all Syria." Also, 9:26.

[15] Matthew 4:24, by the Nr: "They brought him all the sick, those afflicted." Matthew 8:16 as well.

[16] Matthew 9:8, the Nr: "When the crowds saw it, they were afraid, and they glorified God, who had given such authority to men." Also, 9:33; 12:23; 15:31.

[17] Matthew 4:25, the narrator's information: "And great crowds followed him from Galilee and the Decapolis and Jerusalem and Judea and from beyond the Jordan." Also, 8:18; 12:15; 13:2, 36; 14:14; 15:30; 19:2.

[18] Matthew 7:28-29, by the Nr: "The crowds were astonished at his teaching, for he taught them as one who had authority, and not as their scribes." Also, 13:54.

[19] Matthew 16:14, the disciples reporting the crowds' opinion: "Some say John the Baptist, others say Elijah, and others Jeremiah or one of the prophets"; 21:8-10 and 15, at the time of the triumphal entry into Jerusalem: "Hosanna to the Son of David", and in 21:11: "This is the prophet Jesus from Nazareth of Galilee"; 21:46 the narrator mentions the reaction of the chief priests and the Pharisees to the crowds' opinion: "[they] feared the multitudes, because they held him to be a prophet."

recognition spreading to the point of being known by the political leader[20]. As for the disciples, they themselves also, at crucial moments, give their opinion, when Jesus invites them to make a decision about his identity and at the time of the entrance into Jerusalem[21]. The last two declarations of recognition take place during the Passion and are individual, that of Pilate's wife during the trial[22], then that of the centurion and his men after the death of Jesus[23].

That the recognition is constitutive of the Matthean narrative – as it is for the Markan, which we ascertained in the preceding chapter –, and that the narrative loses its raison d'être without it, Jesus' questions to the disciples in Matthew 16:13-18 eminently show, as well as his repeated reproaches to the Israelites of his generation and his emphasis on the terrible consequences of their rejection[24]. For during Jesus' ministry, the recognition of the crowds is not accompanied by that of the religious elite.

In Matthew, as in Mark, opposition indeed alternates with recognition and is progressively intensified. There are numerous passages in which it is pointed out and even highlighted. The first negative declaration comes from the Pharisees, in Matthew 9:34: "He casts out demons by the prince of demons." A strong accusation that makes Jesus an agent of evil, a *magos*, a magician, and it will be reiterated in 12:24 by the same actors, those who will have already planned having him put to death[25]. Jesus does not ignore the contempt of which he is the object[26],

---

[20] Matthew 14:2 in which Herod declares: "This is John the Baptist, he has been raised from the dead; that is why these powers are at work in him."

[21] Matthew 14:33: "Truly you are the Son of God!" Also, Matthew 16:16, when Jesus asks them to make a decision about his identity: "You are the Christ, the Son of the living God."

[22] Matthew 27:19: "his wife sent word to him, 'Have nothing to do with that righteous man!'"

[23] Matthew 27:54 [RSV]: "Truly this was a son of God."

[24] Matthew 11:21-24: "Woe to you, Chorazin! woe to you, Bethsaida! for if the mighty works done in you had been done in Tyre and Sidon, they would have repented long ago in sackcloth and ashes. But I tell you, it shall be more tolerable on the day of judgment for Tyre and Sidon than for you. And you, Capernaum, will you be exalted to heaven? You shall be brought down to Hades. For if the mighty works done in you had been done in Sodom, it would have remained until this day. But I tell you that it shall be more tolerable on the day of judgment for the land of Sodom than for you." Also, 12:39.

[25] An observation of the narrator in 12:14: "But the Pharisees went out and took counsel against him [Jesus], how to destroy him."

[26] "The Son of man came eating and drinking, and they say, 'Behold, a glutton and a drunkard, a friend of tax collectors and sinners!'" (Matthew 11:19)

that he will progressively characterize as a deadly rejection[27] and that in the end the narrator will present as a plot[28] finding its realization in the Passion and death of Jesus.

One of the last accusations, that of Matthew 27:63, calls for a brief comment. Barely dead, Jesus is accused by the chief priests and the Pharisees of having deceived the crowds by having assumed a false identity, in short, of being an impostor (in Greek, *planos*)[29]. But if Matthew mentions this accusation, it is because during the era when he is writing, it has become current among the Jews. If the actual narrative of Mark had been written after that of Matthew, he, in order to remain reliable, would also have had to mention it and, as needed, refute such an accusation[30] – a probable, supplementary clue to the anteriority of his macro-narrative.

The numerous mentions of recognition and opposition that were just noted are scattered throughout the Matthean macro-narrative and show that, like the narrator of Mark, that of Matthew neither has forgotten nor avoided the question of the *anagnôrisis*. But the declarations of recognition that he accumulates during Jesus' ministry do not suffice, for one could object that these repeated recognitions are those of the crowds and that they were obtained by seduction. For in no way does Matthew point to a final recognition – from the beginning of the Passion to the death of Jesus – on the part of the elite or the crowds, but much rather the opposite, a massive rejection. How to interpret this final situation?

The preceding chapter on the Markan Passion narrative has shown that the narrator took from the holy Scriptures of Israel the model of the individual supplications of the persecuted faithful, which excludes the recognition by other men of the righteousness of the supplicants. But how is this done, in other words: what model does the Matthean narrator use to honor the problem of the recognition, in order to show that the final rejection of which Jesus was the object does not disqualify his biography?

---

[27] Matthew 16:21; 17:22-23; 20:18-19; 23:37; 26:2. Already implicitly in 16:4.

[28] Matthew 21:45-46; 26:3 and 14-16. In Matthew, unlike in Mark and Luke, the Pharisees are reported as participating in the plot.

[29] The word means "deceitful". Deceitful, for he would have caused believing that he was a prophet, king/Messiah, Son of God, etc. The accusation will be repeated and amplified in the IInd century in the disputes between Jews and Christians. Cf. note 32 in the preceding chapter on this accusation raised by Justin (*Dialogue with Trypho*, 69:7).

[30] In the Markan narrative of the appearance before Pilate, the implicit accusation, related by Pilate in the form of a question, concerns the kingship of Jesus. But there Jesus' coreligionists do not say the words *magos* or *planos*.

The Matthean Model of the Passion/Death of Jesus

If one reads and compares the three narratives of the Passion/death of Jesus in the Synoptics, one cannot fail to note that Matthew and Mark are very close to each other: the arrangement of the episodes is exactly the same[31], and the vocabulary is on this point so identical that one cannot but wonder which one copied the other. It is, moreover, the vocabulary that merits our attention, for the motifs of the supplications that irrigate and constitute the semantic structure of the Passion narrative in Mark are also found in that of Matthew. It is now up to us to ascertain whether Matthew, like Mark, describes the Passion and the death of Jesus by using as a model the figure of the persecuted righteous from the Psalms of supplication.

The tables that follow repeat those from the chapter on Mark and show how many of the same motifs of the supplications run throughout both narratives; two relationships, the one between the supplicant and other men as well as that between him and God, are treated in Matthew as in Mark, up until the final cry of Jesus:

a) The Supplicant and Other Men

- plot of the enemies: Ps 30/31:14; 63/64:5-7; 70/71:10-11	Mark 14:1-2	Matthew 26:3-4
- betrayal of a friend: Ps 40/41:10	Mark 14:10-11	Matthew 26:14-16
- estrangement or abandonment of the friends: Ps 30/31:12; 37/38:12; 68/69:9; 87/88:19; - isolation of the faithful:	Mark 14:50-52	Matthew 26:56

---

[31] Gethsemane, Matthew 26:26-36 = Mark 14:32-42; arrest, Matthew 26:47-56 = Mark 14:43-52; appearance before the Sanhedrin followed by insults, Matthew 26:57-68 = Mark 14:53-65; Peter's denial, Matthew 26:63-74 = Mark 14:66-72; the trial before Pilate, Matthew 27:11-26 = Mark 15:1-15; soldiers' insults, Matthew 27:27-31 = Mark 15:16-20; crucifixion, Matthew 27:32-44 – Mark 15:21-32; death of Jesus, Matthew 27:45-54 – Mark 15:33-39. A single supplementary episode in Matthew, that of the death of Judas in 27:3-10. On the other hand, and for reasons that we will see, two episodes are not in the same order in Luke: Peter's denial and the insults precede the session before the Sanhedrin; Luke has inserted as well an appearance before Herod (23:6-12) in the midst of the trial before the Roman governor.

Ps 24/25:16; 70/71:11; 141/142:5		
- false testimonies, false accusations: Ps 26/27:12; 34/35:11; 37/38:21; 108/109:4, 29	Mark 14:53-59; 15:3	Matthew 26:59-62
- the enemies want the death of the faithful: Ps 12/13:4; 21/22:16; 69/70:3	Mark 14:64; 15:13-14	Matthew 26:66; 27:22-23
- insults, sarcasms and provocations: Ps 21/22:7-9; 30/31:14; 101/102:9	Mark 14:65; 15:16-20, 29, 31	Matthew 26:67-68; 27:27-31; 41
- the supplicant does not respond to the accusations nor to the sarcasms of the enemies	Mark 14:60-61; 15:4-5	Matthew 26:62-63; 27:12-14
- the supplicant is contested in his religious identity: Ps 3:3; 41/42:4, 11	Mark 15:31-32	Matthew 27:40-43
- poison, etc.: Ps 68/69:21	Mark 15:36	Matthew 27:48

b) The Faithful and His God

- the supplicant assiduously turns towards God only (and not towards his enemies): all the supplications of the innocent	Mark 14:32-42	Matthew 26:36-46
- God declared deaf, aloof or absent: Ps 6:4; 10:1; 12/13:2; 21/22:2	Mark 15:34	Matthew 27:46
- the supplicant declares himself to be honest and righteous: Ps 7:9; 16/17:3-4; 25/26:1-8; 58/59:4-5; 85/86:2		
- the supplicant does not offer his sufferings to God for the conversion and forgiveness of enemies		
- the supplicant does not know if God loves him and considers him as His faithful: Ps 76/77:8-11	Mark 15:34	Matthew 27:46
- the stakes are divine, for the death of the faithful places God Himself in question, He who has promised to protect His faithful. He must save		

them, so that they may praise Him – the praise being necessary so that God may be known as a righteous and all-powerful savoir: Ps 6:6; 87/88:11-13; 141/142:8		

What was said concerning the Markan Passion narrative is valid for Matthew's, and the reader can reread in the preceding chapter the commentary on the tables of the motifs of the supplications. May it suffice to repeat here that, from the mention of the plot until the cry of Jesus on the cross, Matthew himself also echoes the motifs of the supplications of the unjustly persecuted faithful and strings them together like pearls. For the Matthean narrator, as for the Markan, Jesus entirely submitted to the persecution and the temptation to which the faithful of the Psalms were submitted.   Like Mark, he gave to the motifs of these Psalms the chronological cadre of the Passion, and, similarly, his Jesus experienced the same dereliction, the same rejection, but also the same faith as the innocent of the supplications.

Of course, just as in Mark, the death of Jesus in Matthew is not only that of the unjustly persecuted faithful, for the narrator emphasizes as well that the crucified is the Christ/Messiah, the king of Israel[32] – which for Matthew worsens the responsibility of those who handed him over[33] –, that his death causes the *eschaton* to occur[34].   But the psalmic model covers the others.

The Psalmic Model and the Question of the *anagnôrisis*

The dominant model followed by Matthew is thus that of the supplications in which the innocent is not recognized by any one; all his friends, and God Himself to whom he appeals, have abandoned him. For this model, as already seen in the preceding chapter, prohibits the protagonist Jesus from being recognized by his people: *the non-recognition by all other men is an integral part of the model*. In fact, a *collective* recognition of any kind is absent from Matthew, since the disciples have fled and the entire people have asked the governor for his

---

[32] Matthew's emphasis on the messianic identity of Jesus is well-known. See the following passages that are proper to it: Matthew 1:1, 18; 16:18, 20; 23:10; 27:17, 22.

[33] Cf. the response made to Pilate by the people in Matthew 27:25; "His blood be on us and on our children!" (RSV).

[34] Cf. the earthquake and the resurrections of the dead in Matthew 27:51-53.

death. There is actually the recognition of Jesus' innocence by Judas[35] and
that of his fidelity to God by the centurion and the few soldiers present at
the foot of the cross[36]. But there are only these, and they do not suffice for
disrupting the model.

In short, in Matthew and in Mark, as in the supplications of the
persecuted righteous, it is not the human characters who determine the
value and the status of the protagonist, *but God alone*. The sole
recognition that the model calls for and requires is divine. In Mark and in
Matthew, it happens only after the death, with the resurrection of Jesus.
The Matthean Passion narrative, in a manner similar to that noted in the
preceding chapter regarding the Markan narrative, has not eliminated the
final recognition; thanks to the model chosen, Matthew caused it to pass
from human characters (a horizontal recognition) to God (a vertical
recognition). The final recognition is thus really there. The genius of Mark
and of Matthew is not to have eliminated it, but to have modified its
nature, thanks to the model chosen for developing their characters, this
model being that of the supplications of the persecuted innocent of the
Psalms.

The Particularities of the Matthean Narrative

The preceding results invite asking several questions.
1.   Do Mark and Matthew use the model of the supplications
independently of each other or has one of them been inspired by the other?
And which one? The Passion narratives of Mark and Matthew do not
authorize an immediate response. If one can speculate on the anteriority of
Mark and the use of his Passion narrative by Matthew, it is for other
reasons, as was said above, and as we will see regarding the resurrection.
2. By using, like Mark, the model of the supplications, but without the
explicit citations, the Matthean narrator certainly assumes that his reader
knows the holy Scriptures of Israel and can/must notice the allusions that
he makes to them in order to admit their pertinence. In other words, the
narratives of the Passion/death of Jesus in Mark and Matthew are
addressing (1°) Christians who will find in them keys for reading, thanks to
the explanations of homilists who will comment upon them, (2°) but also

---

[35] Matthew 27:4: "I have sinned in betraying innocent blood."
[36] Matthew 27:54: "When the centurion and those who were with him, keeping watch
over Jesus, saw the earthquake and what took place, they were filled with awe, and said,
'Truly this was a son of God!'."

Jews not yet disciples of Jesus, who, nevertheless, desire to know him better than from the accusations of their fellows and to see if he was the awaited Messiah. The model of the Psalms of the persecuted righteous indeed allowed responding to the Jewish objections and suspicions concerning the identity of Jesus and the scandal of an ignominious death: like the identity and total fidelity of the faithful of the supplications, that of Jesus was misunderstood and rejected. The typology at work has an undeniable apologetic function; it is addressing Jewish or non-Jewish readers who are, nevertheless, convinced of the veracity of the holy Scriptures of Israel. However, it is not certain if a model excluding a final collective recognition would have been able to persuade Greeks not yet believers: one will see in the following chapter, that if the Lucan narrator chose another model, it is probably for this reason.

3. In his narrative of the Passion/death, the Matthean narrator proceeds by allusions. This means that the reference to the Old Testament figures has for its sole addressee the reader, for the characters of the narrative – the disciples, oppositional Jews, the governor and soldiers – did not know that they were living the drama recounted many times in the supplications. These allusions to the persecuted righteous have the same function as the explicit citations made by the same narrator in the preceding chapters: to show that Jesus fulfilled the prophecies and brought the biblical figures to their fulfillment. But in passing from the explicit (infancy and ministry) to the implicit (Passion/death), the references to the Scriptures elicit some questions: why did the Matthean Passion narrative not intersperse citations of fulfillment as in chapters 1 to 21? Since the narrator's project is clearly to show that Jesus fulfills the prophecies, could he not have facilitated his reader's route through his Passion narrative by *explicitly* pointing out for each psalmic motif that Jesus and the other actors were living the drama of the supplicants of the Psalms: "Thus was fulfilled what had been said by the psalmist..."? For such is the paradox: unlike Mark, little inclined to explain typological relationships, Matthew helps his reader by recalling for him, when he judges it opportune or necessary, a passage from the Scriptures capable of shedding light on an episode of his narrative. Yet, when with the Passion and the death on the cross everything seems to be totally upended into nonsense and it could have been possible to help the reader with explicit references, the narrator ceases to provide them for him, only proceeding by allusions not immediately perceptible to those who have little familiarity with the Scriptures.

The Why of the Allusions to the Psalms

Before outlining a response, let us briefly recall that in Matthew the number of explicit references to the fulfillment of the Scriptures is impressive[37], for the most part made by the narrator in a uniform manner[38], the others by Jesus[39], and they all aim, except for one[40], to relate what Jesus says/does/lives to the prophecies. Let us return to the question: why beginning with the entrance of Jesus into Jerusalem does the narrator not use citations of fulfillment in order to show that Jesus' ordeal echoes that of the persecuted righteous of the Psalms?

1. If the Matthean narrator does not explicitly mention the supplications, it is perhaps because the style and the nature of his narrative change. Up until the mention of the plot and the preparation for the Passover (Matthew 26), the macro-narrative is indeed episodic, and the citations of fulfillment allow regrouping episodes into sections more or less unified thematically[41]. With the Passion, the narrative ceases being episodic: the plot of the action (is Jesus going to be condemned and put to death?) and that of the revelation (will his prophetic and messianic/royal identity be manifested and how?) progress continuously, and the dramatic tension prevails over the didactic redaction to which the scriptural citations belong.

2. To this first reason, probable but not restrictive, is added a second, determined by the type of scriptural texts appealed to. Indeed, the explicit

---

[37] Matthew 1:22; 2:15, 17, 23; 3:15; 4:14; 5:17; 8:17; 12:17; 13:35; 21:4; 26:54, 56; 27:9. In total, 15 times. In another passage, Jesus speaks of fulfillment – of all righteousness, Matthew 3:15 – but without referring to the Scriptures. On the subject, see Jean MILER, *Les citations d'accomplissement dans l'Évangile de Matthieu. Quand Dieu se rend présent en toute humanité* (AnBib 140 ; Rome, Pontificio Istituto Biblico 1999).

[38] Matthew 1:22; 2:15, 17, 23; 3:15; 4:14; 8:17; 12:17; 13:35; 21:4. The verb is uniformly *plèroô* in the passive ("in order to fulfill" or "thus was fulfilled"), followed by "the word" (in Greek, to *rèthen*, a passive participle, literally "the saying") and from the instrumental circumstantial complement "by the prophet(s)" (*dia tou/tôn prophètou/prophètôn*).

[39] In Matthew 5:17, "I have come not to abolish them but to fulfil [*anaplèrôsai*] them"; 13:14, "with them indeed is fulfilled [*anaplèroutai*] the prophecy of Isaiah"; 26:54 "how then should the scriptures be fulfilled [*plèrôthôsi*]"; 26:56, "that the scriptures of the prophets might be fulfilled [*plèrôthôsi*]".

[40] The only explicit mention of the fulfillment of the Scriptures in the narrative of the Passion does not concern Jesus but Judas; cf. Matthew 27:9.

[41] On the subject, see J. MILER, *Les citations d'accomplissement dans l'Évangile de Matthieu, passim*.

citations made by the narrator refer to prophetic oracles, in other words: to divine statements (from God to Israel), whereas, even if they can be called *Word of God*, the supplications are above all human statements, from human voices addressing God. What the supplicants describe with their voice has become in the Gospels a voice-over narration. Explicit citations would in some way have weakened the dramatic tension and the mystery of the relationships described.

3. A third reason exists, more well-founded than the preceding two but not in opposition to them: if the narrator does not take the initiative to insert scriptural citations into the narrative of the Passion/death of Jesus, it is because he left it to Jesus to do in Matthew 26:31, 54 and 56 before the violence erupts: in Matthew 26:31, Jesus says to the disciples during the Last Supper: "You will all fall away because of me this night; for it is written, 'I will strike the shepherd, and the sheep of the flock will be scattered'"; in Matthew 26:54, he says to the crowds that came to arrest him: "But how then should the Scriptures [*hai graphai*] be fulfilled, that it must [*dei*] be so?"; in Matthew 26:56, to the same crowds: "But all this has taken place, that the Scriptures [*hai graphai*] of the prophets might be fulfilled".

It is Jesus himself who invites all the men who came to arrest him, but also the disciples still present – and the reader, clearly – to read the events in relation to the Scriptures. The narrator thus no longer has to intervene, nor Jesus either, for, like the persecuted righteous of the supplications, he is going to remain silent until the final cry, led here and there by capricious whims, silent except when it is necessary for him to answer about his identity. Two stages are thus clearly drawn on either side of the arrest: the first, in which Jesus announces the events – betrayal, rejection, denial, dispersion of the "sheep" – that gives one of the keys for reading, essentially biblical, and the other stage, in which he is the prisoner, manhandled, living his agony in silence until the cry of death on the cross.

The Matthean narrator has not chosen the model of the supplications by chance. A Jew, a member of the Jewish community who recognized in Jesus his Messiah, the narrator is addressing his coreligionists, who have rejected Jesus and seen in him a blasphemer, and is proposing to them to read the events of the Passion in order to discover in them the opposite of what they are for them, not the punishment of an impostor, but the necessary ordeal of the innocent par excellence, rejected, persecuted and put to death, an ordeal crowned by the resurrection...

IV. THE RESURRECTION AND THE FINAL "ANAGNÔRISIS"

If Mark did not need to describe where and how the disciples were able to recognize Jesus resurrected, Matthew had to do it, for, when he is writing, the Jews are beginning to accuse the disciples of announcing the resurrection of their master, even though they had removed his body – incidentally, if Mark had been written after Matthew, he could not have ended without speaking about these questions: a supplementary reason for considering his redaction as anterior[42]. These accusations will be believed in the IInd century as witnessed to by a passage from the *Dialogue with Trypho* in which the apologist is questioning his Jewish interlocutor:

Not only did you not do penance when you knew that he was truly resurrected, but, I had already reproached you about it, you assigned men of your choosing to broadcast throughout the land that Jesus, a Galilean and impostor [in Greek, *planos*], had formed a sect [in Greek, *hairesis*] of impious and lawless men; that this Jesus had been crucified, and that his disciples had removed him during the night from the tomb where he had been placed after he had been taken down from the cross; that they deceived [Greek verb *planaô*] mankind by saying that he was resurrected from the dead and ascended into heaven[43].

G. Stanton points out that these accusations come from the pen of Celsus, who had a Jew speak in his name and ask why the Resurrected One did not appear to his opponents, for all could have seen him and would thus have been able to believe in him[44]. In the IInd century, the majority of

---

[42] In Acts 25:19, Luke himself also points to the accusations of the Jews reported by Festus: "They [the Jews] had certain points of dispute with him about their own superstition and about one Jesus, who was dead, but whom Paul asserted to be alive."

[43] JUSTIN, *Dialogue with Trypho*, 108:2. Also see the Testament of Levi, 16:3, where, without being named, Jesus is said to be a deceiver/magician (*planos*). G. STANTON mentions as well *The Acts of Thomas*, 96:102, 106-107 (with the two words *magos* and *planos*).

[44] One knows the ideas of Celsus thanks to ORIGEN, *Contre Celse*, II, 63:67 and 77. Cf. G. STANTON, *Jesus and Gospel*, 148-161. On the criticism of which the Christians were the object on the part of pagans, see S. BENKO, "Pagan Criticism of Christianity during the Frist Two Centuries A.D.", in *ANRW* 2.23.2, (1980) 1054-1118; R.L. WILKEN, *The Christians as the Romans Saw Them* (New Haven, Yale University Press 1984).

Jews and Greeks thus declare themselves as not believing in the resurrection of Jesus proclaimed by Christians.

Unlike Mark, Matthew points out the final recognition of the disciples (Matthew 28:9, 16-20) and, its opposite, the lie of the Elders of the people, according to whom the body of Jesus would have been removed (Matthew 28:11-15). The manner in which the narrative recounts the story aims at showing that a removal was impossible given the presence of the soldiers before the tomb: by mentioning these refusals to believe, the narrator ends his narrative as he began it, by repeating that if his coreligionists have refused to believe in Jesus, it is not by chance or by misunderstanding, but because they, like their ancestors, are deaf to the appeals of the envoys of God[45]. In short, by ending with the problem of the recognition and its opposite, the Matthean narrator suggests that this is what has arranged and unified the diverse components of his narrative.

V. CONCLUSIONS

1. It was possible to suggest, without having to compare all the pericopae of Matthew/Mark, that the narrative of Mark is prior to that of Matthew. Not that the comparative study of the ancient Greek witnesses is not necessary, but, by raising the questions and the accusations formulated by the surrounding world in the second part of the I[st] century of our era, one can see if and how each macro-narrative is located in relation to this context. The advocates of Matthew's anteriority will possibly respond that in some pericopae this Gospel clearly seems to have been used by Mark. Without here entering into the heart of the matter, let us only say that, for some episodes, Mark was able to know a pre-Matthean redaction and to use it. But if one compares the definitive redactions, the problems to which Matthew responds are subsequent to those confronted by Mark.

2. Matthew, no more than Mark, does not provide raw, anecdotal facts but much rather keys for reading, and it is first as elements of meaning – and not as historiographic components – that the facts of the text must be interpreted. In short, in order to grasp the narrator's strategy, exegesis must first go in search of the literary and semantic models.

3. The route undertaken has shown as well Matthew's belonging to the biographical genre, not only because of the infancy narrative – the *genos*

---

[45] The accusation is previously and explicitly formulated by Jesus himself in the parable of the rebellious winegrowers in Matthew 21:33-43.

section –, but also because of the narrative of the Passion/death of Jesus in which the problem of the *anagnôrisis* and the solution that is provided by it, thanks to the Psalms of supplication of the persecuted righteous, constitute the central thread of the narrative. The place granted to the *anagnôrisis* indirectly shows that the Matthean narrator wanted to honor the Greco-Roman requirements of the biographical genre. We are far from thinking that the problem of the *anagnôrisis* exhaustively explains all the components of the Markan and Matthean narratives, but if it is ignored, one cannot account for either their writing or their theology in a totally satisfactory way.

4.   This chapter has shown as well that Matthew's narrative of the Passion/death of Jesus is very close to Mark's and has allowed determining the reason for this proximity. The model of the supplications could indeed help the Jews, for whom the death of Jesus was scandalous, to enter into the mystery of a Messiah dying like a criminal and impostor. The paradox, but also the genius, of the narrators of the Passion/death in Mark and Matthew was to honor the requirements of the Greco-Roman biographical genre by having recourse to an Old Testament model – the formal cadre is Greco-Roman but the content, biblical.

It remains for us to see if and how Luke was able to overcome the difficulties that the project of a biography of Jesus posed at that time.

CHAPTER IV

THE NARRATIVE OF LUKE
AND GREEK BIOGRAPHIES

I. INTRODUCTION

It has been accepted, for two or three decades, that, of the three
Synoptics, the Gospel of Luke is the closest to Greco-Roman biographies,
principally because of its preface (Luke 1:1-4) and its introduction,
generally called the *Gospel of the Infancy* (Luke 1:5 – 2:52), which
corresponds to the *genos* of the biographical canons of that time. The
question of the final collective *anagnôrisis* has been worked on less, and
this is regrettable, for it is possibly this question that determined not only
the writing of Luke 23 – 24 but also, and above all, the general disposition
of the Lucan macro-narrative.

II. THE PREFACE AND ITS RAISON D'ÊTRE. LUKE 1:1-4

What Type of Preface?

Many studies have been devoted to Luke 1:1-4. The most well-
known and widely used by commentaries is that of L. Alexander[1], for
whom it is not a historical type of preface[2], for the closest parallels belong
to the Greek scientific tradition. Luke 1:1-4 is indeed distinguishable from
historical prefaces in several regards: (1) the text is markedly shorter and
does not clearly state the contents of the book (the name of the protagonist,
etc.); (2) it is anonymous as well, whereas Greek historians give their

---

[1] L. ALEXANDER, *The Preface to Luke's Gospel. Literary Convention and Social
Context in Luke 1.1-4 and Acts 1.1* (SNTSMS 78; Cambridge, Cambridge University Press
1993).
[2] In Greek, *prooimion*, translated as preface or prologue.

name; (3) it contains a dedication that is lacking in these prefaces, (4) which, moreover, do not use the first person singular (the "I").

The objection to Alexander's conclusions has been that Luke is not a scientific treatise – of geography, medicine, botany, etc. – and that, for this reason, Luke 1:1-4 could not be a preface of the same type[3]. One can also ask if, instead of being due to the subject treated, the anonymity comes rather from the biographies of Jesus that had already been written and diffused – at least Mark – being themselves anonymous – and thus Luke is doing as his predecessors had done. In the discussion on the scientific/historical alternative, the biographical genre seems to have been forgotten by Alexander, for the preface of Luke resembles, at least in length but with an added dedication, that of the *Vita Mosis* of Philo (1:1-4).

Still according to Alexander, Luke 1:1-4 cannot be a historical preface, for it does not name Jesus, the protagonist of the macro-narrative. In order to outline a pertinent response to this objection, it is necessary, however, to take account of the clues provided by the narrator in the first chapters of the Gospel (Luke 1 – 2). Indeed, the first episodes do not begin by speaking about Jesus but only about the events related to the birth of John the Baptist; furthermore, as narrator, Luke calls Jesus by his name only after his circumcision (2:21), thus obeying, with Mary, the angelic order (cf. 1:31): why would his name not have been mentioned before this episode if it were a preface? But if this rhetorical vagueness is due in part to the scrupulous respect for the angel's words and the usages reported by the narrative, this indicates that the narrator is showing discretion: the characters will speak, and the events themselves will manifest the soundness, the truth of a message already familiar to Theophilus.

The Narrator's Project

At the end of the preface, Luke says to Theophilus that he is narrating "that you may know the truth concerning the things of which you have been informed" (Luke 1:4). The formulation is sufficiently vague so that each may make of it whatever he wants. It is possible to see in it an apologetic project, for if the narrative shows the soundness of the teaching and thus of the apostolic testimony, is it not in order to respond to possible detractors, Jewish or pagan? The first criticisms concerning the apostles'

---

[3] Cf. D.E. AUNE, "Luke 1:1-4: Historical or Scientific *Prooimion*?", in ID., *Jesus, Gospel Tradition and Paul in the Context of Jewish and Greco-Roman Antiquity* (WUNT 303; Tübingen, Mohr Siebeck 2013) 107-115.

fidelity to the teaching of their master indeed began before the end of the I[st] century, and, as one knows, Luke set about showing that there was a total continuity from the master to the disciples[4]. The hypothesis is thus not to be excluded, but the preface writer names no one nor does he mention possible grievances made against the apostolic doctrine that would enable identifying with certainty the adversaries being fought against and the subject of the dispute. On the other hand, the verification of the soundness of the message is not necessarily prompted by exterior attacks; it is a part of the growth of faith, as Luke conceives it. The dynamic of the Lucan narrative in some way reflects that of a *fides quaerens intellectum*[5]. The IIIrd Gospel does not just present the life of Jesus with meticulous care and objectivity; it goes further, unceasingly relating the events lived by the master and his disciples to the biblical past: allusions of the promise/fulfillment type structure the narrative. For Luke, to narrate indeed means to show the logic of a history, in its most remote preparations. Let us thus not believe that the search for coherence begins only in Luke 24, with the systematic explanation of the Scriptures: if the goal of the narrative is only explained at the end, it remains no less true that the connection between the two series of events – those lived by the witnesses mentioned in Luke 1:2 and those from the biblical past – has principally determined the birth of the narrative and Luke's choices.

The Lucan narrative is thus the manifestation, indeed the revelation, of a coherence on all levels, as the term "teachings" (or "information") in Luke 1:4 suggests, sufficiently vague to encompass everything. But at no time, in this preface itself and in what follows, does the narrator call his narrative Good News (*euaggelion*[6]), the way, for example, that Mark does (Mark 1:1). An oversight or a deliberate silence? It cannot be an oversight since Luke knows and uses the word *euaggelion* in Acts. By not describing his narrative as Gospel, Luke implies that for him the Good News cannot be reduced to his narrative. A valuable distinction, even if it remains implicit: it is anticipating the one that will become classic, between Gospel and Scripture.

---

[4] He did it thanks to the *synkrisis*, by showing in Acts that the apostles were a copy conformed to Jesus. Cf. J.N. ALETTI, *Quand Luc raconte. Le récit comme théologie* (Lire La Bible ; Paris, Cerf 1998), *passim*.

[5] *Faith seeking understanding* (translator's note).

[6] The term *euaggelion* is, moreover, absent from Luke. One only finds it twice in Acts (15:7; 20:24). Luke, in contrast, massively uses the verb *euaggelizomai* ("to evangelize"), in both books.

If the preface (Luke 1:1-4) is already pointing out that the narrative is going to follow Greek literary models in an original way, its function goes well beyond this, since it is not primarily aiming to highlight the narrator's culture or capacity for imitation but to confirm the value of the eye witnesses, the apostles, and their testimony, implicitly indicating from the first lines of his work that what Jesus said and did was truly transmitted and taught. But the preface writer is also announcing the reliability of his own writing, for through his narrative the actual credibility of the Christian movement was being exposed to the judgment of the prevailing Greek culture.

III. THE INTRODUCTION OF LUKE AND THE BIOGRAPHIES OF THAT TIME. LUKE 1 – 2

As with Matthew, it is above all because of its first two chapters that one sees in Luke a Greco-Roman biography. With most of the biographers of his era, Luke describes the origins and the birth (in Greek, *genos*) of his protagonist.

The task of the Lucan narrator was not simple. On one hand, indeed, in the *genos* of Jesus there was (almost) nothing to praise: his village was not famous[7], and his family was poor[8]. The narrator alludes to Mary and Joseph's humble situation, even if he does not go so far as to reveal the reaction of the inhabitants of Nazareth who recognize in Jesus a carpenter (Mark 6:3) or a carpenter's son (Matthew 13:55). Without risking the loss of his reliability, the Lucan narrator cannot but echo this lackluster social and familial background. So why did he write this first part even though there was apparently nothing to praise? His genius was to contrast this earthly human poverty and Jesus' royal and divine dignity, his exceptional *genos* revealed by a celestial messenger, for he will be the Messiah, will have the throne of David his father (Luke 1:32), and, above all, will be Holy, Son of God (Luke 1:35). More than the titles' connotations, ably analyzed since the Fathers of the Church up to recent commentators, one should here point out the manner in which, like the

---

[7] Nathanael's statement in John 1:46 ("Can anything good come out of Nazareth?") reflects the common opinion of the Jews – it thus had to be the same for the Greeks and Romans.

[8] Cf. Luke 2:7: the lack of room at the inn where Jesus is born; 2:24: the doves, the offering of the poor.

narrator of Matthew 1 – 2, that of Luke was able to get around the difficulty that in principle prohibited him from writing, following the Greco-Roman biographies, this encomiastic part.

Luke 1 – 2 does not only provide the titles that are revealed by the angel and that state Jesus' unique origins (*genos*). To this revelation, for which he is not responsible, the Lucan narrator adds his own contribution in order to emphasize this very origin; a technical contribution, since it is the comparison (the *synkrisis*[9]), already mentioned, that parallels John the Baptist and Jesus in order to show both the similarities that exist between them as well as, and especially, the second's superiority. These parallels being more or less known by readers, it suffices to enumerate them without commentary:

JOHN		JESUS	ELEMENTS OF THE *SYNKRISIS*
1:5-7	//	1:26-27	presentation of the parents
1:8-11	//	1:28	appearance of an angel
1:12	//	1:29	trouble of Zechariah/Mary
1:13-17	//	1:30-33	discourse of the angel on the infant
1:18	//	1:34	question of Zechariah/Mary
1:19-20	//	1:35-37	response of the angel
1:24-25	//	1:38,39-55	reaction of Elizabeth/Mary

JOHN		JESUS	ELEMENTS OF THE *SYNKRISIS*
1:57	//	2:1-7	time of the birth
1:58	//	2:8-20	the entourage hears, praises and rejoices
1:65-66	//	2:17-18	reaction of fear/astonishment
1:59-64	//	2:21	circumcision
1:67-79	//	2:22-38	human interpretations and prophecies
1:80*a*	//	2:40,52	growth of the child
1:80*b*	//	2:39,51	dwelling place desert/Nazareth

The John/Jesus *synkrisis* even goes up to Luke 4:13, indeed 4:15, that is, to before the episode at Nazareth (4:16-30), which clearly begins a new stage in the life of Jesus[10]:

---

[9] A technique learned by schoolchildren in the *progymnasmata*. Cf., for example, the *progymnasmata* of Theon and Hermogenes, in G.A. KENNEDY, *Progymnasmata*, 52-55 and 83-84.

[10] Cf. C.H. TALBERT, *Literary Patterns, Theological Themes and the Genre of Luke-Acts* (SBLMS n° 20, Missoula, Scholars Press 1974) 45-48.

JOHN		JESUS	ELEMENTS OF THE *SYNKRISIS*
3:1-6	//	3:21-38	presentation of John and of Jesus
3:7-17	//	4:1-13	their respective missions
3:18-20	//	4:14-15	summaries of end/beginning of respective missions

Let us conclude this brief presentation on Luke 1 – 2, by saying that this exordium was not written solely or principally in order to respect the cadre followed by the biographies of its time. Luke took advantage of the cadre in order to begin with a revealed and inspired Christology, proceeding by accumulation and progressive specification, in order to arrive at a unified portrait that is going to serve as a model and a reference point for the remainder of the narrative. Without a doubt, this initial part is essential, for, as none of the characters of Luke 1 – 2 reappear in what follows, the Christology of these two chapters is clearly for the reader, so that being aware of the authoritative revelations of the angels (Luke 1:31-32,35; 2:10-11), of Simeon (2:29-32), and lastly of Jesus (2:49), he may see how the latter is going to work so that humanity may be saved and recognize him as a true envoy of God, royal Messiah and Son of God.

In short, if the Lucan narrator takes up the formal cadre and follows the conventions of Greek biographies, the next chapter will show that the semantic allusions, quite numerous, are essentially biblical and will try to highlight their raison d'être. What now remains is to see if Luke was influenced by the problem of the *anagnôrisis* and if, in this regard, he follows in the footsteps of the Markan narrative.

IV. THE FINAL RECOGNITION OF JESUS IN LUKE 22 – 24

The difficulty of the Lucan Passion narrative comes from how it is both close to and different from Matthew/Mark. As in them, some motifs of the Psalms of supplication are easily noted because of the vocabulary – the division of clothes (Ps 21/22:19 in Luke 23:34), Jesus' cry (Ps 30/31:6 in Luke 23:46) – and the situations: Jesus is dying, alone, reviled and does not respond to the insults. But other traits denote a different perspective: if the Psalms of supplication and the narratives of Mathew/Mark in no way mention an intercession, the Lucan narrator, on the contrary, retains the request "Father, forgive them, they know not what they are doing" (Luke

23:34*a*)[11]. The filial address ("Father", twice, in verses 34 and 46) implies an attitude that has nothing to do with the insistent demand for the immediate liberation from the threat and death. God is neither absent nor deaf: He is there, very close, and Jesus trustingly abandons himself into His hands, without ever asking Him to come quickly, not to abandon him. Clearly, in Luke, Jesus' attitude refers to that of the Psalms of trust, where at every possible moment the one praying repeats that he is hoping for and does not doubt the help of the Lord. Jesus' speech to the criminal crucified with him: "Truly, I say to you, today you will be with me in Paradise" (23:43), indicates as well a certitude that nothing will be able to overturn: God is on his side and remains the well-beloved Father.

In faithfully following to the end the model of the supplications of the persecuted righteous, the dual recension Matthew/Mark highlights, as was noted over the course of the preceding chapters, the situation's dramatic and enigmatic aspect but, above all, the refusal of recognition, utilizing for this the Psalms of the persecuted faithful: Jesus cries out and questions God about his apparent abandonment. Admittedly, he is recognized as "Son of God" (Matthew 27:42; Mark 15:39) by the centurion, right after his death, but all the other witnesses, in particular the Jewish authorities, maintain their positions, confirming the psalmic background of the faithful persecuted. In the IIIrd Gospel, the scenes at the foot of the cross, on the contrary, highlight the progression that goes from scorn and insults to the final twofold confession, of Jesus' innocence – "Certainly this man was *innocent!*" (Luke 23:47) – and the responsibility of all the others. On the road to Calvary, only the women bewailed and lamented him (Luke 23:27 RSV), but, at the very end, after Jesus is dead and recognized as innocent by the centurion, it is no longer only the women who are beating their breasts, but *all the crowds assembled* in order to see the spectacle (23:48). Jesus dies with trust, recognized innocent not only by the women, the criminal who asks him to remember him, and the centurion but also (in an implicit way) by the crowds. The recognition of his innocence is inseparably a confession of their responsibility. In short, the narrator contrasts the trusting innocence of Jesus with the *avowed* sin of the crowds. *The actors of the narrative are*

---

[11] Jesus' prayer is missing from some very reliable witnesses: the problem of textual criticism is thus real. Nevertheless, whether or not one keeps verse 34*a* changes nothing about the conclusions of the narrative analysis, as one will be able to realize by what follows. If there is an addition, it is in conformity with the line taken by the narrator of Luke.

recognized for who they are: Jesus innocent, and the others – at least the crowds – repentant sinners. A schema clearly shows the passages in Luke where the final recognition of the innocence of Jesus is highlighted:

explicit recognition
Luke 23:4,14 by Pilate, governor and Roman judge[12],
Luke 23:15 by Herod
    (Herod's point of view interpreted and made known by Pilate),
Luke 23:40-42 by one of the thieves crucified with Jesus,
Luke 23:47 by the centurion who is at the foot of the cross.

implicit recognition
Luke 23:27 the women who bewail and lament,
Luke 23:48 all those present go away beating their breasts.

Jesus Proposes the Key to Reading His Passion/Death

Following the example of Matthew/Mark, Luke never intervenes as narrator in order explicitly to propose the biblical template for reading the Passion/death of Jesus. The latter is the only one to make a reference to the Scriptures, but *only once*, at the very end of the Passover celebration (Luke 22:37 RSV):

For I tell you that this scripture must [in Greek, *dei*] be fulfilled [*telesthènai*] in me, "And he was reckoned with transgressors"; for what is written about me has its fulfilment [*telos*].

This announcement, which at the same time is a reminder of Isaiah 53:12[13], merits the reader's attention, for it is the only episode in the IIIrd Gospel where, speaking of his fate, and thus of himself, Jesus explicitly mentions the Scriptures and precedes the citation with a formula of fulfilment. The case of Luke 4:18-20 is indeed different, for the passage from Isaiah at the synagogue was the reading of the day, and the mention of fulfilment does not precede the citation: in Luke 22:37, Jesus *chooses* the text that, according to him, allows reading the events to come. But compared to Luke 24 where, after his resurrection, the same Jesus will emphasize the necessity of the suffering and the death through which the

---

[12] Let us not forget that at no time in Mark 15:1-15 does Pilate declare the accusations false nor does he express an opinion on the innocence of Jesus. In this regard, the contrast with the parallel episode in Luke (23:1-5 and 13-22) is striking.

[13] In technical terms: analeptic prolepsis.

Messiah must pass, and where he will open the prophecies of the Scriptures to his disciples, this unique citation seems insufficient: would not a substantial presentation of the Scriptures have been better placed during the Passover meal, before the events deteriorate and seem to collapse into nonsense?

It will, of course, be necessary to respond to this difficulty. Let us note, however, that if, before the Passion, Jesus only once calls upon the Scriptures in order to point out how far his road of suffering and rejection will go, everything that follows in the Lucan narrative, from the voice of the characters or that of the narrator, seems to be a fulfillment of the prophecy of 22:37. May it suffice to mention the passages, several proper to Luke, where it is a question of thieves and criminals:

22:52 (= Matthew/Mark) Jesus to the men who came to arrest him: "...as against a robber, with swords and clubs?"
23:2 (only Luke), the Sanhedrin to Pilate: "[Jesus] perverting our nation, and forbidding us to give tribute to Caesar."
23:5 (only Luke), the Sanhedrin to Pilate: "He [Jesus] stirs up the people..."
23:14 (only Luke), Pilate repeating the accusations from v.2 and 5 "perverting the people."
23:19 (= Mark 15:17), the Nr. "[Barabbas] ... thrown into prison for an insurrection ... and for murder."
23:25 (only Luke), the Nr: "[Pilate] released the man ... thrown into prison for insurrection and murder."
23:32 (= Matthew/Mark), the Nr: "Two others also, who were criminals, were led away to be put to death with him."
23:33 (= Matthew/Mark), the Nr: "there they crucified him, and the criminals"
23:39 (only Luke), the Nr: "One of the criminals who were hanged railed at him ..."
23:41 (Luke only), a criminal "And we indeed justly; for we are receiving the due reward of our deeds, but this man has done nothing wrong."

Such then is one of the paradoxes highlighted by Luke: Jesus, placed among criminals, treated as such, is finally declared innocent, explicitly by the centurion and indirectly by the crowds, who leave while symbolically indicating their fault. The more the fate of Jesus is that of the thieves, the more, paradoxically, will his innocence emerge.

The prolepses made by Jesus during the last Passover – announcements of betrayal, of Peter's denial, of his own fate, identical to that of the lawless – thus call for the events and form the dynamic of the Lucan narrative of the Passion. Jesus, nevertheless, does not say that he will be recognized as innocent, and that is where it is necessary to recognize the mark of Luke: he did not wait for Calvary in order to stress Jesus' innocence, an innocence *recognized by the narrative's characters*.

An Initial, Official Recognition. Luke 23:2-25

The recognition of Jesus' innocence by the judicial authorities clearly is very important: an official recognition, proclaimed by the judge in front of all the people!

1. The Jewish Religious Authorities: An Undeclared Recognition?

The scene where Jesus appears before the High Council (22:66-71), before the episode at Pilate's, is short and gets directly to what is essential; in two stages[14], the assembly wants to hear from Jesus' mouth a clear declaration of identity: "If you are the Christ, tell us!" (v.67*b*), and: "Are you the Son of God, then?" (v.70*a*). Knowing that they are hoping for a clear response in order to accuse him, Jesus retorts in an ambiguous manner: "You say that I am!" An ambiguity, for the phrase can mean: "See! You yourselves sensed it!" or, on the contrary: "It is you who say so, and I leave to you the responsibility for this title that I reject." Jesus is not answering as simply as they would like; he refers them to their own question and to what it implies: how could they ask him these questions if they did not have reasons for responding positively? The reaction of the interlocutors, nevertheless, shows that they wanted to see in the prisoner's statement a clear declaration of identity. But the Lucan episode is not an official trial[15]: Jesus is not a person being charged, and the narrator mentions neither the judge, nor the witnesses, nor any kind of sentence, like "He deserves death!", to such an extent that the reaction of the members of the High Council itself also becomes ambiguous.

Ambiguous or not, the position of the religious authorities is narratively interesting, for the High Priest and his confederates do not say to Jesus: "Tell us who you are!" or even "Whom are you pretending to be?", but *themselves* state the two titles that constitute Jesus' real identity.

---

[14] Is it necessary to remind the reader that this Christology in two stages, and thus progressive, is not new in Luke's macro-narrative? It occurs very early on, in the episode of the Annunciation, when the angel first declares that Jesus will be the son of the Most High, an epithet of the king, son of David (Messiah), and then that he will be Son of God.

[15] Compare with Matthew 26:57-68 and Mark 14:55-65.

In spite of the final declaration of v.71[16], it is not Jesus who pronounced the two titles (in vv.67 and 70), but they themselves! Is it not a recognition that does not want to be admitted to? If, in terms of the macro-narrative, the Jewish religious authorities are not the only ones who do not recognize, even implicitly, their responsibility, the nocturnal meeting really stresses what these authorities perceived of Jesus' identity and the awareness that the latter had of their goal of non-reception.

2. The Recognition of the Political Authorities

The ambiguity of the situation disappears at the moment when the narrator reports the accusations of the High Council, all ("the whole company of them" 23:1) having arrived before the Roman governor. But the difference between the accusations made before Pilate and the statements from the preceding scene jump out: whereas it had only been a question of Jesus' identity, the same High Council now carries the debate to a political level: revolution and refusal to pay taxes (23:2). The reader, who has had ample time to read and be familiar with Jesus' statements, immediately sees the lying character of the accusations. Why does the narrator thus not point it out? Why, unlike Matthew/Mark, is he silent as well about the reason that caused them to hand over Jesus: jealousy[17]? Perhaps it is not necessary to clarify that the accusations are false: the narrator, convinced of his reader's perceptiveness, omitted a self-evident observation. But if he is silent as well on the reason or reasons that cause the Jewish religious authorities to lie, is it from ignorance, a lack of interest or by design? What we know of the narrator allows opting for the third hypothesis: during the episode, Luke allows the truth and the lie to be manifested through the dialogues, without himself mentioning the profound reasons for the choices and wishes. But a careful reading of the passage shows the reasons for Luke's discretion.

If he is happy to allow just the characters to speak, it is because the lie will not prevent the truth from being revealed, on the contrary. The setting is, moreover, ideal: the two supreme authorities come face to face, the High Council of the Jews and the Roman magistrate, showing the official nature of the proceedings. An official nature that the

---

[16] "And they said, "What further testimony do we need? We have heard it ourselves from his own lips."

[17] Cf. Matthew 27:18; Mark 15:10.

circumstances confirm: Pilate really emphasizes that he did not interrogate the accused in private, in order to come to an agreement with him or to find an expedient, but that *everyone*, absolutely *everyone*, from the chief priests to the country's humblest inhabitants, heard the questions and the answers (v.13-14). And if everyone heard everything, then Pilate's words acquire a testimonial power and a maximal extension: "This man as one who was perverting the people" (v.14, echoing v.2 and 5) has done nothing for which one may accuse him. The supreme judicial authority recognizes, in front of all the gathered population, that the reasons put forward in order to condemn Jesus are false and thus proclaims his innocence: "I did not find this man guilty of any of your charges against him" (v.14).

But does not Pilate declare a little too quickly that Jesus is innocent? He has not listened to his teaching and is not even informed about it! The three reasons given by the members of the Sanhedrin (v.2) indeed aim at provoking the reaction of the Roman authorities: if, as the accusations say, Jesus asks the crowds not to pay the tax to *Caesar* and if he calls himself *Christ-King*, it is that he rejects the imperial authority and wants to be substituted for it. The governor cannot but make the connection between the titles "Caesar" and "King". His question to Jesus: "Are you the King of the Jews?" (v.3), shows, moreover, that he knows what is at stake. But the prisoner's response remains ambiguous, at least as Luke recounts it: the Greek *su legeis* can mean: "You say it, and you speak truly" or "You yourself say it, not me!" The reader, moreover, easily perceives why Jesus responds in that way rather than with "I am" (*egô eimi*): given what the accusers have said, Pilate can give to the title only a political sense, which implies a rivalry with the Roman power and thus a condemnation, and as Jesus never gave a political connotation to his kingdom, the *su legeis* thus acquires a negative resonance ("It is you, and you only, who say it"). But by asking the prisoner: "Are you the king of the Jews?", Pilate is saying something true, for Jesus is King, in the sense that during the journey towards Jerusalem, he had implied it, and he was acclaimed by his disciples, while he was mounted on the ass (Luke 19:35-38): his response "*Su legeis*" then takes on a positive coloration: "You say it, and you say well".

The rest of the narrative shows that Pilate understood the *su legeis* as a rejection of the political kingdom, and the accused immediately becomes innocent of it. That is why the members of the Sanhedrin, who absolutely want to obtain satisfaction, subsequently no longer maintain only the accusation of insurrection, which the reader – as well as the Jews in the Lucan narrative – knows will provoke the merciless reaction of the governor (cf. Luke 13:1). But they pronounce the word "Galilee", which is going to allow Pilate to send Jesus to Herod's, for the reason indicated by the narrator (v.7a).

The function of the scene at Herod's is really intriguing. For, if with Pilate it is a matter of an official trial, here, on the contrary, no sentence whatsoever of acquittal or of condemnation is pronounced: the scene seems to have neither the form of a trial nor a determinative role for the outcome of the debate, since Herod sends the prisoner back to Pilate without commentary. The narrator has kept it only to mention the beginning of the friendship between Herod and Pilate – but why does he not give the reason for this about-face?

Actually, if the narrator does not himself point out the importance of the appearance before Herod, it is because he wants to make it known to the reader *by the characters of the narrative*, more precisely by Pilate (v.15): the latter refers to what happened at Herod's in order to support his own judgment. That Jesus had been returned to him without any declaration demonstrates the inability of the tetrarch himself to deliver the least condemnation and emphasizes the accusations' lack of grounding; Pilate's reaction was thus not arbitrary: the *two judicial authorities* are in agreement in recognizing, one explicitly and the other implicitly, Jesus' innocence.

But the narrator could have drastically summarized the scene, by saying for example: "Pilate sent Jesus to Herod, who, finding nothing in Jesus that merited death, sent him back to Pilate." We have already seen why the narrator again evokes the vehement accusations of the Jewish leaders: so that the scene may not be close-ended, that the accusers may not speak of forfeiture. Another element remains to be explained: the mention of the outrages inflicted upon Jesus (v.11). The reader has, however, all the clues needed to find its function. He already knows that Herod is a malefactor (cf. Luke 3:19-20); if Herod, in spite of all his villainy, shown here by contempt and outrages – this character has not changed since the beginning of the macro-narrative and confirms the truth of Luke's words –, can then find nothing in order to hold Jesus, indeed to put him to death, it is because the latter's innocence is total.

Is it necessary to interpret the narrator's thinking on the friendship of Herod and Pilate (v.12) as one of the first beneficial effects of the Passion of Jesus: the reconciliation of enemies? Or as an additional ironic trait: a shady friendship, based on a misdeed – the failure to take responsibility or the collusion of both powers? Perhaps, but in order to be plausible the response must be based on the narrative dynamic. Yet, Luke does not recount this friendship at the beginning of the scene (before v.8), as if Pilate had done so by showing Herod that he recognized his authority, but he recounts it at the end, *after* Herod sent Jesus back to Pilate's. By having the prisoner returned to the governor's palace, the tetrarch shows that he recognized Pilate's supreme jurisdiction – the recognition thus became reciprocal, the two powers no longer ignoring each other. But the reader has another reason for appreciating Herod's gesture: by sending back the prisoner – got up in his striking clothes –, the tetrarch confirms the governor's diagnosis of the accusations as unfounded and leaves him the task of deciding as a last recourse Jesus' fate. A paradox of the scene, since it is Jesus' innocence that allows the two judges to recognize their respective powers. There is more: it is their recognition of Jesus' innocence that allowed another recognition, that of their respective authority.

3. The People: Recognition or Rejection?

The prisoner having returned, Pilate convokes *everyone*: the members of the Sanhedrin and the people (in Greek, *laos*), who appear for the first time in the Passion episodes. His statements will thus have a maximal extension: no one will be able to ignore the events and say that they had nothing to do with them. The fate of Jesus becomes the affair of all.

The question of the people has existed from the beginning of the interrogation since, according to one of the main accusations, Jesus "stirs up *the people*" (v.5 RSV). It is perhaps for this reason that Pilate calls together everyone, including the people, in order to make known his decision to release a man unjustly accused. That Jesus had not attempted to incite the multitudes, all the episodes of the preceding sections fully prove; this, however, had not prevented this same people from listening fervently and enthusiastically to Jesus every day that followed his entrance into the Temple (Luke 19:45 – 21:38). Yes, the people had always treated Jesus favorably and considered him to be a prophet. Yet, what does the multitude say at the decisive moment of the trial, when it is necessary to testify in favor of the one that it admires? That Jesus never attempted to incite anyone against the Roman authorities? The narrator laconically notes: "But they all cried out together, "Away with this man, and release to us Barabbas!" (Luke 23:18).

The people clearly know that the accusations of their religious authorities are false, but they cry: "Away with him". And here, in this complex episode, is a new paradox: the people testify to the falsity of the accusations at the very moment when they cry "Away with him!" How indeed could Jesus have incited against the Roman occupation this people who, far from being seduced by him and recognizing him as leader, call for his death?

But the itinerary of the people during the Passion of Jesus does not stop there, contrary to that of the religious authorities. After the official disavowal of the trial, the immense crowd will follow Jesus up to Calvary and, after the death of the victim, they will return repentant, conscious of their fault, of their cowardice[18].

4. The Contradiction of the Religious Authorities of Israel

The narrator thus allows the characters to speak: the contradictions in which they become imbued are strong enough so that there is no need to highlight them. He does intervene all the same to take to task that of the Jewish religious authorities. In the beginning of the trial, the members of the Sanhedrin indeed attest that Jesus urged the nation to revolt (v.2). Yet, during the second audience at Pilate's (v.13-25), the one where they ask for the Jesus' death, their bargaining chip is a certain Barabbas, about whom Luke twice emphasizes that he was in prison "for an insurrection started in the city and for murder" (v.19,25). The reader will have perhaps noted that the name of Barabbas is spoken only by the opponents and that the narrator only uses pronouns to designate him (v.19a,22a). This is one

---

[18] The characters "the people" and "the crowds" have traits in common in the scenes at the foot of the cross: in 23:35 the "people" are there and look on, but do not mock Jesus as the Jewish religious leaders and the soldiers do (cf. 23:35-37), and after the death of Jesus, the crowds that are gathered for the spectacle and look on leave beating their breasts (23:48). Are the people a part of these crowds that repent, in other words, does the last multitude include the people who cried "Away with him!" at the trial, or rather are these crowds composed solely of pilgrims who came in order to celebrate the Passover in Jerusalem and have gathered in order to take advantage of the spectacle and return disrupted? The narrator is not clear. It seems that although the repentance may be that of all the spectators present – thus of the people (laos) mentioned in 23:35 – the term "crowds", in the plural, includes everyone. Whatever may be, what is essential, for the veridical process, is the effective recognition of the innocence of Jesus and the guilt of all by the greatest possible number of witnesses – which the term crowds indicates.

of the rare times that the narrator intervenes in order to give a character's
negative ethical profile[19]. But it is not difficult to see why he is forced to
do so: the high priests and the scribes themselves are quite careful not to
mention his past, and this is truly their contradiction. For, if there is a man
for whom the High Council had to ask for death, it is Barabbas, who had
incited the people and had killed!   Yet, although Pilate may have
proclaimed Jesus' innocence for all to hear, the leaders reject the latter's
being released and demand the freedom of a rioter, precisely what they had
reproached Jesus for being. To accuse an innocent man of wanting to
incite the people and to end by asking for the freedom of another, who had
killed and had wanted the people to rebel: this episode clearly manifests
the accusers' incoherence.

Where, except at an official trial, must the revelation of the truth and
the lie occur? The goal is reached: the falsity of the accusations is
established, the accusers' lie confirmed and Jesus' innocence recognized
by the judicial authorities. Must everything thus not be at an end?

5. The Proclaimed Innocence in Spite of the Outcome of the Trial

In verse 22, Luke observes that Pilate says for *the third time* that he
has found nothing in Jesus that merits death. The reader does not need this
information from the narrator in order to know that Pilate is repeating
himself: mentioning it three times obviously emphasizes the judge's
conviction, a conviction all the more firm for being affirmed not only
before Jesus but in front of an entire people and its highest religious
authorities[20].

But if Pilate is also convinced of the prisoner's innocence, why does
he accede to their request? From fear of a riot: are not their howls aimed at
intimidating the judge?   The narrator's words authorize a similar
interpretation when he notes that Pilate frees Jesus "to their will" (v.25*b*):
the judge abdicated before the tenacity of the multitude. Fear and
cowardice.

The situation's profound irony emerges from between the lines: a
crowd that is itself bordering on revolt wants the death of a man that it
accuses of agitation. But whatever may be the reasons that cause Pilate to
comply, he finds himself as well imbued in the contradiction: he wanted to

---

[19] Cf. Luke 3:19-20 (on Herod).

[20] Compare the Lucan narrative with the corresponding episode in Matthew 27:11-26
and Mark 15:2-15, where Pilate does not say that he sees nothing in Jesus that merits death.

release Jesus whose innocence he understood and proclaimed and ends by releasing a prisoner who rose up against the Empire.

The episode's revelatory function is more important than the drama. Assured of the truth and the realization of Jesus' prolepses, in particular of those relating to his sufferings and his death, the reader already knows the final outcome; his interest is rather concerned with the *how*, with the circumstances and the recognition. All the actors of the drama being present at the trial, the episode acquires a decisive importance: before *all*, and *from the mouth of the official judicial authority*, Jesus' innocence is recognized. But at the same time as it seals the innocence of Jesus, this episode reveals the contradictions that dwell within the other actors: *all* without exception – the members of the Sanhedrin, the people, Pilate, Herod as well – contradict themselves, without the narrator ever needing to point it out explicitly.

But as important as they may be, the scenes of the appearance before Pilate and before Herod do not conclude the process of revelation that is at work during the Passion. For, if the reader knows that the characters are contradicting themselves, the latter still do not seem to realize it. Putting Jesus to death on the cross will be necessary for the crowds to beat their breasts. The lie does not prevent the truth from being revealed, on the contrary. That Pilate may have ceded to the demand of a crowd bordering on revolt is not at all contradictory with the process of the recognition of Jesus' innocence. The narrator's technique is only to show that the recognition of innocence is going to prevail over its opposite, the rejection.

Recognition and Characterization of the Characters in Luke 22 – 23

The Lucan narrator seems more interested by the when and the how of the recognition than by the drama. Jesus announces that he will suffer, that he will be considered a criminal, and this happens. But by substantially reducing the drama of the righteous whom the enemies refuse to recognize up to the end – a drama that the two other Synoptics wanted to recount in all its intensity by following another model –, does not the Lucan narrative remove from the situations and the characters their weight of humanity?

It is first necessary to admit that Luke is attempting to minimize the responsibility of some of his characters – that of the disciples, for example. During the agony at Gethsemane, they slept... "from sadness", out of sympathy, one would say today, whereas in Matthew and in Mark, especially, they strictly understand nothing of the gravity of the hour. In Luke, they do not flee when the armed band comes to arrest Jesus[21]. In the other three Gospels, Peter's denial follows Jesus' interrogation at the High Priest's, which greatly accentuates the seriousness of his statements that they do not have in the IIIrd Gospel. We indeed know that in Matthew/Mark/John the disposition of the text itself indicates that the reader must read the two interrogations, that of Jesus by the authorities and that of Peter by the servants, as if they were concomitant[22], in order to compare[23] the questions and the answers:

a Jesus is led to the High Priest's	Matthew 26:57; Mark 14:53; John 18:13-14
b Peter is seated outside	Matthew 26:58; Mark 14:54; John 18:15-18
A Jesus' interrogation	Matthew 26:59-68; Mark 14:55-65; John 18:19-24
B Peter's interrogation	Matthew 26:69-75; Mark 14:66-72; John 18:25-27

What is more, for Judas' betrayal, Luke does not keep the terrible sentence pronounced by Jesus: "It would have been better for that man if he had not been born." (Matthew 26:24; Mark 14:21). Moreover, does not the final prayer include all the actors of the drama in this semi-responsibility tainted by ignorance: "Father, forgive them; for they know not what they do" (Luke 23:34)? But is it because God is the agent who is directing the events, because it "was necessary" that Jesus die? Such a necessity would seem to reduce the role of the opponents, of all the actors of the Passion.

The Lucan characters, nevertheless, do not become flimsy, simple puppets useful for demonstrating the thesis of Jesus' innocence. From Peter, who is caught up in his denial and then weeps, to Herod, whose sadism does not disappear, as if by magic, before Jesus' innocence, they keep all this trait of mystery that the external focus, almost always adopted by Luke, clearly highlights.

---

[21] Luke 22:53. Compare Matthew 26:56; Mark 14:50-52. Like Luke, John 18:1-12 does not speak of the flight of the disciples.

[22] On the meaning to give to this disposition, see the work already cited of A. BORRELL I VIADER, *The Good News of Peter's Denial*.

[23] The comparison, in Greek *synkrisis*, is a technique very much used by Luke but also by Plutarch (cf. his *Parallel Lives*). If the Lucan narrator does not use it for this episode, although he knows the disposition of Mark and he would thus have had an ideal occasion to do so, it is really because he does not want to charge Peter.

The case of the people is perhaps the most typical: if Jesus had been followed assiduously and with devotion, it is really by the people; yet, during the trial, without warning and without the reader knowing why, the people place themselves on the side of the religious authorities and demand the death of Jesus. If Luke had wanted only to highlight Jesus' innocence, without implicating the people, it would have been easy for him to say that the people had heard and seen everything from the trial, without crying out or demanding Jesus' death: this would not have lessened the testimony for establishing the truth of his narrative. Yet, he causes all the multitude to cry out, without exception. A strange reenactment, perhaps explainable by sociological laws, but narratively inexplicable. It would not have mattered in the least, in the Lucan narrative of the Passion, if Jesus' life had been spared: if the people had not shouted with the high priests and the scribes, would Pilate have freed him? The narrator says nothing more on this because he knows nothing more about it! And this makes his narrative more opaque, at the very moment when the contradictions of the accusers and the innocence of the accused are revealed. The episode of the appearance perhaps reflects more than the others the way in which Luke presents his characters during the Passion: layers of feelings, reasons and declarations. Decisions and hearts thus keep all the mystery of their humanity – of obstinacy but also of fragility. A mystery, certainly, but in agreement with the narrative logic, if one is really willing to keep in mind the problem of the *anagnôrisis*. Indeed, during his Passion, Jesus was not recognized by his coreligionists, and, in this regard, Mark and Matthew clearly reflect the reality. If the Lucan narrative had taken the opposite option of mentioning the explicit recognition of the crowds during the trial, it would have certainly obeyed the canons of the biographies of that time, but in doing so, it would have forfeited being seen as reliable by its readers. An implicit collective recognition, of the gestural type (Luke 23:48), *post mortem*, respected the Greek biographical canons, without however ignoring the rejection of which Jesus had been the object during his Passion.

Truly, the problem of the characters' consistency is raised less by his enemies or by his disciples than by Jesus himself. His silence before Herod, his promise made to the thief, his familiarity with God, his indefectible trust: so many traits that seem to make up a smooth character, without depth, playing a role that he knows must soon end. Where is the weight of humanity, of dereliction, reported by the scenes at the foot of the cross in Matthew/Mark? Certainly, during the proceedings and the circumstances that surround the death of Jesus, Luke almost exclusively keeps the elements that lead up to the double recognition – the innocence of Jesus and the remorse of the crowds. But it is necessary not to forget the evening before in Gethsemane, where the narrator speaks of Jesus' agony (Luke 22:44) and of the comfort (22:43) that is necessary for him to face the suffering and death. A strange episode, at the least unexpected on the part of a narrator who, above all, carefully highlights the way in which Jesus announces and dominates the events. If the narrator has not omitted it, it is really because his protagonist has actually passed through the throes of an agony, the intensity of which is suggested by the mention of sweat. Certainly, Luke is silent about the reasons for this agony, but his writing resonates with this battle: Jesus does not appear as a good schoolboy who does as he is told but as a man who offers his freedom, without which the "it is necessary" (in Greek, *dei*) loses its pertinence. One may thus not say that the character of Jesus is lacking in humanity in the episodes of the Passion of the IIIrd Gospel: given the Lucan perspective, the reader rather had to be astonished that he still has it!

The episode of the trial shows, moreover, how to understand this "it is necessary"; the having-to-suffer (in order to enter into glory), which drives the narrative's logic, does not erase human freedoms, but only indicates their limits: faults, resistance, rejections do not prevent God from causing His salvation to happen. The "it is necessary" cuts through human rejections in order to manifest them and purify them.

Rejection and Final Recognition

In preceding sections, Jesus was proclaimed by the disciples as Christ (Luke 9:20) and King (Luke 19:38). Without going this far in their recognition, the crowds had seen in him a great prophet. During the trial and the scenes at the foot of the cross, the recognition of his identity will be less. Pilate, who sees in him neither a prophet nor the king of the Jews, however, proclaims that he is innocent, and the centurion confesses that he is righteous (Luke 23:47). The crowds present at the placing on the cross and at the death also share, although implicitly, the centurion's opinion, since all go away beating their breasts – the recognition of their fault is correlative to that of Jesus' innocence. Thus, there are degrees to the confession and the recognition; on the other hand, for the narrator, what matters is not the degree but that at the trial and after his death Jesus' innocence be *recognized in one way or another by the greatest number of characters*.

Let us go further! Paradoxically, the rejection is in the service of the recognition. Two categories of characters, the religious leaders and the soldiers, indeed refuse to see in Jesus the One Sent by God, and the narrator attempts neither to be silent about nor erase their resistance, their provocations (Luke 23:35-37). The reason for it is simple, narratively speaking, of course: if there had not been opponents up to his death, Jesus would not have been able to go through to the end the ways that *had* to be his: to support the outrages without responding to them, even to ask God – whom he calls his Father – to forgive, in order thus to be recognized as righteous, innocent. It is really the intimacy of which Jesus is the object, that highlights his trust and his abandonment to the tenderness of God and that allows the crowd of witnesses to discover in the end their own fault.

What remains is that the narrative consistency of the Jewish authorities in the Lucan narrative causes difficulty. During the journey towards Jerusalem, Jesus already had opponents: the Pharisees, the legalists and the scribes; but there is no more mention of the legalists and the Pharisees after Luke 19:39. And the narrator does not say what became of them. As for the religious leaders, high priests and guards that the narrative highlights only after the entrance of Jesus into the Temple (19:47), their life and death opposition gives the impression of being as sudden as it is violent: how were they able to decide to deliver to death a man that they had never encountered? But, will one object, do not the scribes form a bridge between the first series of opponents and the second, since they follow Jesus from the beginning of his teaching[24]. Certainly, but after Luke 22:2, thus before the Passion, they also disappear; then only the priests, the strategists, the leaders and the elders remain as opponents. Actually, what it is necessary to accept is less the narrative's coherence seen in the reasons that the religious authorities were able to find in order to get rid of Jesus than in the narrator's wanting to make them the ones principally responsible for his death. This, moreover, is what the two disciples will repeat on the road to Emmaus (Luke 24:20): "Our chief priests and rulers, delivered him up to be condemned to death, and crucified him." In short, the reader must not look for the narrative's

---

[24] The term *scribes* (in Greek, *grammateis*) is always used by Luke in the plural. For the sections of the itinerant ministry, cf. 5:21,30; 6:7; 9:22 (Jesus' prolepsis); 11:53, 15:2. For the episodes that take place in the Temple and where the plan to put Jesus to death is clearly expressed, cf. 19:47; 20:1,19,39,46.

coherence in the sustained opposition, from the beginning to the end, by the same characters, but in the progressive accession of the truth and the lie: the contradictions of the religious leaders are shown in the break between the accusations that they formulate at the encounter with Jesus and the freeing of the rioter Barabbas, which they demand from Pilate. For an objection could be formulated: certainly, the people saw in Jesus a prophet, but the authorities charged with good doctrine and responsible for order have not given in to seduction! The appearance before Pilate shows that it is necessary to make such an objection.

To show the truth and/or the lie of the different actors of the drama that he is describing, without removing their aura of mystery and opacity, such is the tour de force to which the Lucan narrator has reached in the episode of the trial and in the scenes at the foot of the cross. All the actors know – more or less – who they are respectively and end by saying so. But if the narrative of the Passion is in some way the *Who's Who* of the IIIrd Gospel, it seems to seal the failure that the two disciples of Luke 24 deplore while they walk to Emmaus.

The Final *anagnôrisis*. Luke 24

In Luke 23, there really is a collective and final recognition… that of the crowds present around the cross upon which Jesus, dead, remains hanging until he is taken down. A lesser recognition than that of the disciples in Luke 9:20 and 19:37-38, but a recognition all the same. According to the literary canons followed by the Greco-Roman biographies, this recognition suffices, for it indicates that Jesus' coreligionists, on the whole, have recognized with gestures their fault, their responsibility (Luke 23:48) and, at the same time, the innocence of the one whom they had declared guilty of sedition.

Such a recognition on the part of the crowds, nevertheless, does not exhaust the project that the Lucan narrator settled on, for the disciples are excluded from it. For them, the recognition of innocence does not suffice. What is important is to see Jesus alive, to recognize him in a way that is not mistaken about the person but also to know, now that he is alive, why he had submitted to an ignominious death. If they neither encountered nor recognized Jesus resurrected, how would they be able to testify and do so in a way that others might, in their turn, be able to recognize in him the Messiah promised and announced by the Scriptures? This is one of the functions of Luke 24: to describe how the disciples came to recognize Jesus and why they had to recognize him.

Although insufficient, for it involves only two of the disciples and thus does not constitute a final collective recognition, the episode of Emmaus, so many times commented upon, is interesting for the subject that we are dealing with, for it clearly shows that it does not suffice to see in order to recognize. The narrator does not say: "Their eyes were prevented from *seeing him*: (v.16), nor "Their eyes were opened and *they saw him*" (v.31), for the two disciples saw him *without recognizing him*[25]. Thus, are clearly indicated the limits of physical seeing for recognizing the Resurrected One. The time that separates the "seeing" from the "recognizing" permits the exegetical lesson that the two men will later (v.32) confess had transformed them. They will then understand why Jesus had not wanted to cause them to recognize him at once: their desire to see him was strong, but they now know that physical sight is no longer an absolute; even invisible to their fleshly eyes, the Resurrected One will remain present: *invisibility* is not/is no longer the equivalent of absence. The sudden disappearance of Jesus, after the recognition, could have left them sad, stunned, paralyzed. Yet, they do not even speak of it, as if it neither affected nor worried them. It is rather the time that preceded the recognition – the time of the journey, the time of listening – that holds their attention: they mention only their radical transformation, their burning hearts, and attribute it to the words of Jesus when he was expressing the coherence of his life and theirs.

By not making himself known immediately, Jesus allows the two disciples to understand that recognition is not the equivalent of physical sight, but it must integrate all that had prevented the Messiah and Son of God from being *recognizable* and had made him *unrecognizable* to the eyes of all. Yet, this recognition is identical to that of the ways of God, so that one may say, along with Jesus resurrected: "Yes, it was necessary that the Christ suffer in order to enter into his glory." And this recognition goes well beyond the Greek biographical canons.

---

[25] Luke 24:16 ("But their eyes were kept from recognizing him") and 31 ("And their eyes were opened and they recognized him") use the verb *epiginôskô* (to recognize). The same verb in JUSTIN, *Dialogue with Trypho*, 69:6 (Jesus did miracles in order to be recognized). The problem of Luke 24 is really that of the *anagnôrisis*. The synonymous verb *anagnôrizô*, which is found in Genesis 45:1, when Joseph made himself known to his brothers, is literally repeated in Acts 7:13, by Stephen ("Joseph made himself known to his brothers").

The process of recognition reaches its end with *all* the disciples (Luke 24:36-49). It was indeed necessary that *all* recognized him in order to be able to testify to his resurrection and to justify the necessary passage through the sufferings and the death on the cross. In short, even if Luke 24 seems to end with an *Acta est fabula* [= the End], it is clearly preparing for the book of Acts.

V. CONCLUSIONS

The differences that exist between the narratives of the Passion/death of Jesus in Matthew/Mark and in Luke come from the models by which they have respectively been inspired. If one uses the facts without seeing that they belong to a structure or that they form the elements of different models, one will say that one or the other of the Synoptics is awkward or mistaken[26], even though different models required different facts. Just like Mark and Matthew, Luke does not provide raw, anecdotal facts, but those with meaning, as keys to reading, and it is, above all, as elements of meaning – and not as historiographic components – that the facts of the text must be interpreted. May the presentation of the Passion according to Luke that has just been made have sufficiently shown this!

Regarding the skill of the Lucan narrator in the matter of literary formation, in particular of narrativity, commentators are divided[27]. In *Le Jésus de Luc*, I tackled the question of the style and the allusions to Greek literature. The preceding paragraphs on the Passion and resurrection of Jesus in Luke do not seem to me to require changing the thoughts formulated at that time: through his art of developing a narrative, of recounting the characters' points of view, of using the *synkrisis*, Luke demonstrates a technical and cultural level that school exercises (the *progymnasmata*) would not have necessarily given to him.

In the studies on the biographical genre of Luke, it has been more a question of the prologue and Gospel of the Infancy – that correspond to the *genos* of the Greek canons –, for it is principally these passages that confirm the genre in question. But the importance that the Lucan narrator gives to the final recognition and the way in which he presents it have not received enough attention. The next chapter will show how much the question of the recognition additionally influenced the typological writing of Luke.

---

[26] Did or did not the disciples flee at Jesus' arrest? Etc.
[27] J.N. ALETTI, *Le Jésus de Luc*, 14-16.

CHAPTER V

THE BIOGRAPHICAL GENRE
AND TYPOLOGY IN THE IIIRD GOSPEL

I. INTRODUCTION

In the Gospel narratives, Jesus is quite often described with traits that recall those of biblical figures from the past in order to show the unity and the fulfillment of the divine plan of salvation. The phenomenon is called *typology*. But if the four Gospels have recourse to it, it is neither with the same frequency nor in the same manner. We may unmistakably state from the outset that the prophetic typology developed by Luke is thematically more continuous than in the other Gospels, to the point of its practically covering the entire narrative.

The present chapter is proposing to show (1°) that the use of typology is firmly linked to the question of the *anagnôrisis*[1], (2°) that the typology of the Lucan narrative is principally prophetic, and we will try to determine the reason for this, (3°) that this prophetic typology begins with Luke 1 – 2, in which it is the work of the narrator and remains implicit, then with Luke 4 it is taken over by Jesus, who sets it out and develops it in an explicit manner and continues it up to the end of his ministry.

---

[1] Perhaps it is good to recall once again that the recognition (of the hero in narratives, of the guilty in tragedies) in general announces the denouement of the tension in ancient dramas and narratives. One encounters similar scenes of recognition in the Gospel narratives, in particular after the resurrection. The recognition is almost always preceded by a non-recognition, like that of Mary Magdalene at the tomb, who sees Jesus but confuses him with the gardener before recognizing him. But there is also the *anagnôrisis* of the protagonist whose moral and religious qualities or status were previously ignored, rejected, like the Jesus of Luke, who was, as we have seen, implicitly recognized innocent by the actors present at the foot of the cross.

II. TYPOLOGY AND RECOGNITION

Before showing that typology, in the Gospels, has the function of responding to the demands of the *anagnôrisis*, let us recall that one wrote only the lives of men known and recognized for their teaching and their actions – military leaders, political men, philosophers and orators. As has been pointed out in the preceding chapters, the biography of an unknown, like Jesus of Nazareth, was unthinkable, *a fortiori* if he had been rejected by his contemporaries and remained so for subsequent generations.

The challenge of the first Christian generations was thus to write biographies of Jesus by showing that he had been recognized during his ministry, assiduously followed and acclaimed by the crowds. Some Gospel episodes end with the stupefaction or acclamation of those who are present at his miracles and hear his teaching. But, as we explained at length in chapter II, the final *anagnôrisis* was lacking: Jesus died alone, abandoned by his disciples, accused of blasphemy and put to death. How to interpret the contrast between the admiration of so many during the itinerant ministry and the ignominious death, that of criminals? To the Christian group for whom his death was salvific, the representatives of Judaism of that time could object that, if Jesus had succeeded in seducing the crowds, he was not able to deceive the country's religious elites and had, moreover, been abandoned by the God whose messianic envoy he had claimed to be.

We have already seen how the Gospel narratives were able to show that the recognition of their protagonist Jesus had not taken place only in light of his miraculous acts during his ministry and how they were able to propose a coherent reading of his Passion and his death that was capable of bringing about their readers' recognition. During Jesus' ministry in Galilee and through the ascent to Jerusalem, the recognition of Jesus' prophetic identity by the crowds was possible thanks to the type of acts performed, for they recalled those of the great prophetic figures from ancient times. This connection of Jesus to the biblical figures from the past is what constitutes the typology of the New Testament narratives[2]. This chapter is proposing to show that prophetic typology is what best accounts for the Lucan narrative material.

---

[2] The typological reading of the New Testament is not the most ancient, as shown by M. FISHBANE, *Biblical Interpretation in Ancient Israel* (Oxford, Clarendon Press 1985) 281-440, but is the most well-known.

Before seeing how the Lucan narrative elaborates its typology, it is important to provide some clues about the voice that, in Luke, states the typological relationships. (1) Some correspondences are made by the narrator in the form of allusions. Thus, the first episode of Luke, that of the announcement to Zachariah, is entirely typological[3], for it places the divine promise and Zachariah's response in line with the divine promise of numerous descendants and Abraham's corresponding response in Genesis 15, but it is an allusion, not an explicit reference. It is the same in Luke 7:15, where the narrative voice says that Jesus restores the living child to his mother, like Elijah at Zarephath and with the same words as in 1Kings 17:23 (*edôken auton tè mètri autou*). These typological allusions are made by the narrator and have for their sole addressee the readers – those clearly having a sufficient knowledge of the biblical books. (2) In other passages, as we are soon going to see, it is Jesus himself who states the typological relationships, and he does so for the listeners of that time, the disciples and the crowds that listen to or follow him. One can thus diagram this allocation:

	ALLUSIVE STATEMENTS	EXPLICIT STATEMENTS
Speaker	narrative voice (Nr)	Jesus
first addressee second addressee	reader	disciples and crowds reader
sections of Luke	Luke 1 – 2 (+ Luke 3)	Luke 4 to 19

To the two principal speakers, the narrator and Jesus, correspond two series of typological statements in Luke 1 – 3 and Luke 4 – 19, respectively. In other words, the typology of Luke is split into two groups, the first that precedes the episode of Jesus at Nazareth (Luke 4:16-30) and the second that takes its point of departure from there.

III. PROPHETIC TYPOLOGY BEFORE LUKE 4

As was just said and will be fully demonstrated by what follows, the Lucan narrative is typological all the way through, but in its first chapters

---

[3] Cf., for example, M. COLERIDGE, *The Birth of the Lukan Narrative, Narrative as Christology in Lukan 1-2* (JSNTSS 88; Sheffield, Academic Press 1993), 33-41, who points out the range of the Old Testament allusions and the most probable parallels – in Greek, *synkrisis*.

(Luke 1 – 2), which are its introduction, the prophetic typology applied to Jesus is the work of the narrator and not the narrative's characters.

For a long time, it has been admitted that the vocabulary and the style of these chapters are anthological. Throughout the episodes, the narrative indeed echoes words, expressions, stylistic turns and schemas of the Greek Bible, in particular the first three chapters of the first book of Samuel. But what is borrowed is not only lexical and stylistic, for in 1Samuel 1 – 2 and Luke 1 – 2 the situations and the reactions of the characters are analogous, the narrator implicitly tracing a parallelism between Samuel and Jesus:

1 SAMUEL	LUKE	COMMON ELEMENTS
1:1-20	1:5-25	barrenness of Hannah/Elizabeth, prayer, fulfillment
2:1-11	1:46-56	canticle of Hannah/Mary and the return home
2:18-21	2:22-35	presentation of Samuel and Jesus in the Temple, an elderly man blesses the parents, the return home
2:21,26;	2:40,52	for Samuel and Jesus, growth and grace before God and humans
3:1	2:43,46	Samuel and Jesus remain in the house of God

In Luke 1 – 2, the narrator thus shows by repeated allusions that Jesus will be like Samuel and that, still a child, he is *recognized by all those who have close contact with him* as being filled with the grace and wisdom of the Lord. The narrative of the childhood and the introduction of the Lucan macro-narrative thus end with a (collective) *anagnôrisis* that at the same time establishes a typological relationship of a prophetic nature. Jesus will be a prophet and, if Samuel was the first great biblical prophet, Jesus will be the eschatological prophet. Will Samuel still be the prophetic figure used in order to describe Jesus' actions during his ministry? In other words, will the narrator take up other traits from the character of Samuel in order to describe Jesus in his teaching and in his actions? It is clearly impossible to respond before Jesus begins his ministry in Galilee. What it is necessary to keep in mind is the artful way with which the narrator has used, without making explicit citations[4], some

---

[4] The sole exception: Luke 2:23-24

passages from the Old Testament for the unfolding of his narrative and for describing Jesus' prophetic identity[5].

The Lucan narrative's manner of proceeding is already identifiable in Luke 1 – 2. The narrative voice (the narrator) constructs his typology with discretion and works behind the scenes, effectuating numerous correlations between actors and between events, but without saying so. And, will one ask, why does he not say so clearly? His discretion is not the equivalent of a rejection of typology, rather it reveals, as we are going to ascertain, a technique, that of giving Jesus the task of *explicitly* undertaking the typological route.

IV. THE TYPOLOGY IN LUKE 4:16-30

The first part of the episode at Nazareth recounts the ritual of the reading of the text from Isaiah 61. As commentators note, the composition aims to show indirectly that Jesus is the prophet of whom the text is speaking, the one upon whom the Spirit of the Lord rests and who is sent to announce the Good News. This indirect designation is clearly made for the reader (alone), who knows that Jesus received the Holy Spirit at baptism (Luke 3:22). The text thus functions on two levels: (1) the one in which the narrator suggests to the reader that Jesus is the prophet of whom Isaiah 61 is speaking; (2) that of the connections between the characters, in other words, between Jesus and the Nazarenes, his listeners, who are still ignorant of Jesus' being the prophet of whom Isaiah 61 is speaking. In Luke 4:16-30 the reader of Luke is thus not in the same position as the listener to Jesus in the synagogue, who does not know what happened at the baptism… and even well before, at Jesus' conception (Luke 1:35).

The narrator's typology has up to this point remained discreet, and for a simple reason: it is to Jesus that, henceforth, is reserved the role of explicitly saying what his relationship is to the prophets from the past. In the second part of the episode, he interprets the text of Isaiah 61 and reveals his prophetic identity by appealing to the figures of Elijah and Elisha.

In Luke 4:24-27, Jesus announces that he is a prophet and will, like his predecessors, be rejected, but he also names the Old Testament figures

---

[5] As all the commentators point out, there are many other allusions to the Old Testament in Luke 1 – 2; only those that construct a prophetic typology are considered here.

with whom he will be in a typological relationship and implicitly indicates by what signs one will thus be able to recognize him. This is one of the characteristics of the Lucan typological relationship: the prophet must be recognized as such, but he must also be rejected: there cannot be one without the other. By saying that *no* prophet is acceptable in his homeland, Jesus is not just claiming to describe the situation of the prophets of his time, in particular that of his predecessor John the Baptist[6]. He is referring, in the form of a saying, to the whole of the prophets from the biblical past grasped as a unified totality: the past of prophetic history sheds light on the events in Nazareth and prepares for the whole of Jesus' itinerary. The two examples in verses 25 to 27 are interesting because the prophetic activities of Elijah and Elisha are described in narratives that already suppose a rereading of Moses' thaumaturgical activity. Then, because the Jewish tradition itself held Elijah to be an eschatological figure (cf. already Sirach 48:10-11); all the prophetic history can thus be summarized in him: he refers back to the past model, Moses, and he is the promise of the future time, a time of anger and of salvation. But it is by following the IIIrd Gospel that one will see the profound reason for the choice of Elijah and Elisha. The two prophets are thus no simple passing illustrations: thanks to them, Jesus is proposing a reading of his entire ministry as one of continuity. He will do analogous signs and will thus be able to be recognized as an authentic prophet. It is thus not only the rejection (v.24) that makes Jesus a true prophet but the whole of his salvific activity (and, in consequence, the whole of the IIIrd Gospel), which will give the same message, coming from the same God.

From the episode of Nazareth on, Jesus thus sees the prophetic history and his own as one of universality and rejection, thus tracing a way through the Scriptures to him, the prophet of the eschatological day. One can, henceforth, reverse the terms: if the Scriptures provide the means for understanding the fate of Jesus, they in fact become a model and a norm through Jesus' word that thus acquires its maximal extension, since the

---

[6] That Luke places Jesus in relation with these two figures does not prevent John the Baptist from also having Elijah's traits (Luke 1:17,76). The traditional link between John the Baptist and Elijah has paradoxically allowed the Lucan narrator to emphasize the difference between John (prophet: 1:17,76) and Jesus (Son of God: 1:32,35; Messiah, savior, etc.) in the so called "Infancy Narrative" (Luke 1-2) and, in the remainder of the Gospel, to connect what is said of Elijah and Elisha entirely to the person and the work of Jesus. For the function of Elijah in the IIIrd Gospel, cf. also R.J. MILLER, "Elijah, John and Jesus in the Gospel of Luke", in *NTS* 34 (1988) 611-622.

prophetic history is found to be summarized, unified in him at the very moment when it is called upon in order to shed light on the present.

One also sees that the prophetic figures from Isaiah 61:1-2 and the books of Kings are complementary. The passage from Isaiah determines some new relationships but says nothing of the modalities of the fulfillment of the prophet's mission, namely of the concrete recipients and conditions in which the envoy will accomplish his mission, nor above all how he will be recognized by his hearers. Thus is necessary a template of reading, of criteria that make this recognition possible: this is the function, in verses 25-27, of the recourse to the Elijah and Elisha cycles. The text of Isaiah indeed lays out some roles and is found, by what Jesus says, to be confirmed as a prophecy of last events, but it says nothing of the whole of the history of salvation in its events and its great figures. As to the passage on Elijah and Elisha, it could only state a law of continuity and discernment concerning the non-recognition of the prophets, but without the text of Isaiah 61 and its confirmation as eschatological prophecy it would not be a culminating point in the series.

What to retain from this episode for our subject? The confirmation that in Luke the prophetic typology prevails, since in this programmatical narrative it is Jesus himself who will take charge of it and designate the two principal figures who will serve for recognizing him. But there are also the two sides to prophetic typology: positive with the necessary recognition and negative with the rejection, for it is these two dimensions that allow recognizing a true prophet, Jesus, who, being the ultimate link in such a series, must thus himself also be recognized *and* rejected. What remains is to verify that this double dimension structures the ministry of Jesus.

V. THE TYPOLOGY OF JESUS AFTER LUKE 4 AND ITS REASONS

We just said that Luke 4:24-27 kicks off the application of the typology of Elijah and Elisha to Jesus. Even a quick reading of the passages evoking the figure and the deeds of the two prophets confirms this[7]:

---

[7] The numbers in italics indicate the passages proper to Luke. For the details, see J.D. DuBois, "La figure d'Élie dans la perspective lucanienne", in *RHPR* 53 (1973) 155-173.

	LUKE	BOOKS OF KINGS
Jesus in the desert	4:1-13	1 Kings 19:1-8
healings of the lepers	5:12-14; *17:11-19*	2 Kings 5
healings of the blind	*7:21*; *14:13*; *14:21*; 18:35-43	2 Kings 6:17,20
miracles with food	9:10-17	1 Kings 17:7-16; 2 Kings 4:42-44
resurrections of the dead	*7:11-17*; 8:40-56	1 Kings 17;17-24; 2 Kings 4:18-37
the encounter with God on the mountain or the episode of the transfiguration	9:28-36	1 Kings 19:9-18
the destructive fire	*9:54*	2 Kings 1:10-12
the call of the disciples	9:57-62	1 Kings 19:19-21
the ascension	*Luke 24* and *Acts 1*	2 Kings 2:1-18

If Elijah and Elisha are the principal figures used by Luke, the typology is not limited to them, for it is employed to show that what is at stake remains the recognition of Jesus' prophetic identity. And this problem is going to be developed in two complementary parts. In the first, it is the aspect of being recognized that is going to be favored, for Jesus is going to be recognized by his countrymen as a prophet, and, in the second, it is the rejection that is going to constitute the principal leitmotif. Jesus' ministry can thus be divided into two parts that take up and develop the proleptic statements of Luke 4. The first part goes *grosso modo* up to Peter's confession, and the second runs throughout the journey to Jerusalem, up to Luke 19:27, which we can represent in a diagram:

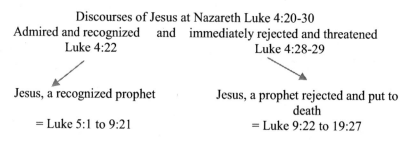

Discourses of Jesus at Nazareth Luke 4:20-30

Admired and recognized   and   immediately rejected and threatened
Luke 4:22   Luke 4:28-29

Jesus, a recognized prophet   Jesus, a prophet rejected and put to death

= Luke 5:1 to 9:21   = Luke 9:22 to 19:27

Recognition and Prophetic Typology

That the recognition prevails in the first part of the ministry, the accumulation of questions on the identity of Jesus amply proves:

REACTIONS OF CHARACTERS	VERSES	IDENTITY OF JESUS BY AFFIRMATION/QUESTION
the crowd	7:16	"a great prophet"
Jesus	7:19-22	describing John the Baptist in connection with him (a reprise of Isaiah 61:1, a passage read in Luke 4:18-19)
Jesus	7:24-27	describing John the Baptist in connection to him = to prepare his way
persons present at Simon's home	7:49	"Who is this, who forgives sins?"
the disciples	8:24-25	"Who is this, whom the elements obey?"
a demoniac	8:28	"Jesus, Son of the Most High God"
the people	9:7-9	John the Baptist, Elijah, a prophet of old
Herod	9:7-9	"Who is this?"
the crowds	9:18-20	"Elijah or one of the great prophets"
Peter	9:18-20	"the Christ of God"

The characters' reactions are also distributed throughout the first chapters of the ministry and come from all the population, from the humblest to the most elevated (Herod). Many follow Jesus in order to listen to him or to be healed by him, and his identity leaves no one indifferent. That the recognition and prophetic typology are strongly associated may not be denied. An episode like Luke 7:11-16, proper to Luke, clearly emphasizes this association, for it echoes Jesus' statement in Luke 4:25-26 and ideally summarizes this section of the Gospel devoted to the question of the recognition of the identity of Jesus. Let us briefly see how and why[8].

Entering into the city of Nain, Jesus encounters a widow in tears, accompanied by a large crowd that is leaving the city with her to bury her only son. Moved by pity, he asks those who are carrying the child on a stretcher to stop, asks the dead to rise and returns him alive to his mother. In light of Jesus' deed, all the people present, whether they were accompanying the widow or Jesus, begin to praise and exclaim: "A great

---

[8] One will find a more developed narrative analysis of this episode in J.-N. ALETTI, *Le Jésus de Luc*, 115-120.

prophet has arisen among us!" and "God has visited his people!" (7:16), the second part of the sentence literally repeating a verse from Zechariah's canticle (1:68). In what way can Jesus' deed be able to spark such a reaction and in some way cause all to have recognized him as a *great prophet* and understood that by him the eschatological visit of the Lord had come? Why do all those present declare Jesus "a great prophet"? The allusions to the narrative of Elijah reviving the only son of the widow of Zarephath provide an initial explanation. Let us recall the words that echo 1Kings 17:17-24 (LXX)[9]:

1KINGS 17:17-24	LUKE 7:11-17
the widow (v.20)	a widow (v.12)
her dead son (v.17,20)	a dead only son (v.12)
the child cried (v.22)	the dead began to speak (v.15)
[Elijah] gave him to his mother (v.23)	[Jesus] gave him to his mother (v.15)
you are a man of God (v.24)	a great prophet has arisen (v.16)

Have the characters made the connection between Jesus' deed and that of Elijah? The text does not say, but this is not impossible, regarding the other miracles already performed by Jesus – a subsequent passage (Luke 9:19) will indeed say that many saw in him Elijah at the end of time. For the reader, on the other hand, the recognition is facilitated by the verbal correspondences, in particular that of Luke 7:15 with 1Kings 17:23 ("he gave him to his mother"), but especially in Luke 4:26-27 where it was already a matter of the widow of Zarephath. These are the signs that allow recognizing the visit from God. But these analepses call for reading the passage in context, which will enhance this episode.

After the discourse on the plain, Jesus enters Capharnaum where he heals a slave on the point of death. A progression can thus be seen in the two episodes, for in Luke 7:10, at Capharnaum, Jesus heals *someone dying*, and in 7:11-17, at Nain, he revives a *dead* young man, son of a widow. These two miracles are not isolated from what follows: in his response to John's envoys, Jesus refers to the resurrections of the dead performed by him: "The dead are raised" (7:22). The function of the episodes at Capharnaum and Nain then appear clearer: with them the narrator is preparing for the question of Jesus' identity and the response of the latter. Thanks to these two acts of power and to the other healings –

---

[9] Cf., among others, T.L. BRODIE, "Towards Unraveling Luke's Use of the Old Testament: Luke 7:11-17 as an Imitatio of 1 Kings 17:17-24", in *NTS* 32 (1986) 247-267.

those that preceded them and those that the narrator enumerates in the summary that follows in 7:21 –, Jesus will be able to say simply and implicitly "See what I have done"! But the recognition is possible because these signs correspond to an expectation, itself inspired by a promise: in his response, Jesus echoes the text of Isaiah already read during the episode at Nazareth and others, mentioned above, indicating once again that it is necessary to see in all this the fulfillment of prophecies.

The presentation of Luke 7:11-17, an episode proper to the IIIrd Gospel and where the Lucan redaction appears with even more clarity, thus allows seeing how the prophetic typology gives form and profundity to the Christology. Jesus' initiative, his compassion, the power of his intervention and especially the resurrection of the child – that heralds the final resurrection and God's victory over death – actually demonstrate that the God of Israel is and will be victorious over evil and death. By giving a son back to his mother, by recreating bonds and identities, Jesus is conjointly manifesting a new and decisive trait of his own identity, that of giving life, like God Himself. Luke 7:11-16 thus summarizes this section of the Lucan narrative dedicated to the manner in which Jesus makes himself known and identifiable as the eschatological prophet.

What it is above all necessary to retain for our subject is the relationship existing between the episode of the widow of Nain and the statement of Jesus at Nazareth on the sending of Elijah to the widow of Zarephath: this typological relationship reminds us that it is Jesus who, from the beginning of his ministry, has inaugurated the typology concerning himself and that he has himself executed it by his deeds and his words in Luke 7 and, from there, in the entire first part of the ministry.

Rejection and Prophetic Typology

Once the process of the recognition of the prophetic identity (for the crowds) and the messianic identity (for the disciples) reached its conclusion with Peter's confession, Jesus initiates the second part, henceforth negative, of the prophetic typology. As the rejection is not going to be effective until the entrance into the Passion, it is only a matter of announcements explicitly formulated by Jesus – and by him alone.

If these announcements are not disseminated throughout the journey, they are, nevertheless, found in some of the passages that recall for those who listen to Jesus and the reader the importance of the composite *rejection*, by which Jesus is able to be recognized as a true prophet:

ANNOUNCEMENTS	VERSES	REJECTION, SUFFERINGS AND DEATH
Jesus	9:22	1st announcement of the Passion
Jesus	9:43b-44	2nd announcement of the Passion
Jesus	11:29-32	"an evil generation… like that of Jonah"
Jesus	11:47	"you build the tombs of the prophets"
Jesus	11:48	"your fathers killed the prophets"
Jesus	11:50-51	"the blood of the prophets"
Jesus	13:33-34	"Jerusalem, you killed the prophets"
Jesus	17:17	"Where are the other nine?"
Jesus	18:31-34	3rd announcement of the Passion

As Luke 7:11-16 was the representative episode of the recognition section in the first part of the ministry, Luke 17:11-19, itself also proper to the Lucan narrative, is representative, for the second part of the *rejection* section. Let us see why and how[10].

While going up to Jerusalem, Jesus passes through the borders of Samaria. There, ten lepers implore him from a distance and ask him to have pity on them. Jesus sends them to the priests, and the ten immediately obey him. While they are on their way, they are healed and purified, and one of the ten, a Samaritan, returns to give thanks at the feet of Jesus, who is surprised to see only this stranger returning and asks all present: "The other nine, where are they?"

Commentators rightly highlight the incongruity of Jesus' injunction to the ten lepers ("Go show yourselves to the priests"), for it assumes that these men are no longer leprous, even though they still are[11] – one went to see the priest, not in order to be healed by him, but in order to have him certify an already effectuated healing and ask him to celebrate the rite of purification[12]. In short, by obeying and by accepting an apparently crazy order, the ten lepers show their entire trust. Thus, it is hard to see why, at the end of the episode, Jesus seems to stigmatize the lack of faith of those who did not return "to give thanks" in his presence. He had not asked them to return, and they have quite certainly obeyed his order by going to show themselves to the priests. If the faith of the ten is not placed in doubt, the difference is indicated by the Christic coloration of the

---

[10] For a more developed analysis of this episode, see J.N. ALETTI, *Le Jésus de Luc*, 92-96.

[11] Compare with Luke 5:13-14 and the parallels, where it is only after the healing that Jesus sends the healed man to the priest in order to celebrate his return to normal life.

[12] See Leviticus 14.

Samaritan's; the latter judged it more important to return to praise God at the feet of Jesus without his having even suggested it to him. By acting in this way, the Samaritan makes known that, for him, to praise God and "to give thanks" to Jesus are, henceforth, inseparable. There is thus a *plus*: if the ten have totally trusted in the word of Jesus, the Samaritan's faith is, henceforth, expressed christologically, in that it associates God and Jesus, through whom the salvation of God happens. It is thus this *plus* that Jesus highlights and about this *more* that he questions his coreligionists, the Jews: will they be able or will they want to make the same move, to praise God in and through Jesus, to recognize in him their savior? By asking the crowds, who are present at the Samaritan's act of thanksgiving, where are the other nine healed lepers, Jesus is implicitly raising the question of his identity, and this, to his own people: only a Samaritan, a man considered as a bastard and schismatic by the Jews of that time, understood that for him it was, henceforth, impossible to separate the praise of God and the act of thanksgiving to Jesus. To the subject with which we are dealing, Jesus' final question connects the announcements of rejection mentioned above: which of his people will recognize him?

Just as the theme of recognition was earlier linked to prophetic typology, that of rejection is here going to go hand in hand with prophetic typology. One has for a longtime hesitated to recognize in Luke 17 a probable Elishian typology, but a careful reading shows that the parallels are quite numerous[13]:

2KINGS 5	COMMON OR PARALLEL ELEMENTS	LUKE 17:11-19
v.3	Samaria	v.11
v.1	afflicted with leprosy (*leprômenos*)/ lepers (*leproi*)	v.12
v.8,9,15	question to the prophet (Elisha / Jesus)	v. 13,17
v.10	sent elsewhere (*poreutheis / poreuthentes*)	v.14
v.10,12,13,14	was purified (*ekatharisthè / ekatharisthèsan*)	v.14,17
v.15	returned to the prophet (*hypestrepsen*)	v.15,18
v.15	confession of faith to the true God / praise and thanksgiving	v.15,18
v.1	Syrian / Samaritan, foreigner	v.16,19

---

[13] On the passage's typology, see W. BRUNERS, *Die Reinigung der Zehn Aussäzigen und die Heilung des Samariters. Lk 17,11-19. Ein Beitrag zur lukanischen Interpretation der Reinigung von Aussätzingen* (FzB 23; Wurzbourg, Echter 1977).

The drama described in this episode is that of non-recognition, of indifference or of rejection with which the people of Jesus are confronted. Let us recall that in more than its typological nature, the episode of the ten lepers makes an allusion, with the same discretion, to the discourse at Nazareth, where Jesus declares to his compatriots: "And there were many lepers in Israel in the time of the prophet Elisha; and none of them was cleansed, but only Naaman the Syrian" (Luke 4:27). In this way is fulfilled Jesus' prophecy regarding the type of ministry to which he knows himself to be called, at the same time that the composition of the Lucan diptych is outlined, where the discourse at Nazareth has a proleptic function that covers Jesus' ministry and extends up to the passion of Paul in Acts 21 – 28[14]. Let us point out, for the Gospel only, just those episodes concerned, where emblematically the two components of the Lucan prophetic typology, recognition and rejection, are noted:

| 1Kings 17 | Luke 4:25-26 | Luke 7:11-17 | recognition |
| 2Kings 5 | Luke 4:27 | Luke 17:11-19 | non-recognition |

Let us lastly point out that the beauty and subtlety of Luke 17:11-19 comes from the manner in which the Lucan narrator unites and articulates the two Christological components, royal / messianic and prophetic, that were only contiguous in Luke 4. The typology is Elishian, but by falling at the feet of Jesus, the Samaritan at the same time initiates the royal/messianic theme that is progressively going to take over what follows in the macro-narrative. Discretely, throughout the narrative's signifiers, Jesus becomes the point of convergence of the expectations and hopes from the past.

It is, henceforth, possible to describe how the Lucan narrator proceeded in order to construct his typology beginning with the episode at Nazareth. First, with concentration, by focusing on Jesus' prophetic identity; then by accumulation, in other words, with allusions or declarations repeated throughout Jesus' ministry. The following table uses these facts and shows how the narrative sets out the two components, positive and negative, of the prophetic typology as a key for reading the identity of Jesus:

---

[14] On the link between Acts 21 – 28 and Luke 4, see J.N. ALETTI, *Quand Luc raconte*. 149-153.

Discourse of Jesus at Nazareth, Luke 4:20-30
Admired and recognized and, after, rejected and threatened
Luke 4:22   Luke 4:28-29
       ↓   ↓

JESUS, A RECOGNIZED PROPHET = Luke 5:1 to 9:21	JESUS, A PROPHET REJECTED AND PUT TO DEATH = Luke 9:22 to 19:27
7:16 (the people: a great prophet) 7:19-22 (Jesus: v.22 = Isaiah 61:1) 7:24-27 (Jesus: John the Baptist to prepare the way) 7:49 (all the guests: who is this, who even forgives sins?) 8:24-25 (the disciples: who then is this, that the elements obey?) 8:28 (the demoniac: Jesus, Son of the Most High God) 9:7-9 (Herod: who is this?) 9:18-20 (the crowds: Elijah, one of the great prophets) 9:18-20 (the disciples: The Christ of God)	Many announcements of the Passion by Jesus (9:22; 9:43b-44; 18:31-34) 11:29-32 (Jesus: evil generation... Jonah) 11:47 (Jesus: you build the tombs of the prophets...) 11:48 (Jesus: your fathers killed (put to death the prophets...) 11:50-51 (Jesus: the blood of the prophets) 13:33-34 (Jesus: Jerusalem, you who kill the prophets) 17:17 (Jesus: where are the other 9?)
representative episode = Luke 7:11-17	representative episode = Luke 17:11-19

The Raison d'être of the Lucan Typology

One now sees why the Lucan narrative developed a typology with two parts. The component of *recognition* was indeed necessary; it was necessary that Jesus' identity be recognized by most of his coreligionists. But, as the elites recognized in Jesus neither the prophet of the end of time nor the Christ nor the Son of God, it was important to show that this refusal to believe in no way threatened the truth of Jesus' prophetic and messianic identity; thanks to its two parts, the Lucan typology will honor this necessity. The Lucan typology is thus in the service of the problem of the *anagnôrisis*.

VI. THE TYPOLOGY OF THE NARRATIVES OF THE PASSION

Up to now we have noted that it was by having recourse to prophetic typology that the Lucan narrative was able to respond to the challenge of a biography in which the *anagnôrisis* of the identity of the protagonist by the other characters of the narrative could not be lacking. The prophetic typology has indeed provided a valuable key for reading the ignominious death of Jesus.

But if the Lucan narrative of the Passion brings the prophetic typology to its end, if it is also the effectuation of the announcements of the prophet Jesus and confirms the truth of his statements, it has another characteristic, that of showing that there is a recognition at the very moment when the protagonist is reviled and rejected. One will perhaps object that this motif is also encountered in Matthew/Mark, since right after the death of Jesus the centurion exclaims: "This man was a son of God / righteous". Actually, in Luke, as already noted, the recognition is described more systematically and extends to all the characters – except for the Jewish religious authorities –, from the trial to Jesus' death. And what was recognized? Jesus' innocence. The reader can easily notice through the scenes that the respective characters, more and more numerous, are aware of this innocence and show it more or less explicitly and directly, by their words or their gestures:

CHARACTERS	TYPE OF RECOGNITION	
Pilate	explicit and repeated	"I did not find this man guilty of any of your charges against him" 23:14 and 23:22
Herod	indirect	"neither did Herod, for he sent him back to us" 23:15
the women of Jerusalem	indirect	"the women who bewailed and lamented him" 23:27
Criminal	explicit and direct	"this man has done nothing wrong" 23:41
Centurion	explicit and direct	"certainly this man was innocent" 23:47
all those who came to Calvary	indirect	"all the crowds… returned home beating their breasts" 23:48

The recognition is not as great as that of the crowds and the disciples in Luke 9, but it undeniably exists, and, paradoxically, it is with it that the section in which rejection dominates concludes. If it was important that the ministry began with the search for Jesus' identity and went up to his recognition, varied but real, it is just as important that the section of the Passion end with that of his innocence:

MINISTRY		PASSION	
recognition = prophet	announcement of the rejection	rejection	recognition = innocence
by the crowds and by the disciples	by Jesus	by the religious authorities	by everyone except the religious authorities

The scenes of recognition in Luke 24 bring to an end the problem of the *anagnôrisis*. However, the reader cannot but note that the allusions to the prophetic figures from the biblical past are less numerous during the narratives of the Passion than during the ascent to Jerusalem. One encounters only a single explicit mention from the mouth of the guards who ridicule Jesus: "Prophesy! Who is it that struck you?" (Luke 22:64). This cannot be interpreted as an absence, for the narrator makes the events of the Passion the effectuation of Jesus' announcements on the death of the prophets (cf. Luke 22:37 as well). The Lucan narrative of the Passion cannot be read without that which precedes it, announces it and justifies it.

If one encounters the vocabulary of prophecy only once in the Lucan narrative of the Passion, one must, nevertheless, ask if Luke 23 does not indirectly allude to the accusation of false prophecy. In verses 2 and 5 of this chapter, the religious leaders indeed say to Pilate that Jesus misleads[15] and incites the people. If the accusation can be understood politically, for those who formulate it, the members of the Sanhedrin, it is also implicitly religious: by his teaching's diverting the people from the ways of God, Jesus would thus be a false prophet[16]. By emphasizing the explicit recognition of Jesus' innocence (by Pilate, the judge, by the criminal crucified with him, by the centurion at the end) and the implicit (the women of Jerusalem, all the crowds present at the foot of the cross), the Lucan narrator thus makes the Passion and death the proof through which the prophetic identity of Jesus finds its ultimate confirmation.

VII. CONCLUSION

Although quick, the journey taken highlighted the continuous usage of prophetic typology in the Lucan macro-narrative. It is thus possible to

---

[15] A Greek verb *apostrephô*, used by Pilate in verse 14.

[16] For G.N. STANTON, *Jesus and Gospel*, 141-142, at the time of the evangelists and of Luke in particular, the Jewish accusation of Jesus' being a false-prophet was already circulating.

respond to a question concerning the choice of Old Testament figures. Indeed, if in Luke 1 – 2 the narrator is largely inspired by 1Samuel 1 – 2 and presents Jesus in relation to Samuel, beginning with the episode at Nazareth (Luke 4), it is the characters Elijah and Elisha who are Jesus' and the narrator's explicit and implicit references. If the reasons for the choice of Elijah and Elisha appeared to us clear, it was not the same for Samuel – the Scriptures not speaking of his being persecuted, threatened or put to death like most of the prophets. We can, nevertheless, grasp why Samuel was chosen for Luke 1 – 2: undoubtedly because he is the only prophet whose birth and childhood were told to us, but also because he inaugurates a decisive stage in the history of Israel, that of the kingdom.

The route taken in this chapter can as well be summarized by a few statements: the Lucan narrator chose prophetic typology in order to characterize Jesus because for him the recognition and the rejection are inseparable. Constituting an essential component of the prophetic identity, the rejection in no way threatens the truth of the prophetic (and messianic) identity of Jesus. The choice of prophetic typology also assures the continuity with the biblical past and shows *a contrario* that there is no discrepancy whatsoever between Jesus and the tradition which he is recommending. This chapter also intended to show the importance of Old Testament semantic models in Luke, as in Mark and Matthew. The Lucan narrator did not conceive of his text as an anecdotical narrative, purely descriptive of the events, whose information one could critique, but as a narrative providing meaning and keys for reading. To forget this, the historian would, put succinctly, miss what is essential. The breaks in the narrative of the Passion between Mark/Matthew and Luke are essentially owing to the choice of different models, themselves responding to different difficulties and constraints.

As this chapter proposed to show this, it was important to emphasize the genius of the Lucan narrator who used prophetic typology in order to respond to the requirements of the *anagnôrisis*.

No doubt, this issue cannot account for all the components of theology, especially the whole of Luke's Christology. It, nevertheless, allows ascertaining how decisive the recourse to typology was for the Lucan claim of an authentic testimony. May the readers be convinced of its importance.

CHAPTER VI

OVERTURE

I. INTRODUCTION

Thus comes to an end our voyage through the three synoptic Gospels, Mark, Matthew and Luke. We, of course, have not said everything – nor wanted to say everything – on the anteriority of one or the other, on the similarities and differences of their Christology, their ecclesiology, etc. The issue dealt with is a prior one, its subject being the reasons why the first Christian generations thought themselves obliged to transform the words and deeds of Jesus that were useful for catechesis and liturgical gatherings into continuous biographical narratives with Jesus as the protagonist. For, let us once again repeat, the Greco-Roman requirements for biographies were such that the Christians of that time would have had to refrain from writing one on Jesus. But popular biographies could be widely disseminated; so they presented the opportunity to respond to the accusations of the Jews and, later, the pagans and thus provided a true and reliable image of Jesus – the biographies of Jesus that are Mark, Matthew and Luke have an undeniable apologetic tone. The will to write, nevertheless, did not suffice; the genius of the Markan narrator was necessary for finding a model capable of showing why and how one could do without a final collective *anagnôrisis*. Thanks to Mark, the first Christian generations could finally attempt the biographical genre.

In addition to the importance of the genre, the current essay has shown that of the final *anagnôrisis* and the effects that it had on the choice of episodes, on their arrangement, but also on the Old Testament models used for narrating the Passion/death of Jesus. Without repeating, in order to summarize, the development of the points dealt with, our conclusion, based on methodological reflections, will open the hermeneutical horizon.

II. LITERARY GENRE AND HISTORICAL RESEARCH[1]

The Biographical Model

In recent decades, the research on the genre of the Gospels has progressively reached the conclusion that the narratives were biographies. Burridge, cited several times over the course of this essay, noted the characteristics that show this was so: (1°) the opening of the narratives, (2°) the focusing on an individual, the *protagonist*, (3°) the sequence of events, on the whole chronological, (4°) the brevity of the *genos* and *paideia* sections in comparison to the *praxeis*, (5°) the existence of several sub-genres (teachings, disputes, miracles, etc.), (6°) the demonstration of the protagonist's value by his words and by his deeds.

Without denying the pertinence of these traits, it is necessary to add that the Gospels are popular biographies and that the description of their protagonist Jesus is made in reference to the holy Scriptures of Israel. In short, the formal cadre is Greek, and the content, biblical.

Implications for Interpretation

The presentation on Mark, Matthew and Luke recalled that the narrators are not interested in the anecdotal but want to provide keys for reading and that they do it by using semantic models that most often refer to the OT. In order to interpret the narrative facts correctly, it is thus essential to research the models used by the narrators and to determine their exact function. We hope to have also shown that the deeds and events narrated cannot be interpreted separately from the models that give them a precise function. In other words: to interpret the facts without first identifying the models that give meaning to them often causes errors; or, if one prefers: to use the facts historically without seeing that they belong to literary and semantic models is methodologically erroneous and not without risks.

Thus, in the narratives of the Passion of Mark/Matthew, Jesus' cry is not the same as in Luke, and we have seen that because of the model chosen by the first two and that chosen by the third it was important for them to be different. But then, will one ask, which of the two cries reflect the reality? Without any doubt, each narrator made his choice and only

---

[1] J.A. DIEHL, "What Is a "Gospel"? Recent Studies in Gospel Genre", in *Currents in Biblical Research* 20 (2010) 1-26.

kept the events of the Passion that corresponded to the model that was followed. This certainly does not mean to say that in order to reconstitute the events it suffices to add up the motifs of the three stories – or even four, if one adds John –, for these are not all compatible; if the four narratives indeed mention that there was a cry, it is difficult, if not to say impossible, to know what it was historically. History is devoted to reading through the literary genres and the semantic models: no narrative element is directly usable historically. Not that it is necessary to renounce getting to the historically real, but the way that leads to it is longer than is often thought.

III. JESUS AND THE GREEK AND ROMAN HEROES

Jesus and the Heroes of Biographies

By proposing to write a biography and to confront the question of the necessary *anagnôrisis*, the Markan narrator and those who followed in his footsteps wanted to show that Jesus merited being recognized for who he was, the Messiah and Son of God, savior of humanity. Did they also want to show that he had the stuff and traits of the Greek and Roman heroes? To do so, have they given him the physical, intellectual, moral and religious qualities that the Greek readers were expecting to find in the biographies of that day? We have noted that at no time do the Gospels dwell on the physical beauty, the intellectual capacity, the moral virtues or the religious piety of Jesus. They rather confine themselves to the question of his messianic and filial identity, the reasons for which it was or was not recognized... and by whom. Moreover, if the narrators relate the praise of the crowds throughout the ministry of their protagonist, they themselves remain astonishingly discreet about his physical, moral and religious qualities. The praise of the Gospel narratives remains the feat of the characters and not of the narrators; in other words, it is intra-diegetic and not extra-diegetic.

All the while being a protagonist, the Jesus of the Gospel narratives does not resemble the heroes of Greco-Roman biographies: the narrators do not focus on his personal qualities but on the recognition of his religious and salvific role.

Jesus and the Heroes of Greek Tragedies

So is it possible to compare Jesus to the heroes of Greek tragedies? The latter are out of the ordinary, kings or tyrants, in charge of cities and peoples, and their decisions have dramatic consequences for their subjects. It is not only a matter of the drama of a man or a family but of the effects that the hardships of the heroes have for a people or an entire city. Can the same thing be said of Jesus who, being a king/Messiah and the Son of God, is out of the ordinary? Similar to the heroes of tragedies, if the Gospel narratives focus on him, it is not only because his fate and recognition arc at stake but because the salvation of Israel and the Nations is as well. If "[t]he tragedies exceed the present in order to connect to the type[2]", would it not be the same in the Gospels, in which it is not only the "in that time" that is important, but also, and above all, what is typical in the characters and the situations for all times?

What is necessary for events to appear as tragic? According to J. de Romilly, in order for murders and disasters to be such, it is necessary for them to be "connected to causes that exceed the individual case and that make them *necessary* because of the circumstances imposed on the man[3]". Do the "must", "was it not necessary" of the narratives of the Passion allow saying that it is the same for Jesus and that tragedy and fate are linked? Whether it is a matter of Tyche, for the Greeks, or of God, in the Gospel narratives, the protagonists of tragedies and the narratives of the Passion obey forces that exceed them: as J. de Romilly notes, "Greek tragedy does not cease to point beyond the man, to divine or abstract forces that decide his fate and decide without appeal. This can be sovereign Zeus, or other gods, or even, the *diamôn*, a mysterious neutral term, or the divine. This can also be destiny, the *Moira*, or even necessity. And the chorus does not fail in each instance to point out the action of these superhuman forces[4]". I have, however, shown elsewhere that the "must" stated by Jesus in the Gospel narratives, in particular in Luke, owes nothing to fate, and that in them, Jesus is not described like the heroes of tragedies: death is not the last word of these narratives, and the drama is

---

[2] J. DE ROMILLY, *La tragédie grecque* (Quadridge/Puf, Paris, 2012) 167.
[3] *Ibid.*, p. 168. My emphasis.
[4] *Ibid.*, p. 169.

much rather that of a non-recognition and of a rejection that are in no way imposed by the divinity[5].

Jesus and the Great Figures of the Holy Scriptures

If one is to find similarities and models for the Jesus of the Gospel narratives, it is necessary to go to the holy Scriptures of Israel, which is one of the theses that emerges in chapters IV and V devoted to Luke's narrative. If this author has placed such emphasis on typology and on the continuity existing between the figure of the prophets and that of Jesus, it is because of the reproach that at that time was made against Christians for inventing a new religion, an extremely serious reproach, because for Socrates, the subject of the same indictment, that of introducing new gods, the result was condemnation to death[6].

If the prophets and the other Old Testament figures serve to describe Jesus, it is not primarily for their moral and religious qualities but for the signs that they perform and for the fate that was theirs: the problem of the *anagnôrisis* has prevailed not only in Luke but also in Mark/Matthew.

IV. POPULAR NARRATIVES OR LITERATURE?

By accepting to follow the Greek canons, the Gospel narrators, perhaps without knowing it, approached literature, even if their biographies remain popular. But for a long time, they were considered as minor works. Can one say today they are literary works?

Let us first note the proliferation of narratives of the biographical type having Jesus as the protagonist. It is probably the first time so many biographical narratives – let us not forget the extra-canonical gospels[7] – were written on the same man in so short a time. But during that era, Jesus was not the only one about whom several lives were written: may it suffice to mention Caesar and Alexander[8]. This multiplication of biographies of

---

[5] J.-N. ALETTI, *L'art de raconter Jésus-Christ*, 155-176 and ID., *Le Jésus de Luc*, 157-184.

[6] Cf. Plato, *The Apology of Socrates*, 24b-c.

[7] Quite numerous, as one knows; cf. that of the Hebrews, of Peter, of Thomas, of Pilate, of Nicodemus, etc.

[8] For Caesar, see, for example, Plutarch and Suetonius who take up prior biographical sources. On Alexander the Great, we even possess several more or less complete biographies. See R. PENNA, "Kerygma e storia alle origini del cristianesimo. Nuove

the same man, in its own way, means that their respective authors wrote not to repeat what preceded them nor only in order to add deeds or events omitted by the others but because the project of each was different. By wanting to make known the status and the role of Jesus, and thus to lead the readers to believe in him, the evangelists, of course, do not have the same project as that of the biographies of that time, in which the deeds of illustrious men known by all are narrated. Nevertheless, this does not exclude their narratives from the biographical genre, which leaves open the question of the purpose of each *bios* (life). What was important to determine is how the evangelists' project determines a certain type of biography, and this is what oriented the route that we have taken.

The current essay has not repeated in detail the studies on the biographical genre, some more reliable than others. Only research on the relationship between biography and *anagnôrisis* has been missing, for it is this relationship that for the first Christian generations put into question the possibility of writing a biography of Jesus. We hope to have shown the importance of the problem and filled in a decisive gap for the understanding of the narrative writing of the Gospels.

That the Gospels' intended reader was not the educated man of the era, one with an appreciation of the ancient Greek world, is immediately perceived. For, to be recognized as literary works, the writings of that time had to have an abundance of explicit or implicit references to non-biblical sources. Even Philo does not make an exception of this rule: although treating exclusively, or almost so, the biblical past, he, nonetheless, alludes to Greek philosophers and dramatists[9], for such was the condition *sine qua non* for being read. By never citing nor explicitly referring to the great authors of Greek literature, the Gospels directly renounce all literary pretension. That is, undoubtedly, also why one has catalogued them as low-level literature (*Kleinliteratur*). Reading them, one is, nevertheless, struck by the differences that highlight the quality of their narrative and biographical writing, and one must wonder if this itself is not what makes them literary works.

---

considerazioni su di un annoso problema", in *Annali di Scienze Religiose* 2 (1997) 239-256 (in particular 248-251).

[9] See la *Vita Mosis*, 1:135 (in which some see an allusion to EURIPIDES, *Iphigenia at Aulis*, v. 122) and 2:2 (that refers to PLATO, *Republic*, V, 473d); the *De Josepho*, 125-148, in which PHILO develops an argumentation influenced by Skepticism (as in *De ebrietate*, 155-205). One could increase the examples.

This being said, the recognition of the biographical value and the reliability of the Gospel narratives was not immediately recognized, as attested to by the accusations of pagan authors of the IInd century: if the Gospel narratives had truly convinced their contemporaries, the latter would have no longer accused the Christians of credulity[10]. Like the recognition of Jesus, that of the Gospel biographies occurred slowly.

We can thus conclude.

The Gospels were not immediately considered as literary works worthy of this name: they had no pretension to it, and their language did not have the refinement required during that era to be recognized by cultured or educated readers.

However, beyond the similarities with the biographies of the era, one can today see in the Gospels an actual renewal of the biographical genre and the way of telling the truth proper to this type of narrative, this change being principally due to the manner in which the typology was implemented. A new hermeneutic was born with them.

Many have wondered and still wonder if the Gospel narratives belong to the *Hochliteratur* or to the *Kleinliteratur*. Such a question is of little interest. We have seen that it is not the lack of literary ambition (explicit or not) that determines the appellation but the manner in which the narrators chartered the course relating to the identity of Jesus and that borders on – plainly said – the sublime[11].

---

[10] Cf., for example, LUCIAN OF SAMOSATA, *The Passing of Peregrinus*, 11-13, and, on the subject, D.P. BECHARD, "Paul Among the Rustics. The Lystran Episode (Acts 14:8-20) and Lukan Apologetic", in *CBQ* 63 (2001) 84-101.

[11] On this subject, the reader is invited to reread the beautiful analyses of Erich AUERBACH, *Mimesis: The Representation of Reality in Western Literature* (Princeton, NJ, Princeton University Press 1953; original German 1946), in particular the postface. This author has magnificently shown that the Gospel narratives, with their radical mixture of daily reality and sublime tragedy, were the first to break down the classical rule of styles and, from there, the levels of literature (*hoch* and *klein*).

PART TWO

THE NARRATIVE ANALYSIS OF TWO PERICOPAE

CHAPTER I

A NARRATIVE APPROACH TO MARK 7:24-30
DIFFICULTIES AND PROPOSALS[1]

The episode of the Syrophoenician woman, in Mark 7:24-30, is well-known by specialists of the synoptic problem and has drawn a lot of ink, for neither the theory of two sources nor that of the anteriority of Matthew to Mark explains in a completely satisfying way the dependent relationship that exists between Mark 7:24-30 and Matthew 15:21-28. Exhaustive and meticulous accounts of the synoptic difficulties have been made by J.F. Baudoz and P. Alonso[2]. On this episode, in particular its Markan version, monographs that use the narrative approach still do not exist, only articles[3]. As a narrative, Mark 7:24-30 is not, however, easy and constitutes a challenge for the narrative approach, as will be seen.

The question raised here is itself not narrative. Both exegetes and commentators have indeed asked if it is the Syrophoenician woman who has succeeded in changing Jesus' opinion by her response, or if it is not rather Jesus' reaction, apparently harsh, that calls upon the woman's finesse and faith and has in some way made her response possible. In short, it is Jesus' statement in v.27 that divides the interpreters, as F.G. Downing notes: "Most commentators are embarrassed by Jesus' response. Much of the discussion of other issues often seems at least in part aimed to reduce this harshness. Perhaps the harshness stems from the early church,

---

[1] This chapter originally appeared in French in *Biblica* 93 (2012) 357-376.

[22] J.F. BAUDOZ, *Les miettes de la table*. Étude synoptique et socio-religieuse de Mt 15, 21-28 et de Mark 7, 24-30 (Études bibliques NS 27; Paris 1995); P. ALONSO, *The Woman Who Changed Jesus*. Crossing Boundaries in Mark 7,24-30 (Biblical Tools and Studies 11; Leuven 2011).

[3] See, for ex., C. FOCANT, "Mc 7,24-31 par. Mt 15,21-29. Critique des sources et/ou étude narrative", *The Synoptic Gospels*. Source Criticism and the New Literary Criticism, C. Focant (ed.) (BETL 110; Leuven 1993) 39-75; J.P. SONNET, "Réflecteurs et/ou catalyseurs du Messie. De la fonction de certains personnages secondaires dans le récit de Marc", Regards croisés sur la Bible. Études sur le point de vue. Actes du IIIe colloque international du Réseau de recherche en narrativité biblique, Paris, 8-10 juin 2006, O. FLICHY et allii (eds.) (Lectio divina. Hors série; Paris 2007), 365-377.

from controversies then. Perhaps it is in thick quotation marks: 'You know what they say…' Perhaps Jesus is testing the woman's faith and/or demanding humility. Perhaps he is really just working things out in his own mind. Perhaps with his 'Let the children be fed first' and perhaps, too, with his 'puppies', 'housedogs', he is already softening the harshness of what is to follow and providing a clue for the woman to pick up. There is no widespread agreement"[4].

If the question is not narrative, it will here be treated narratively, after some historical-critical difficulties have been presented and resolved in order to highlight some of Mark's distinctive redactional and theological characteristics.

I. A STAGE PRELIMINARY TO THE NARRATIVE ANALYSIS

So that the narrative analysis may be done on a solid foundation, it is important to determine the meaning of two phrases[5].

1.1. "And (he) entered a house" (v.24)

This is not the house in Mark 9:33 and 10:10 where Jesus retires with his disciples in order to explain everything to them[6]. Are the owners of this house pagan or Jewish? Historians point out that in the rural area located around Tyre (and Sidon) there were also Jewish villages[7] where Jesus was able to find hospitality. But given his statements in Mark 7:6-23, in which Jesus affirms that impurity is not external but comes from the heart, thus indicating that not all pagans are unclean, why would he not have chosen to lodge in one of their homes? If the hypothesis of Jesus'

---

[4] F.G. DOWNING, "The Woman from Syrophoenicia, and her Doggedness: Mark 7.24-31 (Matthew 15.21-28)", *Making Sense in (and of) the First Christian Century*, F.G. Downing (ed.)(JSNTS 197; Sheffield 2000) 109. Also, G. THEISSEN, "Lokal- und Sozialkolorit in der Geschichte von der Syrophönikischen Frau (Mark 7.24-30)" *ZNW* 75 (1984) 204-206. On Jesus' response, almost all think that it is shocking and offensive. Cf., for ex., G. THEISSEN, "Lokal- und Sozialkolorit," 202: "Die Anwort Jesus ist moralish anstössig." How can Jesus, up to this point full of compassion for suffering humanity, compare the young daughter to a dog when her mother was earnestly asking him to save her?

[5] Unless otherwise noted, the translation is that of the RSV.

[6] Also see Mark 7:17 and 9:28, with the substantive *oikos*, without the article, but followed by the mention of the disciples.

[7] G. THEISSEN, "Lokal- und Sozialkolorit," 208, that relies upon, among others, JOSEPHUS, *Bellum*, 2.588ff. The Jews/Judeans were minorities in this region.

lodging in the home of an Israelite seems more probable, it is thus not certain. All things considered, what is more interesting is to know why the narrator mentions this fact, which the narrative analysis must investigate.

1.2. "Now the woman was a Greek, a Syrophoenician by birth" (v.26)

This dual characterization is found elsewhere in the NT: in Acts 4:36[8] and 18:2,24[9] but also in the works of Jewish[10] and pagan[11] authors. According to some exegetes[12], it is for this reason improbable that either of the traits is redactional. But this conclusion is too hasty, for, if the narrator is clearly taking up a twofold model used at that time, he was also surely able to use words that were his own.

The first trait, Greek (*hellènis*), denotes both the cultural and linguistic world to which the woman belonged[13], but also the fact that she is not an Israelite. As for the second, Syrophoenician (*syrophoinikissa*), it is intriguing to exegetes and historians because Syrophoenicia did not yet exist as a province at the time Matthew and Mark were written[14]. If the reason why the narrator has used this denomination remains obscure, one can, however, conclude that Jesus and the woman were able to have an interchange in their respective languages, Aramaic and Phoenician, indeed even in Greek, since the woman, because of her origins and environment could have known this language[15]. Some exegetes have decided against the authenticity of Jesus' proverbial *logion*[16] in v.27 because the play on words *labein/balein* only works in the Greek; to which others have responded (1) that a dialogue in this language was possible, some Galileans and Phoenicians having dealings with Greeks, (2) that, even if

---

[8] Also Barnabas is (1) *levitès*, (2) *kyprios tôi genei*.

[9] In Matthew 15:22 the description is also dual: (1) *gynè kananaia* (2) *apo tôn horiôn ekeinôn exelthousa*.

[10] JOSEPHUS, *Vita*, 427; Philo, *de Abrahamo*, 251.

[11] HERACLIDES CRITICUS, *Descriptio Graeciae*, 3.2.7-8; DIODORUS SICULUS, *Bibliotheca historica*, 26.18.1.7-8

[12] THEISSEN, "Lokal- und Sozialkolorit," 213, this would have also denoted a superior social status.

[13] According to THEISSEN, "Lokal- und Sozialkolorit," 210.

[14] In his *Bellum*, 3.35, Josephus still distinguishes between Phoenicia and Syria. The division of Syria into Coele Syria and Syria Phoenicia seems to have been made under Hadrian. Cf. BAUDOZ, *Les miettes*, 122-132.

[15] Cf. THEISSEN, "Lokal- und Sozialkolorit," 210-211.

[16] Proverbial, especially because the expression *ou (esti) kalon* appears in Proverbs 17:6, 18:6, 20:23, 24:23; 25:27. Also, Tobit 8:6.

the language that was used were Aramaic, the Markan narrator was able to give a Greek form to Jesus' response.

These two traits are not the first by which the narrator characterizes this character, who is first a woman (*gynè*) who has[17] a little daughter possessed by an unclean spirit. If he adds that she is Greek and Syrophoenician, it is due to the way in which she greets Jesus: "she fell down at his feet" (v.25), in a gesture of respect and supplication, as was done before her by sick Israelites[18]. It is because she acts like an Israelite – and she could have been one, since there were Israelite villages in the vicinity of Tyre – that the narrator adds the two traits pointing out that she was not.

These linguistic details being provided, it is now possible to proceed with the narrative analysis. Not every stage will be followed, only those necessary to the thesis being defended here.

II.   THE NARRATIVE'S DIFFICULTIES AND THE NARRATIVE ANALYSIS

Mark 7:24-30 follows the rules of composition of narratives. The only difficulty comes from v.31, which some attach to the episode of the Syrophoenician, whereas others read it as the beginning of what follows, devoted to the healing of the deaf-mute. The first indeed note that vv.24 and 31 have in common the same expressions: *eis ta horia Tyrou* in v.24 and *ek tôn horiôn Tyrou* in v.31, which would make it an inclusion[19]. Let

---

[17] As commentators point out, the construction of the relative *hès... autès* (v.25) is Semitic and corresponds to *asher ... lô/lah*; cf. Mark 1:7 (*hou ... autou*).

[18] Cf. the similar formulations in Mark 5:22,33.   G. THEISSEN, *Urchristliche Wundergeschichten. Ein Beitrag zur formgeschichtlichen Erforschung der synoptischen Evangelia* (StNT 8; Gütersloh 1974) 63, makes this gesture one of the motifs of the miracle narratives.

[19] Cf., for ex., FOCANT, "Mc 7,24-31," 62-63, who even proposes a chiastic disposition based on several lexical parallelisms:
   v.25 *elthousa*
     v.26 *to daimonion... ek tès thygatros autès*
       v.27 *kynaria*
       v.28 *kynaria*
     v.29 *ek tès thygatros sou... to daimonion*
   v.30 *apelthousa*

us not, however, forget that an inclusion is not what allows setting the limits of a pericope, but once the limits have been determined with the help of other criteria, it is what confirms the literary unit through the vocabulary. For, at the narrative level, v.31 clearly begins a new episode.

Before stating the difficulties confronted by the narrative approach, perhaps it is advisable to describe briefly the situational plot. As is known, the composition of a narrative episode can only be effectively determined with the help of the plot, which is its spine. What then is this passage's? After the presentation of the protagonists (vv.24-26a), comes the inciting moment (vv.27-28), which consists of a request from the woman, in indirect speech (v.26b); the complication is developed with Jesus' negative response, in direct speech (v.27), and the woman's retort (v.28); the denouement occurs when Jesus fulfills the request in v.29, and the episode ends with the proof of the daughter's healing (v.30).

In Mark 7:24-30, the plot progresses as in other Markan episodes of miracles and exorcisms in which the miraculous action is not emphasized. Indeed, in several of these narratives, the emphasis is placed on the complication or complications that occur prior to Jesus' salvific act: an event[20], a large crowd[21], Jesus' reaction[22] or that of those who surround him[23] prevent the miracle and require of those who want to be healed or delivered from their misery a durable "doggedness", as has been rightly said[24]. In short, more than Matthew and Luke, Mark stresses the oppositions and the difficulties that put the supplicants to the test and thus manifest the power of their faith, and Mark 7:24-30 is a good example of this.

Having briefly described the plot's main components, it is now possible to examine some of its peculiarities.

2.1   Jesus Unknown in Pagan Territory (v.24)

If, as has been seen, it is not in itself impossible that Jesus had gone to lodge in the home of pagans, given the principle that he himself stated in Mark 7:15, the way in which he is going to respond to the Syrophoenician

---

If these parallelisms are real, they concern the form of the expression of the passage but clearly say nothing about the progression of its plot and are useless if one does not see their respective narrative function.

[20] Mark 5:23-26 (the healing of the woman with the hemorrhage).

[21] Mark 2:1-10.

[22] Mark 4:37-38 (Jesus sleeps); 6:36-39; 6:48; 7:27; 8:2-5.

[23] Mark 10:48.

[24] Downing, "The Woman from Syrophoenicia", 23.

woman seems, nevertheless, to favor an Israelite hospitality. But whether the owner of the house is an Israelite or a Phoenician, the reason that the narrative says that Jesus entered the house is provided by the following phrase: if he is found in a house and not in the public square, it is because he wants no one to know that he is there. The best means of remaining incognito is in fact (1) not to show oneself, (2) to lodge in the home of an Israelite, who will probably not tell the pagans that he is housing a thaumaturge famous in Galilee.

But why does Jesus want his presence to be ignored? This raises a prior question: why did he go to the pagans? The theme developed over the course of the preceding controversy, on the clean and the unclean, allows outlining a response. The declaration in Mark 7:15 and the commentary that accompanies it (7:17-23) indeed affirm that one cannot/must not judge the uncleanness of someone by appearances and that, as a consequence, no one is able to be declared as unclean for physical (uncircumcised) and/or external (rules of cleanliness) reasons. By immediately afterwards going to a pagan territory, in the vicinity of Tyre, Jesus is indicating by his presence, as anonymous as it may be, that it is necessary to apply his statements to the pagans themselves. He goes there by his own initiative: no one has forced nor invited him. If he thus went into the vicinity of Tyre in order to show that the pagans are not necessarily unclean, why does he refuse to release the little daughter possessed by an unclean spirit? Where then is the coherence of Jesus and the Marcan narrative(s)?

2.2 A Contradiction?

More than the episode's coherence, it is that of Mark 7:1-30 and the preceding episodes that then seem to evaporate, for at least two reasons. (1) The daughter is not affected by an illness nor physical defilement but suffers from a more serious evil, that of being possessed by an unclean spirit, and the Jesus of Mark has up to then shown that he wants to deliver those who are prisoners of demons[25]. (2) If he does not want the pagans to come to him in order to be freed from evil spirits and their illnesses, why has he gone into their territory? Merely to let them know that salvation is not yet for them? But that would be a provocation! Jesus would also be contradicting himself, for he has freed the possessed man in Mark 5:1-20[26], himself a pagan, without objecting that the time had not yet come. The

---

[25] Mark 3,22 and 6,13.
[26] Mark 5:2 *anthrôpos en pneumati akathartôi*.

two episodes would then be in direct opposition, for in Mark 5:19-20 Jesus sends the man to proclaim to his own (the pagans) the mercy of God towards him and makes him the first herald of the Good News to the pagans, that of a liberation and of a salvation already at work for them and in them. The statements of Mark 5:19-20 do not allow affirming that Jesus "did not have the intention of being recognized outside of Israel"[27]. Perhaps one will respond that the Gerasenes had asked him to leave their territory (Mark 5:17), and if he is in some way reacting in Mark 7:27, it is because of this prior pagan rejection. But the difficulty remains: was it necessary for Jesus to go to where the pagans lived to point out to them his refusal to free them *in illo tempore*? In short, it will be necessary to choose between the two interpretations: (1) Jesus did not go to the pagan region to actively point out to them the deliverance and the salvation of God; but in that case, it is necessary to explain why he is there and what is the connection of Mark 7:24-30 to Mark 7:15-19; (2) Jesus came to the pagan area in order to announce to them that God is also thinking about them and wants their salvation, but it is then necessary to take into account the anonymity in which he wanted to remain.

2.3   A Recurring Paradox

Jesus' desire for anonymity and his incapacity to preserve it has for a long time puzzled exegetes (and not only narratologists). Most see in it a motif that is present from the beginning of the Markan narrative: Jesus does not want the healings and exorcisms that he performs to be diffused; he requires the silence of those whom he delivers from their maladies, but the latter disobey him and tell those around them what Jesus did for them[28]. One has associated this twofold movement – Jesus' wish for discretion and the diffusion of his fame – to the Markan theme of the messianic secret[29]. Whether or not one accepts this last hypothesis, it is

---

[27] I am repeating here what in "Mark 7,24-31," 52, FOCANT says about Mark 7:24ff, "Mark is emphasizing the fact that, misunderstood among his own to whom he wanted to reveal the Kingdom, Jesus is at once recognized by a pagan woman, whereas he did not intend to be recognized outside of Israel". The statement would also have to be valid for Mark 5, which, however, is not the case.

[28] Cf. Mark 1:44-45 and 7:36. On the injunction to silence in Mark and on the paradox just stated, see the artful and detailed study of S. DE VULPILLIÈRES, *Nature et fonction des injonctions au silence dans l'évangile de Marc* (EB NS 62; Pendé, Gabalda 2010), especially 141-316.

[29] BAUDOZ, *Les mietttes*, 110: "here we find the twofold movement that sets apart this theme of the messianic secret in the second Gospel".

necessary to recognize that if Jesus flees from the crowds that follow him in order to be cured of their miseries, it is because he is refusing a facile messianism. The paradox is, nevertheless, clearly highlighted in Mark: if Jesus heals, it is not in order to seduce or to be adulated but in order to make it known that he has come to deliver from the power of sin those who come to him[30], and, nevertheless, the miracles are performed so that one may recognize him as prophet[31], even more: as Christ[32].

One must not then be surprised to see Jesus, while he is in a pagan region, adopting the attitude that has been his since the beginning of his ministry in Galilee. Among the pagans, he acts anonymously, as he did in the midst of the sinners who came to John for a baptism of repentance. And one must, moreover, not be surprised to see that he cannot remain hidden. Information previously given in Mark 3:7-8 allows recalling that Jesus was also famous among the pagans: "also from Judea and Jerusalem and Idumea and from beyond the Jordan and *from about Tyre and Sidon* a great multitude, hearing all that he did, came to him" (emphasis mine). Being known in these regions, it would have been difficult for him to remain there in anonymity for any length of time.

This being said, if the narrator adds that Jesus "could not be hid" (v.24), it is in order to prepare for the following verse: *the proof that this was so* is that a woman, having heard that Jesus was there, came to find him. The reading provided is *ad sensum*. For if v.25 is related to the last clause of v.24 – normally in Greek, the coordinating conjunction *alla* follows a negation – there can, however, be no opposition between the last clause of v. 24, "he could *not* be hid," and the "immediately a woman heard of him…" from the beginning of v.25. Rather it ought to have a *gar*[33]: "he could *not* be hid; *actually*, immediately a woman heard of him…" If there is an opposition, it is between the preceding negative statement in v.24 and v.25: "He did not want anyone to know [he was there], *but* immediately a woman heard of him"[34]. The Greek in vv.24-25 being neither clearer nor more accurate, it is possible, if one links v.25 to the last statement of v.24, to interpret their connection, as we have done, *ad sensum*, or even to see in this last clause a parenthetical statement made

---

[30] Mark 2:5, 10; also see 2:17.

[31] Mark 6:15 and 8:28.

[32] Mark 8:29.

[33] Cf. BAUDOZ, *Les miettes*, 139.

[34] Cf. BAUDOZ, *Les miettes*, 140: "Jesus wants to remain ignored, but a woman, having heard him spoken about, throws herself at his feet".

in order to recall the Markan paradox – discretion/renown –, and to connect v.25 to the preceding statement. "He did not want anyone to know [he was there] – and he could not be hid – but immediately a woman heard of him..." But then the logic is wrong, which is why the first reading is preferred here. Truly, whatever choice is made, it is clear that the function of the end of v.24 is to prepare for the arrival of the Syrophoenician woman. And it is the dialogue between this woman and Jesus that, henceforth, we are going to examine.

Let us recall the results achieved. To read Mark 7:24-30 in relation to the preceding episode and as an application of the principle stated in 7:15ff implies, without contradiction, that Jesus went to the pagans in order to announce to them that God has not forgotten them and wants their salvation[35]. This interpretation required that one then accounted for the anonymity in which Jesus wanted to remain and which occurred thanks to the Markan discretion/renown paradox. But it still remains to be seen if Jesus, having arrived in the pagan territory in order to apply the principle stated by him in 7:15ff, truly opposed the Syrophoenician woman with the purpose of a non-reception.

III. A REFUSAL AND A PUTTING TO THE TEST

For a large majority of commentators, Jesus, in v.27, initially rejects the request of the Syrophoenician woman and then changes his mind faced with her faith, her intelligence and her obstinacy[36]. We have already questioned the pertinence of this interpretation, for it does not take into

---

[35] E. STRUTHERS MALBON, "Fallible Followers. Women and Men in the Gospel of Mark," *Semeia* 28 (1983) 37, points out as well that the presence of Jesus in the vicinity of Tyre contradicts the principle stated in v.27b: "[A]lthough Jesus' presence in the Gentile region of Tyre (7:24) undermines his statement that 'it is not right to take the children's bread and throw it to the dogs' (7:27), the Syrophoenician woman's clever reply to Jesus' saying is presented as convincing him to change his mind (7:29)". Jesus would thus be saying *grosso modo* this: "I have come to you, but expect nothing from me!" So why did he come?

[36] Let us only cite here two representative opinions, that of BAUDOZ, *Les miettes*, 321, for whom "A reluctant Jesus in pagan territory opens himself to them thanks to a non-Jewish woman. It is indeed because she caused Jesus to fall into his own trap that the woman has a right to the crumbs", and that of ALONSO, *The Woman*, 327: "After giving the bread to the children, Jesus is challenged by a Syrophoenician woman and changes his approach. He starts to seek those who are in exile, to heal and feed everybody." Also, Sonnet, "Réflecteurs et/ou catalyseurs du Messie" 372.

account the sequential progression of Mark 7:1–8:10. Numerous indeed
are those for whom the Markan narrator has placed in a series the episodes
that go from 7:24 to 8:10 and that occur outside of Galilee. But they forget
Mark 7:1-23. If the narrator has indeed linked the controversy over the
clean and the unclean (7:1-23) and Jesus' behavior in the pagan country
(7:24–8:10), it is really because, for Jesus, the pagans are not unclean, and
he is going to them in order to make them aware of this. That is why
another reading of the dialogue between Jesus and the woman will be
proposed here: Jesus' refusal in v.27 is actually putting the woman to the
test.

This is what it is now necessary to show, first with an analysis of
v.27.

3.1 "(Let) the children first be fed/filled" (v.27a)

"The children" (*ta tekna*). The expression designates the Israelites[37].
The statement is reminiscent of the precedence given by Paul to the
Ioudaios in Romans 1:16 and by the book of Acts in 13:46, but it seems in
contradiction with another passage in Mark[38], and especially with the
second principle stated in 27b, as we are now going to examine[39].

3.2 "For it is not right to take (*labein*) the children's bread" (v.27b)

The contradiction has already been clearly described: "If the
children go first and the dogs may follow, why does a prohibition come
later? Or, conversely, if the dogs have no right, why does the text say
'first the children'?"[40] Verse 27a indeed does not say that the pagans
ought not to have access to the blessings granted to the Israelites but that
they will obtain them *after them*, whereas v.27b reasons by exclusion: the
gifts offered to the Israelites ought not to be offered to the pagans. In
order to reestablish the original coherence of the *logion*, some
commentators think that the adverb *first* (*prôton*) reflects the situation of
the early Church, when numerous pagans were adhering to the Gospel, so
that the adverb would thus have been added by the early tradition or by the
narrator himself[41]. If the narrative analysis does not have to reach a
decision on this matter, it must, nevertheless, confront the question of the

---

[37] Cf. Isaiah 30:1; 63:8; Jeremiah 3:19; Hosea 11:1.
[38] Cf. Mark 13:10: "And the gospel must first be preached to all nations".
[39] Cf. BAUDOZ, *Les miettes*, 266.
[40] This is how ALONSO, *The Woman*, 189, summarizes Baudoz's opinion.
[41] Cf., for ex., BAUDOZ, *Les miettes*, 276, for whom the adverb is redactional.

coherence of v.27. Without a doubt, a tension exists between 27a and 27b, but the first principle stated in 27a relativizes the second; it is because, according to Jewish traditions, the pagans have no rights that Jesus asks them to wait so that the Israelites may be *satisfied*. If Jesus had only mentioned the second principle, he would for his part be repeating the idea that the pagans ought not to be substituted for the Israelites and receive the blessings that were destined for them, in short, that the pagans must not harm them. That is why the verb *chortasthènai* ("to be filled", "to be fully satisfied") is here of the greatest importance, for it means that the pagans will in no way harm the already satisfied Israelites. Indeed, it is not good to throw the children's bread to the dogs; on the other hand, once the children are satisfied, the dogs can have what remains. Moreover, it is in this way that the woman has understood the connection of the two principles used by Jesus.

3.3 "[to] throw (*balein*) [the bread] to the (little) dogs" (v.27b)

In this metaphorical verse, the puppies or the little dogs designate the pagans, all those who do not belong to the people of Israel. If, according to other ancient witnesses[42], the appellative dogs (*kynes*) is elsewhere applied to the pagans, the unclean enemies of Israel, does the diminutive *kynarion* (little dog) of *kyôn*, have the same pejorative denotation? Since it is only encountered in Mark 7:27-28 and in the parallel passage, Matthew 15:26-27, it is impossible to be certain with only a single example of the word's use. This being said, in koine Greek diminutives are much more numerous than in classical Greek; the Greek Bible and the New Testament witness to this tendency[43]. But many diminutives were no longer perceived as such. Is this so for the *kynaria* of

---

[42] 1Enoch 89:42 and 46-49, also a metaphorical text, is cited by commentators. ALONSO, *The Woman*, 175, mentions the later witness, *Pirké Rabbi Eliezer*, 29, from the time of the Tannaim (and perhaps later, if it is a pseudepigraphic writing, as some maintain), but just as pertinent, cited here according to the edition of G. Friedlander, *Pirké de Rabbi Eliezer*. The chapter of Rabbi Eliezer the Great according to the text of the manuscript belonging to Abraham Epstein of Vienna (New York; Blom 1971) 208 note 5 (the first edition reads): "He who eats with an idolater is as though he were eating with a dog. Just as the dog is uncircumcised, so the uncircumcised person is not circumcised."

[43] Cf. K. ELLIOT, "Nouns with Diminutive Endings in the New Testament" *NovT* 12 (1970) 391-398. For only the diminutives ending in *–arion*, in addition to *kynarion* (little dog) let us mention, for ex., *onarion* (little donkey, colt) John 12:14, *paidarion* (little child) John 6:9; *ploiarion* (little boat) Mark 3:9; John 6:22,24; 21:8; *ôtarion* (little ear) Mark 14:47; John 18:10. Also, *moscharion* (little calf) that does not appear in the NT but in Genesis 18:7f; Exodus 24:5, etc.

Mark 7:27-28? In other words, is *kynaria* equivalent to *kynes*? The answer is negative, for if there is a diminutive in v.27, it is because there is already one in v.24[44]: the 'little daughter' corresponds to the 'little dogs'. Incidentally, the passage is coherent in its usage of the vocabulary: a little daughter is only a *kynarion*, this term also having a domestic connotation[45]. Thus, the verse is not alluding to roving dogs, unclean because they eat all kinds of animal carcasses that are themselves unclean, and to whom one must, in order not to have unclean contact, throw any leftovers from a distance. Here, another commonplace is used, that of domestic dogs feeding around the table. The diminutive is really a diminutive and tempers the principle stated in v.27b. One may also add that the choice of *kynaria*, and not *kynes*, invites not interpreting the text based on a cynical background[46].

What results have been achieved so far? (1) If it is true that Jesus is expressing a refusal, it is immediately necessary to add that it is provisory. In order to formulate a definitive refusal, the second principle, that of v.27b, *ou kalon labein* etc., would have been sufficient, and Jesus would have then indicated that he shared his coreligionists' opinion on the pagans. (2) The metaphorical designation of the little daughter, and with it, of the pagans, by a diminutive that here preserves its original meaning, also indicates that Jesus does not consider them as unclean and confirms the statements that he made in 7:15ff. The words of Jesus are well-chosen. But why is he responding metaphorically?

3.4 The Function of the Metaphor (vv.27-28)

The discrepancy between the woman's request and Jesus' response is raised by (almost) all commentators, who question the pertinence of the semantic field chosen by Jesus in order to respond: the woman pleads with him to free her daughter from an unclean spirit, and he responds with a food metaphor! Fortunately, they note that the episode is placed in the loaves section and that Jesus is utilizing a semantic field that will find its full raison d'être in Mark 8:1-10: Jesus himself will satisfy the pagans with bread as he has done for the children; the verb *chortazô* (to feed) repeated in 8:4,8, clearly echoes 7:27, but also 6:42, the first multiplication of the loaves. The semantic field is thus in no way inopportune and, given the

---

[44] The little girl will be designated by another diminutive at the end of the episode: *to paidion* (v.30).

[45] Cf. BAUDOZ, *Les miettes*, 263.

[46] As DOWNING does, "The Woman from Syrophoenicia, and her Doggedness".

section's progression, one would have to be blind to believe that the Jesus of Mark has used it accidentally...

That Jesus addressed a pagan metaphorically ought, moreover, to surprise only the readers who have forgotten what the Markan narrator said to them at the end of the parabolic discourse: "With many such parables he spoke the word to them, as they were able to hear it" (Mark 4:33). If metaphor is the language that Jesus usually uses in order to tell the mysteries of the Kingdom to ordinary people, one understands that it is similarly necessary in this episode, if it is true that the Israel/Nations relations are at the heart of the mystery of the ways of God.

Additionally, a metaphor implies, suggests, without imposing itself, and relies upon the understanding and the intelligence of those to whom it is proposed: Jesus has chosen a semantic field that could be understood by the Syrophoenician woman and that, in fact, was. The latter has really seen that the Israelites were the children and the pagans, the little dogs, and that the little dogs, although domestic animals, did not make up a part of the family and had no rights, except that of being fed from the leftovers. She responds by using the same metaphor, but by modifying it *temporally*. Jesus had said to her *grosso modo*: "You, the puppies, wait for the end of the meal, so that the children may be satisfied"; she responds, "but the puppies do not wait, they eat everything that falls from the table during the meal" and no one in the family prevents them from doing so[47]. In short, far from paralyzing the Syrophoenician woman, the metaphor used by Jesus allowed her to respond that an *immediate* assistance would in no way harm the Israelites. Why put it off till *later,* if it is possible *now*?

The question to which the narrative analysis must then respond is the following: has the Syrophoenician woman helped Jesus to envisage a solution of which he had not thought? Has she allowed him to broaden the horizon of his messianism? Or did Jesus only want to put her to the test and probe the strength of her desire, allowing her to say that she absolutely wanted the salvation of her little daughter? A narrative response must return to the beginning of the macro-narrative and see how Mark as up to this point constructed the character Jesus.

---

[47] As has been seen by BAUDOZ, *Les miettes*, 300: "To the temporal schema proposed by Jesus (*ta tekna... prôton*), she contrasts a double schema: that of the simultaneity and that of spatiality; no longer the first and then the others, but both at the same time, the first being at the table and the others being under the table".

3.5 Jesus and Those Who Look for Him or Call Upon Him

Mark 7:24-30 is not the first time that Jesus puts to the test those who come to him to be healed. In his own area, Galilee, he repeatedly flees from the crowds that must make long journeys on foot in order to meet up with him, as soon as they know where he is[48]. Too well-known in the cities and villages, he goes away to deserted places, where he ends up being found. The disciples themselves must also look for him and do not understand why he causes these people who are in such need of relief to travel throughout the region. There is some reproach in the observation that they address to him: "Everyone is searching for you!" (Mark 1:37). Jesus' behavior does not only require those who rely upon him to be patient, it also allows emphasizing (1) the need and the dereliction in which they find themselves: what is at stake is considerable for the one who is suffering and up to then has not found any one capable of giving relief; (2) the faith they have in Jesus' power – they do everything to come in contact with the one whom they are certain is going to deliver and save them.

Mark 6:47-52, an episode that slightly precedes the controversy on the clean/unclean and the journey to the region of Tyre, is itself typical of the way in which Jesus knows humans and connects with them. After the multiplication of the loaves, he makes his disciples cross the lake and wait for him on the other side, while he himself, alone, goes to pray all night. Yet, as the narrator tells us, he sees his disciples toiling, being worn out by the battle against the wind, and only goes towards them in the early morning – "about the fourth watch of the night he came to them, walking on the sea" (Mark 6:48). Jesus sees, knows, and, nevertheless, puts off the moment of going to relieve them. One will clearly exclude all trace of sadism, for the narrator has previously related that Jesus is preoccupied with the health of his disciples and leads them to a lonely place to allow them to rest (6:31). Of the diverse explanations provided by commentators, let us remember the most plausible: the disciples must understand that, even though physically absent, Jesus is watching over them and they no longer have to fear; the multiplication of the loaves has shown that he is able to satisfy a multitude with almost nothing: master of the elements and full of solicitude for the crowds, would he thus not care for those that he has chosen? If the narrator wanted to indicate to his readers the knowledge that Jesus has of humans and situations, it is really in order to point out to

---

[48] Cf. Mark 1:35-38; 1:45; 3:7; 6:32-34; 6:54-55.

them that Jesus does not randomly change his mind because of encounters and that he accomplishes his ministry as he intends. One is thus reasonably able to suppose that it is the same when he goes into a pagan region and when the Syrophoenician woman pleads with him to free her child from the unclean demon that is tormenting her. There is coherence in the narrative of Mark. That is why respect for the narrative logic invites interpreting Jesus' refusal in 7:27 as a putting the Syrophoenician woman to the test[49]: the elements revealed in this paragraph and the preceding ones go in the same direction.

IV. JESUS IN MARK 7:24–8:10

Exegetes point out that Mark 7:24-30 is part of a section – that of the loaves – centered on the search for and, from this, the progressive revelation of Jesus' identity[50]. Is Mark 7:24-30 thus centered on Jesus and his identity or on the character of the Syrophoenician woman?

4.1. 'Lord' (*kyrie*) in Mark 7:28

In the opinion of some commentators, the episode emphasizes the Syrophoenician, her faith, her intelligence and her tenacity. An alternative reading can be recommended by the last words of Jesus in v.29: "For this saying you may go your way; the demon has left your daughter". Even if it is he who has expelled the demon, he does not say so; he attributes the healing to the woman's statement (v.28): it is because she has responded in this way that the demon has fled. A word of faith, clearly, even if, unlike the parallel passage in Matthew[51] and what he declared to the woman with the hemorrhage in 5:34, Jesus does not mention faith in this episode. If Jesus said to the woman with the hemorrhage that her faith had saved her, it is because the narrator is relating his words in indirect speech and that Jesus was not able to declare to her "For this saying..." By highlighting the words of the Syrophoenician woman, Mark is clearly inviting the reader to meditate on the statement of v.28 in order to find in it the reasons for the miracle. For, by her metaphorical response, the woman is in no

---

[49] The wish to remain hidden and the refusal must thus be interpreted in terms of Jesus' behavior since the beginning of the macro-narrative. That is why, *pace* C. FOCANT, "Mc 7,24-31", 52, one cannot say that the healing was extorted by the Syrophoenician woman.

[50] Cf., for ex., ALONSO, *The Woman*, 327.

[51] To the woman with the hemorrhage, Matthew 15:28: *megalè sou hè pistis*.

way putting pressure on Jesus; she is not saying that the children (and Jesus with them) must throw bread to the little dogs, but she means that the crumbs and whatever remains fall under the table on their own. By satisfying the children, Jesus quite naturally, and without being forced, is thus able to feed the little dogs. The Syrophoenician woman could not have said it better: did not the narrator mention the dozen baskets that remained from the first multiplication, that for the children, the sons of Israel (6:43)? And in saying that the puppies can feed on the crumbs, the woman is expressing a desire in which Jesus reads a prophecy: the pagans will be fed with the same bread as the Israelites (8:1-10).

Actually, in their verbal exchange, neither Jesus nor the Syrophoenician woman speak directly of themselves, but of children and puppies: the metaphor clearly raises the question of the connection between Israel and the Nations: will the latter have a part, when and how, in the blessings granted to the former? This is the first time that the Markan narrative tackles the question, and, what is more, does so by connecting it to Jesus and to the purpose of his mission. What is at stake in the passage is quite certainly knowing if Jesus is the Lord of all and is going to manifest himself as such.

In v.28, the Syrophoenician woman apostrophizes Jesus by calling him Lord. Since this is the only time in Mark in which someone addresses Jesus using this word, some think that one must see in it a real title and that the woman, as a believer, is addressing the one who is the Lord of Israel and hers; for others, on the contrary, the appellative is banal[52]. In order to provide a certain response, it is important to see first how, in Mark, those who ask Jesus to save them address him. Yet none of the secondary characters in the preceding Markan miracle narratives give Jesus a title: all of them formulate their request without adding anything[53]. The Syrophoenician woman is the first to do so. Certainly, she is not the only one, for two others will follow her, but with the titles that the Israelites were able to use, teacher (*didaskale*) in 9:17 and Son of David (*hyie David*) in 10:47. The woman does not say teacher because Jesus has not gone to the pagans to instruct them; she does not give him the messianic

---

[52] Relying on the fact that none of the persons asking Jesus to perform a miracle calls him Lord, BAUDOZ, *Les miettes*, 288-289, concludes that this title is pre-Markan. It is possible, but not certain, that the narrator was able to contrast the preceding miracle and exorcism narratives with this one.

[53] Cf. Mark 1:40; 2:5; 3:1-6; 5:23. Only the demons give a title to Jesus, in 1:24 and 5:7. One could put 4:38 on this list, for the title teacher is spoken in it by the disciples in peril, and they are major characters in the macro-narrative.

title of Son of David, for she has just admitted that she is not a part of the children, those for whom Jesus is the Messiah[54]. But *Lord* can be said by a non-Israelite, and the woman clearly sees in Jesus a thaumaturge, powerful enough to give him this title. How then to know if in Mark 7:28 she is giving this meaning to *Kyrie*?

Let us note that before saying *Kyrie* to Jesus, the Syrophoenician prostrates herself before him: a profound gesture of respect already indicating that she does not consider him as just an ordinary man, a gesture undoubtedly owing to what was said about Jesus and that would be more than flattery; the woman sees in him a thaumaturge whose renown is due to his power. The title *Kyrie* is only spoken after Jesus' negative response, the metaphorical field of which could mean that he is a paterfamilias, whereas she herself is only a little dog dependent on his good will: the difference in status itself also justifies the title. By calling him *Kyrie*, the Syrophoenician woman is in the end signifying that she is leaving the initiative to him, that she does not want to force him, for he is the Lord. In short, this title is in no way a banal designation. However, this does not mean that here it is given all those traits that will be declared about Jesus after his resurrection.

4.2. The Acclamation of Mark 7:37

It is not a question of analyzing here, even concisely, the episode of the healing of the deaf-mute[55], only to point out in conclusion the Christological progression that takes shape from Mark 7:24-30 to 7:31-37. Commentators rightly note that the group that was present at the healing expresses its praise by citing Isaiah 35:5-6: the salvation of God is already there, since the sign performed manifests it. Is it possible that some pagans know the Scriptures? What the repetition of Isaiah means is that

---

[54] As is known, exegetes are not in agreement on the denotation of the title *hyie David*. For some, it has a messianic meaning that is accepted by the narrator and by Jesus himself, whereas for others it shows an incomprehension of Jesus' true identity. Cf. E. Struthers MALBON, *Mark's Jesus*. Characterization as Narrative Christology (Baylor University Press; Waco, TX 2009) 90: "Although the narrative does not make clear at the story level just what Bartimaeus means by the term, when Bartimaeus uses it (10:47-48), Jesus seems to ignore it; when Jesus uses it later he seems to do so to dispute the idea that the Messiah could be the son of David (12:35-37)". Actually, Jesus does not reject the title in Mark 12, but he goes beyond only a genealogical and temporal reading.

[55] On the function of this episode in Mark, where is found, in the indirect form, an injunction to silence (disobeyed), see VULPILLIÈRES, *Nature et fonction des injonctions au silence*, 219-230.

the pagans connect with the faith and praise of Israel, that they are the first in Mark to speak of this faith previously expressed by the prophet. There is more here, it is Jesus who is at issue, for they recognize in him the salvation of God that has come to them.

The sequential progression of 7:24-37 can thus be described:

Mark 7:24-30	Jesus frees a young girl from an unclean demon	in a house only one person	Jesus called Lord
Mark 7:31-37	Jesus frees the speech of a man	outside a group	praise to Jesus the Savior

And since these pagans confess God with a faith similar to that of Israel, all – the 4,000 represent everyone – are going to be satisfied by the same eschatological gift, symbolized by the multiplication of the loaves (Mark 8:1-10)[56].

V. CONCLUSION

One was aware during the past years that a consensus in the interpretation of Mark 7:24-30 had been reached. A Syrophoenician woman had succeeded in obtaining from Jesus an opening of his mission's horizons to the pagans, whereas he himself had excluded this eventuality. It seemed necessary to revisit this interpretation and to show that it does not take into account the entirety of the textual facts – those of the passage, those of the immediate context and those of the Markan macro-narrative. One cannot indeed interpret Mark 7:24-30 without the discussion on the clean and the unclean (7:1-23) that informs its meaning and prepares for the journey of Jesus to pagan lands. For the same reason, it has seemed improbable to see in Mark 7:24-30 a radical change in Jesus' missionary project. In this episode, the Syrophoenician woman does not extort a miracle, for it is in putting her to the test that Jesus receives a response thanks to which he is going to be able to manifest the salvific power of God to the pagans and to be confessed as the one by whom the salvation of God occurs.

---

[56] The disciples who are not mentioned in Mark 7:24-37, are once again in 8:1-10, in order to distribute the bread to the pagan crowd. The narrator thus does not make the disciples in this episode the addressees of the gift of Jesus.

Chapter II

NARRATIVE AS THEOLOGY
THE FATHER AND HIS TWO SONS (LUKE 15:11-32)[1]

I. THE COMPOSITION OF THE PASSAGE

It is easy enough to determine the limits of a parable like ours, thanks to the actors' entrance into and disappearance from the scene. In Luke 15 there are in succession three parables on mercy with three different sets of actors[2]: the man and the one hundred sheep (v.4-7), the woman and the ten drachmas (v.8-10), and the father and the two sons (v.11-32).

It is more difficult, on the other hand, to identify the passage's internal composition. For Luke can indeed use several models, having them work together, and the reader is not always able to identify all of them. Luke 24 shows how important the principles of composition are for the work of the Lucan narrative.

An example: Luke 24

The episode called the Disciples of Emmaus, Luke 24:13-35[3], by following the rhetorical rules of that time, recapitulates all of Luke: in answering the man whom they do not recognize and who asks them what they are talking about, the two disciples begin by summarizing the history of Jesus, up to his death (v.19-20): the name (Jesus) and the place of origin (Nazareth) see Luke 1 – 2; – the ministry, especially as described in the first section (Luke 4:14 – 9:50): Jesus recognized as a powerful prophet in

---

[1] This chapter originally appeared in French in J.N. ALETTI, *Quand Luc raconte. Le récit comme théologie* (Paris, Cerf 1998) 219-267.

[2] The terms "actor", "scene" and "episode" originally belonged to the vocabulary of the theater, and they have been taken up by narrative analysis; "character" is only applied to human beings, whereas "actor' is more generic. Both terms are here used indifferently.

[3] See J.N. ALETTI, *L'Art de raconter Jésus Christ*, 178-184.

word and in deed (Luke 4:32; 4:36; 5:17; 6:19; 7:16; 8:26; 9:19); – the
Passion, with the name of the opponents (high priests and leaders) and the
type of death (cross) (Luke 23).

Jesus also echoes the announcements that he made during his
ministry on the necessity of his having to suffer in order to enter into his
glory (v.26): the "it is necessary", Luke 2:49; 4:43; 9:22; 13:16,33; 17:25;
19:5; 22:37; – the sufferings and the glorification, Luke 9:22; 9:44; 13:33;
17:24-25; 18:31-33; 22:16.

This rhetorical model, which makes Luke 24 and this episode, in
particular, a conclusion in good and due form to the entire Gospel, is not
the only one. Another type of composition, this time concentric, also has a
role, for if the rhetorical reprise of themes highlights the past, this one
emphasizes what is extraordinary in the present, by centering on and
taking place around the announcement: "he [Jesus] was *alive*" (v.23)":

(women) frightened (v.5)
[angels] said to them: "Why... ? (v.5), must be crucified, and on the third day
rise" (v.7)

    [two] were going ... from Jerusalem (v.13)
    ---

        women... saying that they had even seen a vision of angels who said
        that he was *alive* (v.22-23)

    ---
    they returned to Jerusalem (v.33)

(disciples) frightened (v.37),
[Jesus] says to them: "why...? (v. 38), must be ... (v.44)... on the third day
rise from the dead" (v.46)

But the narrator does not just take up the past in order to show its
links to the present (the rhetoric of the speeches and the narratives) nor to
announce what is extraordinary (thanks to the concentric disposition), he is
also organizing the episodes according to a dramatic (or narrative, from
episode to episode) ascent noted by several commentators[4]:

---

[4] This point has been really highlighted by J. DUPONT, "Les disciples d'Emmaüs",
1153-1181.

- v.1-12: Jesus is declared alive to the women but is absent and nowhere to be found;
- v.13-33: Jesus is strangely present to two disciples but is not recognized; he finally allows himself to be recognized;
- v.34-53: Jesus, visibly present in the midst of all, immediately makes himself recognizable and remains for some time with them.

The progression is made not only at the level of the encounter and the recognition but also at that of the reflection upon the itinerary and its coherence: in abstruse terms, the dramatic model has a veridical function[5].

The different models are thus each important for the interpretation of Luke 24, and one must, for each episode or each narrative section, look for the principles of composition that are at work, knowing, moreover, that this does not suffice, for it is also necessary to ask whether or not one of the principles (narrative, rhetoric, parallelisms, etc.) reacts with the others. Thus, how is it necessary to proceed for Luke 15:11-32?

The Parable's Composition

Jesus begins in this way: "There was a man who had two sons" (v.11). This opening phrase already indicates a composition in two parts, centered on either one of the sons: verses 12-24: the younger; verses 25-32: the elder. Such a division does not yet say what types of connections the narrative is going to develop, but it is useful, before starting on the analysis, to read the passage being attentive to the relationships and to their direction – from a father to each of his sons and reciprocally, but also between the sons. For the dominant narrative and rhetorical technique continues to be the *synkrisis*. Indeed, Luke does not use it only for the actors in the primary narrative[6] (Jesus and John the Baptist, Jesus and Paul, etc.) but also for those in several parables in order to contrast them – like the priest and the Levite to the Samaritan (Luke 10:30-35), the rich man to the poor man (Luke 16:19-31), the Pharisee to the publican (Luke 18:9-14), the two servants to the third (Luke 18:13-26) –, or, on the contrary, to show the similarity of their reactions and behaviors – like those of the shepherd and the woman, in Luke 15:4-10. By doing this, he invites his

---

[5] On the meaning of this term, see *L'Art de raconter Jésus Christ*, 184-186.

[6] Set within the drama of the Gospel macro-narrative, called for this reason *primary*, the parables are *secondary* narratives.

reader to note the parallel traits and the contrasts so as to determine which ones are emphasized.

But not every parable is constructed around a comparison that allows getting a sense of its composition. Whether or not one notes a rhetorical model, it is always important to begin by determining the different scenes and their arrangement.   To do this, one takes into consideration the following components: the changes of actors, of themes, of setting and of time. After an opening verse (v.11), establishing the cadre (the family), the initial situation (a father having two sons) and the potential relationships (between father and son, between brothers), and another, which initiates the transformations (v.12), the narrative proceeds by stages, easily enough identifiable, to the extent that the younger son and the elder are never together: (I) scenes with the younger (v.13-24), who goes far away and returns to his father; the setting changes (at home – in a distant land – again at home), and the time of the story is quite long: the journey, the prodigal life, the famine and deprivation, the work in the fields, the return. (II) Scenes with the elder (v.25-32), who comes in from the fields and refuses to enter the house; the setting does not change – in front of the doorway – and the time of the story is quite short, that of a brief conversation (with a servant and with his father).

The two subsequent parts have, up to a certain point, the same schema, in two stages, each of the sons being first without his father, then with his father.

	THE YOUNGER	THE ELDER
The sons – without the father	v.13-20a	v.25-28
Father and sons together	v.20b-24	v.29-32

This last division, based on the presence or absence of characters, must obviously be refined in order to get at the other parallels. For the younger, it is thus possible to distinguish between the events narrated or rather summarized by Jesus in verses 13-16 and the monologue of verses 17-19, to the extent that the dramatic situation to which the actor had been led leads him to react: verse 13: a journey and prodigal expenditures; verses 14-16: famine and a situation of want... towards a dramatic outcome; verses 17-19: the envisioned solution to escape the famine and death: to return.

The scenes dedicated to the elder son also have an introduction, verse 25, which is in some way a counterpart to verse 13. In this way, a double parallelism of similarity and contrast is drawn.

	THE YOUNGER	THE ELDER
Introduction – departure for a distant land/return	v.13	v.25
Events – opposite reactions:	v.14-19	v.26-28a
Returning/Not Entering	v.20	v.28b
The father goes out to meet them; speeches of the sons and the father	v.21-24	v.29-32

Can one already draw the parallelism between the scenes? If both begin with facts narrated in the third person, they end with the actors speaking, so that the reader knows their feelings and, especially, their interpretation of the facts; and in the interpretative sections (v.20-24; v.29-32), the last word is each time the father's, a sign that it is his version of the facts that is authoritative. If there are three protagonists, the father and the two sons, the point of view that serves as a reference is no doubt that of the father.

v. 23b-24a	v. 32
let us eat and make merry,	it was fitting to make merry and be glad,
for this my son was dead,	for this your brother was dead,
and is alive again.	he was lost, and is found.

In short, this bipartite composition already allows an interpretation of the two sets of scenes: the facts or the events (v. 13-16; v.27) have no other function than to give rise to the actors' speech and thus to show their respective value systems.

II. THE ACTORS AND THEIR RELATIONSHIPS

The Name of the Actors

None of the human actors – or characters – have a proper name (Lazarus, Zacchaeus, etc.[7]) nor are described with any religious affiliation

---

[7] On the narrative function of proper names in Luke, see the analysis of Luke 19:1-10, in *L'Art de raconter Jésus Christ*, chap. I.

(pagan, Samaritan, Jew, Pharisee, publican, Levite, priest). Perhaps the inhabitant of the faraway land where the younger son finds himself is a pagan, since he owns a herd of pigs – an unclean animal in Israel –, but this is not stated. Values and religious statuses are not mentioned, except from the mouth of the younger in verses 18b and 21 ("I have *sinned* against *heaven*"), and it will be necessary to see why. What is more, the social qualifiers "rich" and "poor" are not used, even if the narrator – Jesus or Luke, here it matters little – succeeds in giving a sense of the situation of wealth or poverty without naming them. One knows as well that the father is wealthy, that the part of the heritage bequeathed to the younger is substantial, that the father has hired workers and servants, that he can organize banquets, offer a fatted calf, kid goats, clothe his children in beautiful garments, etc. As for the younger, he initially is extravagant, then reduced to hunger, but if the cruel deprivation is described (by the narrator) and avowed (by the younger son), it is never called "misery" or "poverty". Let us right away give the reason for this, for it is important for the interpretation of other parables. When Luke begins a parable with the words "a rich man[8]", it is precisely because he is inviting a reflection upon that theme, whereas, in our parable, the wealth – and the misery that is its counterpart – is only a means (social, but also narrative) that allows showing other things at the level of the relationships between father and sons. By not beginning with the label "a rich man", Luke is inviting his reader to move beyond this to the relationship with which his meditation and discernment ought to be concerned.

The three principle actors are respectively called father[9], son (elder, younger) and brother. Not much wisdom is needed to understand that those are the relationships of which it is going to be a question. On the narrative level, it is, moreover, recommended to see how these appellatives are actually used by the various speakers, narrator and actors[10].

	FATHER	YOUNGER SON	ELDER SON
NARRATOR JESUS/LUKE	a man, v.11 his/the father v.20,22,29	the son(s) v. 11,13,21 the younger, v. 12,13	son, v. 11,25 the elder, v.25

---

[8] In Luke 12:16; 16:1,19.
[9] An exception is made in verse 11, where one reads "a man".
[10] The speakers are placed in the column on the left.

FATHER		to the servants: "my son is found", v.24 to the elder: "your brother is found", v.32	"[my] child", v.31
YOUNGER SON	"father", v.12, 18,21 my father, v.17,18	to the father: "no longer worthy to be called your son", v. 19,21 (wants to say to the father) "treat me as one of your hired workers", v. 19	
ELDER SON		to the father: "when this son of yours came", v.30	
SERVANT	to the elder: "your father", v.27	to the elder: "your brother", v.27	

As this table shows, the use that the narrator makes of the names "father" and "son" ("elder" and "younger") is neutral: they are not axiologically significant, since, for him, they only constitute commodious designations. But he is proceeding in this way in order to leave to the actors the task of showing how they are related by having them name each other. Thus, the father is truly a father, for he calls his children "my son" "[my] child", from the beginning of the story to the end, and wants them to consider each other as "brothers". The younger never speaks of his elder brother, even when he is far away, only of his father because his problem is that of attempting to return home in order to eat and only his father can accept or reject his living under his roof; and he is even ready to live without his status of son. But the monologue (v.17-19) is very instructive, for although he wishes to ask the father to consider him no longer as a son, he does not say to him "master" (*kyrie*) in the manner of an employee or a slave but continues to call him "father" – it is for the reader to perceive the reasons for this apparent contradiction and its effect on the meaning. As to the elder son, he never says the words "father" and "brother", a sign that for him the younger is no longer a brother and that he has difficulty in recognizing his father as father. Lastly, the servant charged with informing the elder son uses a neutral and purely designative language, for he uses their familial relationships to designate each: "your brother", "your father". But, when one compares these denominations to those of the elder, their use only takes on more importance: how is it that the servant uses the simple and correct words ("father", "brother") and not the elder son?

The Younger Son and His Itinerary

The younger son is first characterized by a desire, that of having his part of the inheritance. But the narrative does not say why he wants this money: because he has had enough of being with his father and his brother, because he wants to sow his wild oats, etc.? The motivations are not provided, and if the reader is not prohibited from looking for them, it is necessary to avoid responding too quickly: when a narrative is silent about the reasons, it may be (1) because they have no influence whatsoever on the plot, (2) because the narrator is going to have them appear progressively through the words and deeds of this actor or of others, or (3) because it is not on these initial motivations that the reader must reflect. The remainder of the parable will not return to the reason for this demand for the inheritance. At no time does the younger son say that he wanted his freedom, to enjoy life, or to seek out other horizons; the father himself makes no allusion to the reasons that distanced his son; he speaks only of the effects of his decision: "he was lost"; as for the elder son, he also mentions some facts: the squandered money, the debauchery.

One will perhaps object that the desire to leave had unconfessed sexual motivations: it was neither in order to visit other lands, nor to do business, nor to enrich himself and to have profits at his disposal, but in order to misbehave – one will also learn from the elder that he frequented prostitutes. Undoubtedly, his desire had nothing pure about it, and the observations made by the narrator immediately suggest this: "Not many days later, the younger son [...] squandered his property in loose living" (v.13). Yes, this boy was driven to live without constraint and in pleasure. For he could have been able to manage his money, to make it grow, without needing to go far away: the rapidity with which he packs his bags, the distance that he places between him and his family, all this allows presupposing unconfessed motivations, which perhaps for this very reason are suppressed by the narrative. But, let us repeat, if the narrator's observations – the rapidity of the departure, the long distance, the dissipation – clearly show that this son did not leave out of love for his father, they do not say it explicitly. For the narrator's and the actors' silences are entirely functional: the reader is not invited to reflect upon the motivations that took the younger far away and into debauchery but on those that will lead him back to his father.

By asking for his part of the inheritance, has the younger son not committed a fault, and what is it? Should he not have waited for the appropriate time and allowed his father to take the initiative? Actually, even on this point, the narrative remains very functional, in the sense that it invites the reader to question neither the legality nor the morality of the son's demand: he wanted the inheritance that was coming to him (his right), and the father gave it to him, without protesting or recriminating; the reader does not know what the latter is thinking, if he asked questions, made reproaches or expressed warnings: by indicating his agreement, the narrative simply wants to suggest that the son did not leave after stealing the money, in short that the property that was taken was in no way wrongly acquired but received with the consent of the only one who could offer it to him. Up to this point all is said laconically, but nothing is outside the norm – morally understood; very skillfully, the narrator has reached the desired situation: the young man wanted and received the money that was coming to him, from a father who appeared neither niggardly nor jealous of his wealth. To this interpretation, one could object that, later, the boy himself admits that his behavior was peccaminous: "I have sinned against you", he will indeed say to his father. If there was sin, it was not to ask for what he legally had a right to – in fact, if the father had given to him what he had no right to, the elder son would have taken a malicious pleasure in accusing him of it! Verse 12 thus describes a situation that is in no way abnormal. The narrative thus can rebound: how is the younger going to use *his* money?

In the following scene, the narrator's technique can be fully seen: it is necessary that the boy goes to the ultimate extreme, after having lost all, having fallen into misery, and having cruelly experienced hunger. But by indicating that he had squandered his fortune through a disordered life, Luke also wants to recall that, if this is so, it is his own fault. He indeed could have been able to lose his money by incompetence – bad investments, etc., –, or it could have been stolen by dishonest managers (see Luke 16:1); his way of life shows that he wanted neither to manage nor to plan; the famine is only a supplementary complication[11], it is not the true cause of the drama, for even during a drought those who have money can always survive – the owner of the pigs, himself, does not seem to be in

---

[11] This is a technical term designating the events that prevent this or that actor from realizing what he desires, etc.

need (v.15). The son is thus responsible for what happens to him: he only has what he deserves.

More than on the boy's responsibility, the narrator is focusing on the way in which he seeks to get himself out of the situation: not by lying nor by stealing but by going to work for a landowner in order to be able to eat. This situation is axiologically charged, to the extent that it expresses the decline that had occurred, at the level of social status and subsistence: the rich playboy son has become a half-starved swineherd.   Death is not far off, and he himself glimpses this fatal outcome (see the end of v.17).   Then comes the monologue, which constitutes the scene's climax, to the extent that everything that precedes it is done so that the boy may express himself on his past and future itinerary. This monologue is variously interpreted. Many see in it an interior conversion, a sincere repentance, a beginning of a rediscovered relationship with the father – is it not, as always, thanks to distance that the son's eyes were able to be opened? These interpretations, beautiful and edifying, are not, however, narratively based. The present interpretation is clearly going against the flow, all the more so since the sentence "Yes, I will get up and go to my father" is considered to be the very type of a conversion speech and seems to express the true tenderness of a penitent son. Could it not be only a deception?

How to identify the narrator's technique?   By provisionally suppressing[12] the monologue of verses 17-19: "And he [the younger] would gladly have fed on the pods that the swine ate; and no one gave him anything. But when he came to himself, he arose and came to his father. But while he was yet at a distance, his father saw him and had compassion, and ran and embraced him and kissed him.   And the son said to him, 'Father, I have sinned against heaven and before you; I am no longer worthy to be called your son.' But the father said to his servants..."

The words that the boy speaks at the feet of the father then sound like a confession and an act of contrition; it is because he knows that he has sinned against his father, against his tenderness and his goodwill, that he returns. But the speech prepared at a distance completely changes the perspective, for the boy in no way begins with a declaration of sin or an awareness of the pain that he had caused his father. He could have been able to express his repentance in many ways: "I caused pain to my father, who ought to think me dead", "I preferred my pleasure to my father's

---

[12] In order to determine the importance of an observation, it is a good narrative method, initially, to read the text without it so as to determine the resultant effect on the meaning.

love", etc. If the boy truly regrets his independent attitude and his indifference to the paternal feelings, the monologue – and its reprise, in the meeting scene – could have begun differently: Then coming to himself, he says: "I have forgotten my father, his tenderness, his goodwill and his generosity. Yes, I will arise, I will go home and say: 'Father, I have sinned against heaven and against you...'"

Yet, it is not repentance that drives the son to return, but hunger: his point of reference is neither the father's chagrin nor love but the hired workers, who have bread in abundance. The motive is really the will to eat and thus to live, even at the cost of his filial dignity: better to be a hired worker with a full stomach than a debased or dead son! If the hired worker is dependent on his master, he is at least lucky enough to be fed for his work. One then sees that the solution of returning is the boy's last chance in order not to die: he will try to suggest to his father to take him on as a simple hired worker. In order to be honest, the speech that he wanted to recite ought to have begun thus: "Father, I am returning because I am dying of hunger, I can no longer go on, and I prefer to live as a worker, but with a full stomach." This primary truth not being mentioned, the confession of sin serves as a cover story: the utmost thing in the boy's mind is to fill his stomach, and the last thing he wants is to confess to his father that he is returning because of this – the very fact that the first part of the monologue (v.17) disappears from the statements that he wants to make and will make to his father clearly shows this. The lie by omission is flagrant. Whatever may be said, one here perceives the important function that the Lucan narrative gives to monologues[13], to the extent that they allow the reader to go beyond appearances and cause him to enter into the actors' true motivations and to assess what at times is the enormous distance that separates the words from the feelings, walled up in the bottom of the heart.

Those who see in this monologue the sign of a conversion will perhaps object that the boy admits his sin and that he wants to confess it to his father: "Yes, I will arise, I will go to my father and I will say to him: 'Father, I have sinned against heaven and before you; I am no longer worthy of being called your son, treat me as one of your workers.'"

In fact, it is well and truly a confession, however brief: "I have sinned", and why would the son not mean what he says? Let us provisionally accept it. Let us only note that at the end of his statement he

---

[13] On the monologue and its function, see Ph. SELLEW, p.239-253.

wants to add: "Treat me as one of your day laborers." Yet, if he adds these words, it is not in order to demand a status "of penance", – he, moreover, could have chosen something even more lowly, the status of a slave; but the slave is never paid and totally depends on his master, who is able to do with him as he wants, whereas the hired work has more independence and receives a salary for the work he does! If he is proposing to his father to make him a hired worker, it is because, as he himself has admitted, his father's hired workers eat well. The calculation is undeniable! There will thus really be a confession of sin, and perhaps the boy slightly means what he is saying, but this is a self-interested confession, first of all having a rhetorical function, that of a *captatio benevolentiae*, which, in clear terms, means: the son confesses his sin to the father in order to obtain the desired change of status, so that being salaried he may at least eat well. The son's declaration is not glorious, which is the least one may say, even if it saves face. But only those who have never experienced a comedown in the world, misery and extreme hunger will be scandalized or fastidious when faced with such a calculation; as a matter of fact, who, reduced to a similar extreme, would not think of these methods – above all religious – as being capable of getting oneself out of it? It was only necessary to admire in passing the finesse of a narrator with no illusions about some speeches of repentance.

If one more closely examines the reunion scene, the way in which the father welcomes the "returnee" is of the utmost importance. The reader must perceive this description's effect on the meaning. In order to be convinced, it suffices to read the passage without it: "But when he came to himself he said, 'How many of my father's hired servants... I will arise and go to my father, and I will say to him, "Father, I have sinned against heaven and before you; I am no longer worthy to be called your son; treat me as one of your hired servants."' And he arose and came to his father, and he said to him, 'Father, I have sinned against heaven and before you; I am no longer worthy to be your son.' But the father said to his servants, 'Bring quickly the best robe...'"

Without the sentence of the welcome – the father who runs, embraces and kisses him, the son's statements are a gamble: the boy is risking all; what has he to lose at the point where he finds himself? But, on the other hand, his audacity had to be relying upon the knowledge that he has of his father: if he thought he could use this type of speech, is it perhaps because he felt that it would work. There is thus both trust (in the father's goodness) as well as calculation (this should work), and it is with both that he is trying his luck. But if one now rereads the passage with verse 20b – while he was yet at a distance, his father saw him, etc. –, it clearly appears that the boy can say whatever he wants: after all the effusions of paternal tenderness, he has nothing more to fear, and his statement is without risk. How then is it necessary to understand it? Still as a calculation, or, on the contrary, as the expression of a true repentance?

The narrator truly leaves the ambiguity hanging. For, on one hand, the words used sound right: he really has sinned and feels that he no longer is able to remain a son; in any case, he does not have the impertinence to say to his father that he loves him, and he thus completely abandons himself to his will. But, on the other hand, he does not mention the true reason that sent him back, his persistent hunger: "I came back because I was dying of hunger, and I thought I would be able to find food and lodging in your house", and the narrator did not say: "Taken by remorse – or by repentance – the son fell at the father's feet and said to him..." Thus, does the son have any regret? The narrator leaves the reader with his doubts, but, by doing this, he remains consistent, since the father did not need a beautiful speech from the son in order to run and embrace him and to cover him with kisses: *it is not the son's speech that determines the father's behavior...*

Two of the younger son's silences remain to be interpreted: (1) before his father, he does not state the fateful: "Treat me like one of your hired workers": has he abandoned this idea because he, henceforth, knows – thanks to the signs of affection received – that his father will have nothing of it?, (2) the scene ends without any mention of a thank you or acts of thanksgiving: was he ungrateful? Regarding the first silence, the syntax authorizes a sure response: for the son is still in the middle of reciting his speech when the father interrupts him – it is necessary to read the Greek as follows: "*But* the father said to his servants..." The father did not want to hear more: when the boy says to him that he no longer merits being a son, he cuts him short, rejecting this possibility, and impresses upon him the opposite by (re)giving to the son all the signs of his dignity. The narrative here develops a strong contrast: the son: "I am no longer worthy of being called your son"; the father: "Put on him the best robe, a ring on his hand, and shoes on his feet, for this is my son..."

If the boy has thus not stated the last request ("Treat me as a hired worker"), it is because he has not had time, quite simply. As to the second silence, there is nothing about it that points to ingratitude. If the boy states not the least "Thank you, dear papa", it is because the narrator, by composing the first part in this way, wanted to end it with the father's interpretation: what must draw the reader's attention is not that the younger could pass from ingratitude to confusion, then to the act of thanksgiving for the forgiveness received – one will perhaps have noticed that the son's feelings and reactions to the father's effusions, assuming that there may have been some, all occurred in silence. Yes, what is important is that the boy's return gives the father the possibility of showing his feelings and his thoughts. In short, the narrative does not primarily want to describe the itinerary of the boy's conversion or filiation but much rather the father's reaction and interpretation. The initial focus on the son's calculations has no other function than to show in return the absence of calculation on the father's part and finally to focus on it.

The Elder Son and His Reproaches

After the household has begun the celebration, the younger son disappears from the scene, even though he remains a presence in the narrative by what the other two protagonists, the elder son and the father, will say about him. Then comes the elder, who was in the field. With this information, does the narrative really intend to say that the elder son's life is dominated by outdoor work, by the rhythm of the seasons?; that, notwithstanding his status as son, his life is actually that of a hired worker?; that the younger had gone far away in order to escape this laborious and monotonous life?

As in the first part, the narrator laconically reports the facts, but the reader cannot read the information without remembering what was said about the younger son, forced to go into the fields in order to have the slightest amount of money and, as a consequence, to eat.

V. 15 – THE YOUNGER SON	V. 25 – THE ELDER SON
He stayed in the home of an inhabitant of the region, who sent him *into the fields* to watch the pigs	*His elder son was in the field*

If the younger son left in order to avoid working the soil like his brother, his prodigal life had led him to it and in a degrading situation – with unclean animals! But the observation regarding the elder ("he was in the field") also points out, indirectly, that the wealth of the father does not imply *idleness*, even for the sons. The dialogue in verses 29-32 is thus already prepared for narratively.

The surprise of the elder who hears the music and the dancing is not that of the reader, having been alerted by the narrator that the celebration had begun (v.24b). But the same reader cannot but be surprised for another reason, for, if the narrative was up to then full of silences, this one is considerable: why has the father not immediately sent to look for the elder in the fields in order to let him know that his brother had come back? Even worse, why did he want the celebration to begin without him? Is it necessary to see in this a lack of love, of feeling, a forgetfulness owing to the immense joy of the reunion? None of these psychological reasons are to be excluded, but the narrator prevents his reader from deciding which is the best. The rest of the narrative, with the elder's recriminations, could, moreover, favor another interpretation: perhaps the elder son had already told the father what he thought of the goings-on of the younger, and the father, desirous of returning his dignity to the latter, cannot properly invite the other, who neither can nor wants to image a similar outcome. Whatever the hypotheses may be, the elder son's absence can only be a narrative device with the function of showing that the decision came from the father alone and that it is irreversible; the elder can only join the celebration, that is to say, share in the father's choices, or, on the contrary, reject them and rebel. In short, the narrative presents the elder with a fait accompli in order to provoke his reaction, for, as the study of the composition has shown, this parable has proceeded so that the actors' reactions are progressively shown by speech; this is what must interest the reader and force him to wonder about his own values.

The final scene (v.29-32) alternates between the points of view of the elder son (v.29-30) and of the father (v.31-32). The text thus ensures that the elder can express his pique. Thanks to his recriminations, the reader learns how faithful he had been during so many years – especially while the younger led the good life. The technique is actually the one which was highlighted above, the *synkrisis*, which allows comparing both the conduct of the sons and the way in which the father – in the elder's opinion – sanctioned their respective behavior. In the following table, the point of view is that of the elder son.

	THE SONS' CONDUCT	PATERNAL REWARD
ELDER	I have served you for so many years never disobeying your orders	You never gave me a kid to celebrate with my friends

YOUNGER	Your son used his fortune on prostitutes	You killed the fatted calf for him

The elder son begins by speaking of himself; this clearly points out that he takes himself as a point of reference! He summarizes his conduct under three headings: (1) a life of service, (2) exemplary, fully faithful, (3) over a long period of time. One will have, undoubtedly, noticed that he does not view the time as one of closeness to the father, of joy for having been with his father, or even of mutual tenderness and love. He is only considering their relations in terms of the (paternal) law, that is, of obedience to the commandments and the resulting retribution: I have benefitted you, and you owe me the reward; I have harmed you, and I deserve your punishment. Undoubtedly, this vision of family life is partial and biased: here is a boy who describes his existence as a son as that of a slave[14]. Does he himself not need to convert his viewpoint?

Actually, the table shows that the situation is more complicated. If the elder is only considering his relations with his father in terms of his duties and his rights, it is because of what he just heard from the mouth of the servant, that his father has sumptuously treated the one who wasted his fortune. The contrast and thus the injustice of the retributions is clearly pointed out: "I have done everything right, and you have given me nothing, / he did everything wrong, and you gave him everything."

The elder's recrimination is typical of faithful people who wonder what is the point of exerting themselves, if the authority shows itself to be so indulgent towards real criminals and incorrigible swindlers. Virtue requires encouragement, as the proverb says. Is it good and pedagogical to say to a son who, in full knowledge of the facts, has wasted the family's money: "Return, my child, we will no longer speak of it"? Is not mercy in this case the equivalent of weakness? Might it not lead to complacency and license?

Finally, the elder son's protestation is not as badly put as one might think. And the biblical Wisdom writings themselves recommend to the father to punish his children for their own good, for there is no worse education than weakness:

---

[14] The Greek verb used by the son, *douleuein*, connotes, according to the context, servitude or slavery. Here, the narrator is clearly playing on this double connotation.

My son, do not despise the LORD's discipline or be weary of his reproof,
for the LORD reproves him whom he loves, as a father the son in whom he
delights. [Proverbs 3:11-12]
He who spares the rod hates his son,
but he who loves him is diligent to discipline him. [Proverbs 13:24]
Discipline your son while there is hope;
do not set your heart on his destruction. [Proverbs 19:18]
Discipline your son, and he will give you rest; he will give delight to your
heart. [Proverbs 29:17]
But of these things be not ashamed [...]
frequently correct your children [...] [Sirach 42:1,8]

The elder son thus has on his side ancient human pedagogy and the
Scriptures.   The largesse of some parents explains their children's
disorders, and a good lesson never harmed anyone... And, on this point,
whatever may have been said by commentators only slightly familiar with
the Lucan narrative techniques, the elder and the younger are reasoning in
the same manner. When he comes to himself, the younger indeed knows
that the return home will happen only with a subsequent sanction: since he
has abused his privileges as a son – to have the money and to be able to
spend it without reserve –, the remedy is to give him a proportionate
punishment. The elder would have appreciated the younger's reasoning...
The two think according to the same criteria, in the sense that they see
retribution as being proportional to the conduct that it is supposed to
sanction: reward for whatever is beneficial, punishment for whatever is
harmful. The elder is thus right to hope for a reward for his faithfulness,
just as the younger was right to expect to be deprived of his privileges.

Where then is the difference between the brothers? First, on the
level of conduct. Also, the tone that they adopt is not the same: that of the
younger is humble, and that of the elder, arrogant. But in this way, they
are faithful to the character that each represents: the guilty party is always
interested in recognizing his wrongs and lying low, whereas the one who is
in the right claims it loud and clear: how many obedient children, faced
with their parents' weakness towards a licentious brother or sister, have
not repeated the words given by Luke to the elder son in the parable!
Another difference between the brothers: one, with nothing to lose, has the
audacity to return to his father, whereas the second, strong in his fidelity,
refuses to rejoin *his* family. For such is really the radical difference that
separates them: although no longer feeling worthy to be a son, the younger
continues to say "father", portending confusedly – or very precisely – that

he will be treated with clemency, whereas the elder, even if he has always been close to his father, no longer sees him as so. It is his image of the father, an image of paternity forged by the schemas of retribution, that prevents him from understanding the reasons and the choices of his true father... He is thus invited to be open to the ways of this father, and with him, the reader.

The Father, His Reactions and His Values

At the beginning of the parable, the father remains off stage. By dividing his fortune between his sons, he is only enabling the subsequent transformations. But if one learns that he is wealthy, with hired workers, and that one eats abundantly in his house, one still knows nothing of his feelings and his values until the younger arrives in sight of the family estate. It is truly at that moment that the character of the father takes shape. The narrator here reaches the pinnacle of his art, since he discretely knows how to contrast the calculations of the younger son, based on the Law – I am wrong, thus I must renounce past privileges, but I will try to obtain what I can – to the non-calculation of the father who, catching sight of the son in the distance – a clear sign that he was continuously waiting for him –, is moved by compassion, runs to embrace him and covers him with kisses. The promptness and the rapidity with which the actions are executed really emphasize the strength of the interior sentiment indicated in verse 20b: "was moved to pity in his inner parts"[15]. The succession of the verbs is worth being noted, since it shows that it is compassion, and it alone, that dictates the father's gestures – to run, to embrace, and to kiss (v.20):

(although the younger son was still at a distance)
his father saw him
and had compassion [lit. was moved in his inner parts],
and ran
and embraced him
and kissed him.

The manifestation of tenderness has its origin in the depths of his being, and it is through this that the younger is reconnected to the one

---

[15] This is the English of *A Grammatical Analysis of the Greek New Testament* (Pontifical Biblical Institute), p. 244.

whom he calls "father". The narrative, moreover, says nothing about the younger son's feelings: is he so shocked, carried away with tears, stunned by the father's extraordinary tenderness? If the narrative says nothing, it is in order to give to the short speech composed by the younger ("Father, I have sinned...") all the weight of its ambiguity: true repentance, false repentance, calculation? A little of each, perhaps. But it is the absence of calculation in the father that must hold the reader's attention, a father who did not wait for his son's cry of repentance in order to run to embrace him wildly. As the analyses on the younger and the elder have shown, the parable is not proposing a course on being a son, rather it reveals the extent of paternity – but whose? Of which father is it a question? Of all human fathers? Of God the Father and of Him alone? It is still too soon to respond. Let us first listen to the statements of the younger son and the father.

The declaration of the younger: "I am not worthy to be called your son" has an inverse effect, since the father soon reestablishes his dignity, without condition nor compensation. The series of orders clearly aims to provoke astonishment, for not only does the son receive clothing and is going to be able to eat[16], but he also finds everything in excess: the most beautiful clothing, the fatted calf and the celebration. The excess of the gift expresses that of the paternal joy, which is meant to be infectious – all are invited. But it is the reasons, stated at the end, that give all their weight to the father's orders. This point merits attention: it is from the father's mouth – and not the narrator's or the younger son's – that the reader is going to know what is the desire of a father, what is the happiness of a son, etc.[17]: "for this my son was dead, and is alive again; he was lost, and is found" (v.24a RSV).

First surprise: the father does not repeat the word "sin" in order to emphasize it: "If you knew the harm that you did to me!", "Do you repent of your sin?"; or in order to minimize it: "Your sin is forgiven", "Let us no longer speak of your sin". Did the younger son thus not sin? Rather the father focuses less on the offense committed than on its consequences for the son, the death that deprived the father of his son! That is how a father

---

[16] There is no lack of commentators to refer to on the biblical texts where one finds elements of the sequence of verses 22-23; see, among others, 2Chronicles 28:15 (to cloth, to put on sandals, to provide with food and drink) and Daniel 10:3 (where the absence of food and perfume indicate penance and mourning).

[17] On the methodological level, it is always very useful to distinguish who (narrator, which actor) says what, and at what point in the narrative (beginning and/or end), for the effect on the meaning is never the same.

reasons.   Second surprise – consoling as it is –: the paternal speech considers nothing of the suspicious motivations that drove the boy to return; it is of little importance that he may have returned for less than noble motives, by calculation and driven by hunger; a single thing matters for the father: that he is there and that he may lead his son back to life, to the joy of sons. One next learns that, during all the time of the separation, the father never considered the boy as anything other than his son; at no time did he want to reject him, and the marks of affection at the return assuredly indicate that the wait had to be painful, but never bitter or annoyed.   Filiation was thus not linked to merit but came from an intangible paternal decision; it was an incontrovertible status: you are and will remain my son, wherever you may have gone, whatever you may have done. The reader learns as well that the separation was for the son a death; indeed, the father does not say: "I believed him dead, and he was alive", but rather: "He was dead and he has come back to life."   There was a transformation. That is what allows recognizing the paternity of this man, who says he wants life, and declares that the most beautiful gift that his son now has, when he is there, before him, is life, but not just any life, but that of a son returned to his father, of a son who, henceforth, knows that he had remained a son even during his wanderings, loved in spite of his lapses; his return was a long walk towards that life, even without his then knowing it, well beyond his calculations. The text does not say what kind of death affected him – this being one of its silences. But the reader can, without difficulty, figure it out, and I will leave it to him to do so.

The reader lastly learns from the father's mouth that paternity does not consist only in giving life and shelter to children; it has many other dimensions. To be a father is also not to impose his presence, but to wait, to welcome. If the younger knew that he was a son only in the presence of a welcoming father, who thus opened to him true freedom and filial dignity, the father, for his part, was only able to reveal the extreme dimensions of his paternity because the prodigal had returned. Is the father thus in the process of singing the *felix culpa*? Careful, let us not make an error concerning the narrative's logic: at no time does the father declare: "Oh how right you were to go far away and lead the good life, my child, because thus I can show you my mercy." Actually, the accent is placed on the return, on the "he is alive", "he has been found". What the son was right to do is to want to return, to dare to present himself before his father, whatever his reasons were! He did not despair of his father; this is what saved him and opened to him the immensity of the father's love.

To the recriminations of the elder, the father only responds: "My child, you are always with me, and all that is mine is yours" (v.31). He does not reject as unfounded, bad or inappropriate the concept that his elder had of retribution: "You understand nothing", "it is not faithfulness or service that matters to me", etc. No, simply, he says to have been obliged to surpass this type of perspective: "*It was necessary* to celebrate and to rejoice"; and this, because of the return of the brother. The father invites the elder to enter into another logic, that of a father for whom what matters above all is the return to life of his child, that of a brother who had to rejoice in finding the one without whom he himself would no longer be a brother; for the father has returned to him his brother!

If the final motivation teaches us that, for this man, the greatest happiness, the pinnacle of paternity, is to have children who recognize each other as brothers, the preceding ones already enriched the revelation that he made of his being-father. He indeed says to the elder: "All that I have is yours." His being-father consists in sharing everything with his sons, with keeping nothing jealously. Even here, the absence of calculation jumps out. If the image that the elder has of him is that of a man stingy or little aware – "Never have you given me a kid" –, it is because he himself has not wanted or dared to live this liberality, that he was afraid of his father, afraid to ask... But the father indicates to him that now this image no longer has a raison d'être and that they must rejoice, celebrate *together*. By respecting the son's fears and his concepts of justice, the father still shows himself infinitely to be a father; his patience is thus shown to both sons, the one who was absent for a long time, and the one who continually remained present, but, even so, did not know him better.

Character Types and Their Function

The parable thus opens up to both sons – but also and especially to the reader – a type of surprising paternity. Our question may thus rebound: which father is the parable describing? Does it want to give, through this man, an example of what all paternity here below ought to be? But the objections raised by the elder son, who has on his side the good sense conveyed by a secular wisdom and the Scriptures, clearly show that if all fathers of families did as the one in the parable, the results would be disastrous. By putting the past in the past, without explanation, without clarification, without conditions, etc., a human father would be exposing himself, and all the family with him, to ruin; he would also not be helping his child to progress in freedom. Actually, the father described by the parable represents God the Father and Him alone, who rejoices over the return of sinners, who, especially by forgiveness, tries to make them enter into His merciful plan, into this baffling logic, and for this reason, outside of our reach. As for the two sons, who reason according to the same principles about retribution, although based on diametrically opposed conduct, they each represent a part of our humanity, the unfaithful and the faithful, the righteous and sinners. The narrator's technique precisely consists of leading faithful and obedient humans to adhere to the ways of God, to rejoice because sinners have been forgiven and reinstated to their dignity as sons. Let us indeed not forget that the father goes out and exhorts the elder son to rejoin those who are celebrating (v.28): it is to the faithful people that the parable is addressed. This typology of the actors is clearly relying on the narrative analyses that were just made but also on the finale of the two preceding parables (v.7,10) and especially on the first two verses of the chapter where the Pharisees and the scribes murmur while seeing Jesus welcome sinners and eat with them.

Is it really true that the father represents God alone, for the comparison with the two preceding parables seems to indicate the opposite, by appealing to human experiences, that of the shepherd, that of the housewife: "Which one of you, having one hundred sheep..." (v.4); and "What woman having ten drachmas...")? Why would it not be the same with the father of the parable? Certainly, this actor has some of the traits that one encounters in many parents, beginning with patience and mercy. But the narrative is not providing an educational program or strategy. Its presentation of the father, with his reactions and his words, proceeds by excess, precisely in order to overturn our ideas on justice and retribution, placed on the lips of the elder son. For the narrative ends with the father's interpretation and not with the elder's agreement or his entrance into the banquet hall. One will have indeed noted the rupture in the parallelism between the two parts.

v.24	v.32
(the father): "for this my son was dead, and is alive again, he was lost, and is found." *And they began to make merry.*	(the father): "for this your brother was dead and is alive; he was lost and is found."

Did the elder enter, did he embrace his brother, did he celebrate his return? The narrator does not say because this is really the decision that the listeners (Pharisees, scribes) and the reader have to make, without it being forced upon them, for the necessity to which the father is calling leaves us completely free. The "it was necessary" of the celebration and of the joy comes from the very heart of God, who cannot but communicate to His children dignity and joy: that the father may have also urged celebrating, without delay and with his whole household, the return of his son to life shows that the "it is necessary" is that of the love unrelated to any calculation, of unconditional forgiveness. The principles of the elder son and of the younger are based on a concept, that of retribution, a justice that the father does not reject but that he overturns in the name of another principle, which this time is visceral[18]!

If each of the protagonists functions as a type – the father refers to God, the younger to sinners and the elder to the righteous –, it is not, however, uninteresting to note how the narrator, with great finesse, slightly shuffles the cards. Thus, the younger is a playboy ready to do anything in order to survive but who also knows how to use, at the right time, religious speech; the elder, himself, knows more than his father – who, however, represents God – on right retribution and on education: his statements echo scriptural passages from Wisdom and also the Prophets; and the father, representing God, has reactions and statements that are visceral; of the three protagonists, he is the most human – rarely has a narrator shown so well the humanity of God!

One question remains: in our day, the reader cannot but note the absence of the mother; in the parable, the feminine pole is held, in a less than stellar way, by prostitutes: would the narrative thus only view women in connection to pleasure and debauchery? It is clear that the feminine component is not absent from the chapter, since the second parable describes a woman assiduously searching for her lost drachma. And if it uses a father to give an example of mercy, it is not because a mother could not have compassion for her child like a father – and more than he –, but because the cadre described by the parable is that of family law – the juridical context requires it! The father was to tend to the education of his sons, to punish them, and to distribute his inheritance to them, giving more to the elder, to employ and pay the workers, etc., – the law is that of the

---

[18] The Greek verb expresses the upheaval that arises from the depths of being – the viscera –, which is at the same time, compassion, pity, tenderness, and susceptible to every distress.

father, from the family law of that time, and it is in connection to this
paternal law that the narrative is describing the different conceptions that
others have of punishment and reward, principally in terms of the model of
biblical Wisdom. More than the masculine component, the text highlights
the role itself, not, moreover, without subverting the image transmitted by
the tradition[19], to the extent that the father of the parable has a mother's
reactions; may we recall the beautiful passages from Isaiah: could a mother
forget the child that she has borne...? In addition to this cultural aspect,
theological language was also influential, to the extent that God is the
"heavenly Father" who sends the rain upon the good and the bad, the
Father of our Lord Jesus Christ, and, hence, the Father of the baptized. It
is by playing all the possible harmonics of the paternal role that the
narrative is constructed and applied on various levels.

III. THE PARABLE IN THE MACRO-NARRATIVE

The Parables on Mercy in Luke 15

The parallels that exist between the three parables in Luke 15 show
the importance of the *synkrisis* in the Lucan narrative. And, truly, some
analogies, which it is quite necessary to caution against forcing, indicate
another type of composition, this time alternating:

> a : the shepherd with the one hundred sheep – loses one, goes in search of it,
> and finds it;
> b : the woman with ten drachmas – loses one, searches everywhere,
> and finds it;
> A : the father, whose younger son was lost and found;
> B : the father invites his elder son to rejoice over the younger son who was lost
> and found.

The episodes of *a* and *A* have in common a distant wandering,
whereas the episodes *b* and *B* take place in the house or before the
doorway. But narratively, nothing authorizes concluding, with some
commentators, that the elder son was lost, like the drachma. The father
does not say to him that he was – or is – lost, but he invites him, who has a

---

[19] For the same reasons (the cadre of family law, with the questions of inheritance),
one must also not make too much of the absence of daughter(s).

share in all his possessions, to rejoice over the return of the lost brother. The nuance is considerable. Another difference: if, in *a* and *b*, it is the shepherd and the woman who leave to search for the lost actor and say to theirs friend that they have found it, in *A* and *B*, on the other hand, the father does not leave for the foreign land in order to attempt to find his younger son, nor does he say "I have found him", but "he was found"; he, moreover, does not go to the fields to inform the elder; nevertheless, when both sons are on the road to return, at the outskirts of the house, the father each time leaves to welcome them.

This difference, undoubtedly, comes from the sheep and the drachma not being human actors, desiring to return and/or be converted. But then, what is the pertinence of the first two parables, apparently contradictory? How can one choose a sheep or a drachma as examples of "sinners who are converted" (v.7 and 10)? The sheep are stupid – it suffices for one to start running for the all the others to follow –, but certainly not sinful; as to the coins, it is not they that are lost but we who lose them. Exegesis has recently attributed the contradiction between the parables (v.4-6; v.8-9) and their morals (v. 7 and 10) to different redactional layers: the parables to Jesus and the conclusions to the early Church. But, this has little to do with the narrative strategy of these three narratives, where the emphasis is placed not on the desire for conversion but on the desire and the behavior of God, who comes looking for His lost children and who wants to celebrate and be joyful.

Luke 15, Its Antecedents and Its Impact

Jesus narrates the three parables in Luke 15 because the Pharisees and the scribes are scandalized to see him welcome and eat with sinners. But this is not the first time that he finds himself in the company of tax collectors – publicans – and sinners. From the beginning of his ministry, he chose one of them, Levi, and he welcomed the reception that the latter organized in his honor, also provoking the murmurs of the same actors (Luke 5:27-32). The parallel is worth being briefly commented upon.

LUKE 5:27-32	LUKE 15:1-2,7
[Jesus] saw a tax collected named Levi, sitting at the tax office; and he said to him, "Follow me." And he left everything, and rose and followed him. And Levi made Jesus a great feast in his	

house, ……… And there was a large company of tax collectors and others sitting at table with them. The Pharisees and their scribes murmured against his disciples, saying, "Why do you eat and drink with tax collectors and sinners?" Jesus answered them, "Those who are well have no need of a physician, but those who are sick; I have not come to call the righteous, but sinners to repentance."	Now the tax collectors and sinners were all drawing near to hear him, And the Pharisees and the scribes murmured, saying, "This man receives sinners and eats with them." The he [Jesus] told them this parable: There will be more joy in heaven over one sinner who repents than over ninety-nine righteous persons who need no repentance.

Except for Levi's vocation, the actors and the sequence of the events are each time the same: (1) publicans and sinners approach Jesus, (2) which provokes the murmurs of the Pharisees and the scribes, and (3) Jesus' final explanation. Yet, in each of the two situations, it is Jesus' behavior that raises questions: he welcomes and eats with sinners. One will certainly object that the Pharisees and scribes have the arrogance of the self-righteous; perhaps, but if they do not associate with public sinners, it is not because of social rules or class reflexes, it is because the Scriptures demand it: it is necessary not to associate with them, not to come to terms with them, not to take their side in judgements, etc.[20]. It is on this biblical basis that one can understand what is provocative, indeed shocking, not Jesus' response: "I have come to call sinners to repentance", but the way in which he proceeds; for, far from reprimanding them, of blaming them, such as Jonah to Nineveh or John the Baptist on the banks of the Jordan, he is eating and feasting with them!

The parallels in the table raise a question about the rhetorical situation of the listeners and, hence, on the narrative's strategy. For the reader cannot but notice that, from Luke 5 to Luke 15, the elite of the people of Israel seem to have made no progress in understanding Jesus' mission. Does the narrator want to point out that this comes from their blindness and their ill will? Or that Jesus' mission is to this point so extraordinary that it remains outside the scope of all our schemas of

---

[20] The texts are quite numerous, see for example, Exodus 23:1; Psalm 1:1; 26:5; Proverbs 4:14.

retribution? The narrative positively does respond to the two questions. For, on one hand, Jesus stigmatizes the resistance of the elite who, unlike the sinners, have not recognized God's justice: "John the Baptist has come, eating no bread and drinking no wine; and you say, 'He has a demon.' The Son of man has come eating and drinking; and you say, 'Behold, a glutton and drunkard, a friend of tax collectors and sinners!'" (Luke 7:33-34).

What is more, he does not just stigmatize the refusals to repent, with concrete examples; he also tries to get the scribes and Pharisees to enter into the motivations, the effects, and what is at stake from his choices. He does it by drawing upon our most profound and common human experience, in order to radicalize it and to show how it can speak to what is extraordinary about God. Thus does he declare: "What man of you would not leave the ninety-nine in the wilderness and go after the one which is lost?" Of course, a shepherd worthy of this name loves and tends his flock, he calls each of the animals by their name, who, in return, recognize his voice; but, precisely because he does know the extent of their herd instinct, at no time will he abandon or leave so many sheep alone, at the risk of seeing the entire flock scattered and doomed. Why does Jesus thus force the issue and proceed by exaggeration? Quite simply because it alone is capable of reflecting the excess of the divine mercy. The function of Luke 15 – and one will see that the journey to Jerusalem, with the Christologization that it promotes, was an ideal time for this – is thus to invite the listeners and the reader to perceive that one can only understand Jesus' ministry by beginning with this excess, which comes from God Himself. Jesus is thus not only the one who tells these parables; through them he is also speaking of his behavior, of his choices, and asks his listeners to recognize in them those of God his Father.   Luke 15 emphasizes, if there were a need for it, the unity of the Lucan writing, since it is by being himself a herald that Jesus gives testimony to the Gospel of God.

The parables of Luke 15 are thus offered for the meditation of those who know well the Bible and what it says on the way of treating sinners, but it is not the narrator's final word on the question, for the episode of Zacchaeus (Luke 19:1-10) takes up, with a real progression, these parabolic narratives[21]:

---

[21] On these parallels, see *L'Art de raconter Jésus Christ*, chap. 1.

LUKE 15	LUKE 19:1-10
Tax collectors and sinners around Jesus	Jesus was himself invited by a tax collect
Pharisees and legalists murmur: "the one who receives sinners"	Everyone murmurs: "he has gone to be a guest of a man who is a sinner"
Jesus' response: "I have found my lost sheep" "my son" the entire household celebrates	Jesus' response: "I came to seek and save the lost" "son of Abraham" joy (of Zacchaeus)

Between the two episodes, the progression is clear. If in Luke 15, Jesus allows all the sinners to come to him, in Luke 19, he invites himself to the home of a notorious sinner; if, in Luke 15, only the Pharisees and the legalists murmur, in Luke 19, it is all the city, at least everyone present, whatever may be the religious group to which they belong; if, in Luke 15, the one who is seeking and finding is an actor in the parable, in Luke 19, it is Jesus himself who went out, in order to seek and find Zacchaeus, the one who was lost; if in Luke 15, it is still in a fictional narrative that a boy finds his dignity as a son, in Luke 19, it is from the very mouth of Jesus that Zacchaeus hears it said to him that he is a son of Abraham. Undoubtedly, the parables of Luke 15 are preparing for the episode of the encounter between Jesus and Zacchaeus, which emphasizes, if there were any need, how much Jesus' ministry puts into practice the merciful plan of God. The entire section of the journey to Jerusalem[22] is thus proposed as a coming to sinners, as a continual concern for seeking and finding what was lost, as an invitation to enter into the family of God, to receive the dignity of daughters and sons. The reprises of the same motifs – the welcome of sinners, murmurs, the invitation to espouse Jesus' choices, which are the same as God's – are not pure repetitions, but a narrative technique of deepening dear to Luke.

In Luke 15, just as in Luke 19, the sentences that support Jesus' interpretation come from the Scriptures, in particular from Ezekiel 34, which is a diatribe against the shepherds of Israel. The reminiscences[23] are

---

[22] The narrator likes to speak of journeys even though Jesus makes for Jerusalem, in order to indicate that this last journey is not only physical – it is an exodus in every sense of the word.

[23] In order to evoke an event that took place in a time that preceded the point in the narrative, or even in order to refer to prior writings (narratives or not) to which an episode makes an allusion, narratologists use the term "analepsis".

so clear that the well-informed reader will have undoubtedly noted them: "Thus says the Lord God: Ho, shepherds of Israel who have been feeding yourselves! Should not shepherds feed the sheep? You eat the fat, you clothe yourselves with the wool, you slaughter the fatlings; but you do not feed the sheep. The weak you have not strengthened, the sick you have not healed, the crippled you have not bound up, the strayed you have not brought back, *the lost you have not sought...*"

The time spent by the younger in a distant land also has its point of support in Ezekiel 34, in which, after having castigated the leaders of the people who only care for themselves and abandon the flock, the oracle announces, in positive terms, the work of God (v.11f.): "For thus says the Lord God: Behold, I, I myself will search for my sheep and will seek them out... I will rescue them from all places where they have been scattered... I will bring them out from the peoples and gather them from the countries, and will bring them into their own land; and I will feed them on the mountains of Israel... I myself will be the shepherd of my sheep, and I will make them lie down says the Lord God. *I will seek the lost, and I will bring back the strayed*, and I will bind up the crippled, and I will strengthen the weak..."

It would be necessary to cite all the chapter, as so many echoes from Luke 15 and 19 are found there. But more than emphasizing the fault of the religious elite, the Lucan narrator really makes it clear that it is through Jesus that God is, henceforth, coming to seek out the lost sheep and to lead them to life. By recounting these parables, Jesus is thus taking up the entire history of Israel, in its long wait for salvation. But it is also all of Jesus' ministry and even all the narrative that finds their trajectory, in an ever greater extension.

The Two Sons: Israel and the Nations?

The most obvious interpretation of the parable of the father and the two sons, the one that takes into account the situation (Luke 15:1-2) as well as the macro-narrative's broadest context (Luke 5:27-30 and 19:1-10), but also the biblical allusions (Ezekiel 34), consists of making the younger son the representative of sinners and the elder that of the righteous, both being members of the elect people. But historically, as one knows, this parable has been read as well in a broader manner, the younger symbolizing the pagan nations and the elder, Israel. Is such an enlargement authorized by the parable's dynamic, and is it in line with the macro-narrative (Luke and Acts)?

Even if the setting where Jesus' ministry unfolds does not go beyond the borders of Israel of that time, it remains no less true that the question of the addressees of the Gospel and of salvation, and thus of the connection between Israel and the Nations, runs throughout the Lucan work in its entirety. Does one find traces of it in the parable of the father and the two sons?

The parable's immediate and broader context results in a spontaneous application by the reader to the connections between the righteous and the sinners of the elect people. It is, in fact, true that before leaving for a distant land, which is pagan – the presence of pigs unambiguously indicates this –, the younger has the dignity of a son and that his route does not correspond exactly to that of the pagans, of whom the biblical books never say that they were a part of the elect people before they moved away from it and worshiped idols[24].

The narrative of Luke 15:11-32 is, however, narrated in a way that leaves the reader a wide enough margin of freedom regarding the applications that he can make of it. Indeed, Luke removed any explicit reference to the Jewish religious context, to the Mosaic Law; the only religious sentence, that of the younger son – "I have sinned again heaven and before you" – remains generic: of course, heaven designates the divinity, but it is so in all religions. It is not, moreover, on the religious level that the narrative contrasts the two sons, even if, unlike the younger, the elder would make an excellent observer of the Mosaic Law but on the level of one of the two wanting to be independent, away from his father, by profiting from his fortune, without restraints or morals. In fact, it is necessary not to forgot that the parable culminates with the interpretative scenes (v. 21-24 and 29-32), for that is where one may read and meditate upon the values to be corrected or espoused.

The narrator has ensured that the situation is applied to familial relationships, in every culture and civilization, by showing how, in a precise situation, that of one of the children returning after a long flight, the members of the family, brothers and father, react, in order to exclude or, on the contrary, to welcome the one who returns, in order to recognize him or not as son and brother. But, as one knows, what is specific to the familial symbol is its ability to be applied in various contexts, in particular

---

[24] This situation was, according to the Biblical books themselves, that of the Samaritans.

religious, when the members of a group must live in filiation and fraternity. Compared with the whole of the Lucan work describing the progress of the evangelization, the typologization of the roles remains completely coherent: one can indeed say that the father, the true God, wants the two groups, pagans and Jews, to have the same filial dignity, without restriction nor any discrimination, even those who were recognized much later than their Jewish "brothers" (the elder); the challenge presented by God the Father to this obedient elder son – the Jews scrupulously faithful to His will, that is, to the rules of the Torah – is that they recognize as true brothers those who come from afar, from paganism: will they know how to accept the plan of God who wanted the Gentiles to fully be His sons as well, will they know how to bring them in and treat them as brothers, etc.? In short, the techniques used by the narrator show that this interpretation is not only possible, but authorized. A narrative with multiple connotations, this parable shows the constancy with which Luke proceeded and developed the great questions treated and, from there, it opens the reader to his theory of the narrative.

IV. BEYOND THE CONCEPT, THE NARRATIVE

The interest, or better, the importance of the parable of the father and the two sons is in its being the only passage where Jesus does not just say that it is necessary for him to search out those who are lost but explains at greater length the type of necessity that engendered and guided his mission. The impact of this narrative most especially must not be underestimated, for only another narrative, a narrative within the narrative, allows Jesus to say how he himself sees and saw the "it is necessary", the extreme situations where his ministry leads him! That neither he nor Luke summarize nor repeat the experience through a concept, that thus only a narrative may describe the type of necessity which Jesus obeys, emphasizes not only the non-ideological character of the "it is necessary" but also the unsurpassable character that narrative in general, and Luke 15 in particular, has for Luke.

Jesus' itinerary, through the "it was necessary" of mercy, of the celebration for the return of sinners, etc., has no other explanation than this fidelity of a love that can only go to the extreme. It is by continually meditating on this parable that one can enter into the paradoxical logic of the "it is necessary" – "it was necessary", into the logic and coherence –

two words so often linked to conceptualization! – of the paradoxical ways of God. Perhaps one has never said so well or so modestly how much, in Jesus, God recounts His adventure as Father, so that, listening to it, our ears will be opened and we may understand why the Lucan narrative is coextensive to the witness.

BIBLIOGRAPHY

ALETTI, J.-N., *L'art de raconter Jésus Christ*. L'écriture narrative de l'évangile de Luc (Parole de Dieu ; Paris, Seuil 1989).

ALETTI, J.-N., *Quand Luc raconte*. Le récit comme théologie (Lire la Bible ; Paris, Cerf 1998).

ALETTI, J.-N., « Le Christ raconté. Les évangiles comme littérature ? », in Fr. MIES (éd.), *Bible et littérature*. L'homme et Dieu mis en intrigue (Namur-Bruxelles, Lessius 1999) 29-53.

ALETTI, J.-N., « De l'usage des modèles en exégèse biblique. Le cas de la mort de Jésus dans le récit marcien », in V. COLLADO BERTOMEU (éd.) *Palabra, prodigio, poesìa*. In Memoriam P. Luis Alonso Schökel, S.J., Rome, Gregorian & Biblical Press (coll. AnBib 151) 2003, pp. 337-348.

ALETTI, J.-N., « La construction du personnage Jésus dans les récits évangéliques. Le cas de Mc », in C. FOCANT – A. WÉNIN (éd.), *Analyse narrative et Bible*. Deuxième colloque international du RRENAB. Louvain-la-Neuve – avril 2004, Leuven, Peeters (coll. BETL 191), 2005, pp. 19-42.

ALETTI, J.-N., « Analyse narrative de Mc 7,24-30. Difficultés et propositions », *Bib* 93 (2012) 357-376.

ALETTI, J.-N., « Raccontare Gesù. I vantaggi dell'approccio narrativo per la cristologia », *Teologia* 38 (2013) 568-571 (561-574).

ALEXANDER, L., « Luke's Preface in the Contexxt of Greek Preface Writing », *NovT* 28 (1986) 48-74.

ALEXANDER, L., *The Preface to Luke's Gospel*. Literary Convention and Social Context in Luke 1.1-4 and Acts 1.1 (SNTSMS 78; Cambridge, Cambridge University Press 1993).

ALONSO, P., *The Woman Who Changed Jesus*. Crossing Boundaries in Mark 7,24-30 (Biblical Tools and Studies 11; Leuven 2011).

AUNE, D.A., « Greco-Roman Biography », in *Greco-Roman Literature and the New Testament*. Selected Forms and Genres (Atlanta, Scholars Press 1988) 107-126.

AUNE, D.A., « Luke 1:1-4 : Historical or Scientific *Prooimion* ? », in ID., *Jesus, Gospel Tradition and Paul in the Context of Jewish and Greco-Roman Antiquity* (WUNT 303; Tübingen, Mohr Siebeck 2013) 107-115 (orig. 2002).

BAR-EFRAT, S., *Narrative Art in the Bible* (Sheffield, Academic Press 1989).

BAUCKHAM, R., *The Gospels for All Christians*. Rethinking the Gospel Audiences (Edinburgh, T&T Clark 1998).

BAUDOZ, J.F., *Les miettes de la table*. Étude synoptique et socio-religieuse de Mt 15, 21-28 et de Mark 7, 24-30 (Études bibliques NS 27; Paris 1995).

BAUM, A.D., « Biographien im alttestamentlich-rabbinischen Stil. Zur Gattung der neutestamentlichen Evangelien », *Bib* 94 (2013) 534-564.

BECHARD, D., "Paul Among the Rustics. The Lystran Episode (Acts 14:8-20) and Lucan Apologetic", *CBQ* 63 (2001) 84-101.

BECKER, E.M., *Das Markus-Evangelium im Rahmen antiker Historiographie* (WUNT 194; Tübingen, Mohr Siebeck 2006) 64-65.

BENKO, S., "Pagan Criticism of Christianity during the First Two Centuries A.D.", ANRW 2.23.2 (1980) 1054-1118.

BERGER, K., „Hellenistische Gattungen im Neuen Testament", ANRW, II.25.2 (1984) 1031-1432.

BIRD, M.F., Sectarian Gospels for Sectarian Christians? The Non-Canonical Gospels and Bauckham's *The Gospels for All Christians* », in E.W. KLINK (ed.), *The Audience of the Gospels*. The Origin and Function of the Gospels in Early Christianity, (LNTS 353; London, T&T Clark 2010) 27-48.

BIRD, M.F., *The Gospel of the Lord*. How the Early Church Wrote the Story of Jesus (Grand Rapids, MI., Eerdmans 2014).

BORRELL I VIADER, A., *The Good News of Peter's Denial*. A Narrative and Rhetorical Reading of Mark 14:54.66-72 (University of South Florida International Studies in Formative Christianity and Judaism 7; Atlanta, GA, Scholars 1996).

BRODIE, T.L., "Towards Unraveling Luke's Use of the Old Testament: Luke 7:11-17 as an Imitatio of 1 Kings 17:17-24", *NTS*, 32(1986) 247-267.

BRUNERS, W., *Die Reinigung der Zehn Aussätzigen und die Heilung des Samariters. Lk 17,11-19*. Ein Beitrag zur lukanischen Interpretation der Reinigung von Aussätzigen (FzB 23; Würzburg, Echter 1977).

BURRIDGE, R.A., *What Are the Gospels?* A Comparison with Graeco-Roman Biography (Grand Rapids, MI., Eerdmans 2004[2]).

BURRIDGE, R.A., "The Problem of the Markan Genre. The 'Gospel of Mark' and the Jewish Novel", *Expository Times*, 115 (2004) 244-245.

COLERIDGE, M., *The Birth of the Lukan Narrative*. Narrative as Christology in Luke 1-2 (JSNTSS 88; Sheffield, Academic Press 1993).

COX, P., *Biography in Late Antiquity*. A Quest for the Holy Man (Berkeley, University of California 1983).

DIEHL. J.A., "What Is a 'Gospel'? Recent Studies in Gospel Genre", *Currents in Biblical Research* 20 (2010) 1-26.

DE CARLO, F., *"Dio mio, Dio mio, perché mi hai abbandonato?" (Mc 15,34)*. I Salmi nel racconto della passione di Gesù secondo Marco (AnBib 179; Rome, Gregorian & Biblical Press 2009).

DORANDI, T., *Le stylet et la tablette.* Dans le secret des auteurs antiques, Paris, Les belles Lettres (coll. L'âne d'or) 2000.

DOWNING, F.G., "The Woman from Syrophoenicia, and her Doggedness: Mark 7.24-31 (Matthew 15.21-28)", in *Making Sense in (and of) the First Christian Century*, F.G. DOWNING (ed.)(JSNTS 197; Sheffield 2000).

DUBOIS, J.D., « La figure d'Elie dans la perspective lucanienne », *RHPR*, 53, 1973, pp. 155-173.

DUNGAN, D.L., *A History of the Synoptic Problem*. The Canon, the Text, the Composition, and the Interpretation of the Gospels, New York, Doubleday (coll. Anchor Bible Reference Library), 1999.

DUPONT, J., « Les disciples d'Emmaüs », in ID., *Études sur les évangiles synoptiques* (vol.2, Louvain 1985) 1153-1181.

ELLIOT, K., "Nouns with Diminutive Endings in the New Testament" *NovT* 12 (1970) 391-398.

ERLER, M. & SCHORN, S. (eds), *Die griechiesche Biographie in hellenistischer Zeit* (Berlin - New York, Walter de Gruyter 2007).

FARMER, W.R., *The Synoptic Problem. A* Critical Analysis (Dillsboro, NC, Western North Carolina Press 1976).

FISHBANE, M., *Biblical Interpretation in Ancient Israel* (Oxford, Clarendon Press 1985).

FOCANT, C., "Mc 7,24-31 par. Mt 15,21-29. Critique des sources et/ou étude narrative", *The Synoptic Gospels*. Source Criticism and the New Literary Criticism, in C. FOCANT (ed.) (BETL 110; Leuven 1993) 39-75.

FRICKENSCHMIDT, D., *Evangelium als Biographie*. Die vier Evangelien im Rahmen antiker Erzählkunst (TANZ 22; Tübingen, Francke Verlag 1997).

GRIMAL, P., *Romans grecs et latins* (NRF ; Paris, Gallimard 1958).

GUELICH, R., "The Gospel Genre", in P. STUHLMACHER (ed.), *Das Evangelium und die Evangelien*. Vroträge vom Tübinger Symposium 1982 (WUNT 28; Tübingen, Mohr Siebeck 1983) 183-219.

HADAS, M. – SMITH M., *Heroes and Gods*. Spiritual Biographies in Antiquity (Religious Perspectives 13 ; New York, Harper & Row 1965).

HARTOG, F., *Évidence de l'histoire*. Ce que voient les historiens ('Folio' ; Paris, Gallimard 2007) 19-165.

JOHNSON, M.D., *The Purpose of the Biblical Genealogies with Reference to the Setting of the Genealogies of* Jesus (SNTSMS 8 ; Cambridge, UK: Cambridge University Press 1988; origin. 1969).

JOUANNO, C., « La Vie d'Ésope : une biographie comique », *Revue des Études Grecques*, 118 (2005) 391-425.

KAZEN, T., "Sectarian Gospels for Some Christians? Intention and Mirror Reading in the Light of Extra-Canonical Texts", *NTS*, 51 (2005) 561-578.

KENNEDY, G.A., *Progymnasmata*. Greek Textbooks of Prosc Composition and Rhetoric Translated with Introductions and Notes, Leiden, Brill (SBL Writings from the Greco-Roman World 10; Leiden, Brill 2003).

LEDENTU, Marie, « Les Vies de Cornélius Népos. Une nouvelle manière d'écrire l'histoire à Rome ? » *Interférences*, 5 (2009).

LEO, Fr., *Die griechisch-römische Biographie nach ihrer literarischen Form* (Leipzig, Teubner, 1901 – Hildesheim, Olms, 1990^2).

MACFARLANE, J., "Aristotle's Definition of Anagnorisis", *American Journal of Philology*, 121 (2000) 367-383.

MARGUERAT, D., *La première histoire du christianisme* (LD 180 ; Paris, Le Cerf 1999).

MARGUERAT, D., « Luc, pionnier de l'historiographie chrétienne », *RSR*, 92 (2004) 513-538.

MASCILONGO, P., *"Ma voi, chi dite che io sia?"*. Analisi narrativa dell'identità di Gesù e del cammino dei discepoli nel Vangelo secondo Marco, alla luce della Confessione di Pietro (Mc 8,27-30) (AnBib 192; Rome, Gregorian & Biblical Press 2011).

MATTILL, A.J., "The Paul-Jesus Parallels and the Purpose of Luke-Acts", *NovT*, 17 (1975) 15-46.

MILER, J., *Les citations d'accomplissement dans l'Évangile de Matthieu*. Quand Dieu se rend présent en toute humanité (AnBib 140, Rome, Pontificio Istituto Biblico 1999).

MILLER, R.J., "Elijah, John and Jesus in the Gospel of Luke", *NTS*, 34 (1988).

MOMIGLIANO, A., *The Development of Greek Biography* (Cambridge, MA., Harvard University Press 1993).

ORCHARD, J.B., *Matthew, Luke & Mark* (The Griesbach solution to the Synoptic Question 1) (Manchester, Koinonia Press 1976).

PELLING, C.B.R., « Synkrisis in Plutarch's Lives », *Quaderni del Giornale Filologico Ferrarese*, 8 (1986) 83-96.

PENNA, P., «Kerugma e storia alle origini del cristianesimo. Nuove considerazioni su di un annoso problema», *Annali di Scienze Religiose*, 2 (1997) 239-256.

PONTIER, P., « L'Agésilas de Xénophon : Comment on réécrit l'histoire », *Cahiers des études anciennes*, 47 (2010) 359-383.

RADL, W., *Paulus und Jesus im lukanischen Doppelwerk* (Europäische Hochschulschriften. Reihe XXIII, Theologie 49; Berne, Herbert Lang 1975).

RAMLOT, L., « Les généalogies bibliques. Un modèle oriental », *Bible et Vie Chrétienne*, 60 (1964) 53-70.

RAWSON, Elizabeth, *Intellectual Life in the Late Roman Republic* (London, Duckworth 1985).

ROBBINS, V.K., *Who Do People Say I Am ?* Rewriting Gospel in Emerging Christianity (Grand Rapids, MI., Eerdmans 2013).

ROMILLY, J. DE, *La tragédie grecque* (Paris, quadridge/puf, 2012; orig. 1970).

SELLEW, Ph., "Interior Monologue as a Narrative Device in the Parables of Luke", *JBL* 111 (1992) 239-253.

SHULER, P.L., *A Genre for the Gospels*. The Biographical Character of Matthew (Philadelphia, Fortress1982).

SIM, D.C., "The Gospels for All Christians? A Response to Richard Bauckham", *JSNT*, 24 (2001) 23-27.

SMITH, D.M., "When Did the Gospels Become Scripture?", *JBL*, 119 (2000) 3-20.

SMITH, J.M., "Genre, Sub-genre and Questions of Audience. A Proposed Typology for Greco-Roman Biography", *JGRChJ*, 4 (2007) 184-216.

SMITH, J.M., *Why Βίος?* On the Relationship Between Gospel Genre and Implied Audience (LNTS 518; London, Bloomsbury 2015).

SONNABEND, H., *Geschichte der antiken Biographie*. Von Isokrates bis zur Historia Augusta (Stuttgart, J.B. Metzler Verlag 2002).

SONNET, J.P., « De la généalogie au "Faites disciples" (Mt 28,19). Le livre de la génération de Jésus », in *Analyse narrative et Bible*. Deuxième colloque international du Rrenab, Louvain-La-Neuve, avril 2004, C. FOCANT and A. WÉNIN (eds) (BETL 191; Louvain, Peeters 2005) 199-209.

SONNET, J.P., « Réflecteurs et/ou catalyseurs du Messie. De la fonction de certains personnages secondaires dans le récit de Marc », *Regards croisés sur la Bible*. Études sur le point de vue. Actes du IIIe colloque international du Réseau de recherche en narrativité biblique, Paris, 8-10 juin 2006, O. FLICHY et alii (eds.) (Lectio divina. Hors série; Paris 2007), 365-377.

STANTON, G.N., *A Gospel for a New People*. Studies in Matthew (Edinburgh, T&T Clark 1992).

STANTON, G.N., "Matthew : *biblos, euaggelion* or *bios?*"», in F. VAN SEGBROECK et al. (éd.), *The Four Gospels 1992*. Festschrift Frans Neirynck (BETL 100; Leuven, Leuven University Press 1992) 1187-1201.

STANTON, G.N., *The Gospel and Jesus* (Oxford Bible Series; Oxford, Oxford University Press 2002[2]).

STANTON, G.N., *Jesus and Gospel* (Cambridge, Cambridge University Press, 2004).

STERNBERG, M., *The Poetics of Biblical Narrative*. Ideological Literature and the Drama of Reading (Indiana Literary Biblical Series; Bloomington, IND, Indiana University Press 1985).

STRUTHERS MALBON, E., "Fallible Followers. Women and Men in the Gospel of Mark," *Semeia* 28 (1983) 29-48.

STRUTHERS MALBON, E., *Mark's Jesus*. Characterization as Narrative Christology (Baylor University Press; Waco, TX 2009).

TALBERT, C.H., *Literary Patterns*. Theological Themes and the Genre of Luke-Acts (SBLMS 20; Missoula, Scholars Press 1974).

TALBERT, C.H., *What is a Gospel?* The Genre of the Canonical Gospels (Philadelphia, Fortress 1977).

TALBERT, C.H., "Biographies of Philosophers and Rulers as Instruments of Religious Propaganda in Mediterranean Antiquity", ANRW, I.16.2 (1978) 1619-1651.

TALBERT, C.H., "Once Again: Gospel Genre", *Semeia* 43 (1988) 53-73.

TALBERT, C.H., "Prophecies of Future Greatness. The Contributions of Greco-Roman Biographies to an Understanding of Luke 1:5–4:1", in ID., *Reading Luke-Acts in its Mediterranean milieu*, (NovTS 107; Leiden, Brill, 2003) 65-77.

THEISSEN, G., *Urchristliche Wundergeschichten*. Ein Beitrag zur formgeschichtlichen Erforschung der synoptischen Evangelia (StNT 8; Gütersloh 1974).

THEISSEN, G., „Lokal- und Sozialkolorit in der Geschichte von der Syrophönikischen Frau (Mark 7.24-30)", *ZNW* 75 (1984) 204-206.

VILLEMAIN, A.-Fr., « Essai sur les romans grecs », in ID., *Études de littérature ancienne et étrangère* (Paris, Didier,1874).

VOTAW, C.W., "The Gospels and Contemporary Biographies", *American Journal of Theology* 19 (1915) 45-73.

VULPILLIÈRES, S. DE, *Nature et fonction des injonctions au silence dans l'évangile de Marc* (EB NS 62 ; Pendé, Gabalda 2010).

WÉNIN, A., *Joseph ou l'invention de la fraternité* (Le livre et le rouleau 21 ; Namur, Lessius 2005).

WILKEN, R.L., *The Christians as the Romans saw them* (New Haven, Yale University Press 1984).

WILSON, R.R., "The Old Testament Genealogies in Recent Research", *JBL*, 94 (1975) 168-189.

WÖRDEMANN, D., *Das Charakterbild im bíos nach Plutarch und das Christusbild im Evangelium nach Markus* (Studien zur Geschichte und Kultur des Altertums I/19; Paderborn, Ferdinand Schöningh 2002).

YABRO COLLINS, A., *The beginnings of the Gospel*. Probings of Mark in Context (Minneapolis, Fortress, 1992).

YABRO COLLINS, A. – ATTRIDGE H.W., *Mark*. A Commentary on the Gospel of Mark (Hermeneia; Minneapolis, Fortress 2007).

INDEX OF ANCIENT AUTHORS

INDEX OF MODERN AUTHORS

Finito di stampare nel mese di dicembre 2017
presso Printbee.it - Noventa Padovana (PD)